Charitable Giving Law
Made Easy

Bruce R. Hopkins

John Wiley & Sons, Inc.

Library of Congress Cataloging-in-Publication Data
Hopkins, Bruce R.
    Charitable giving law made easy / Bruce R. Hopkins.
       p.   cm.
    Published simultaneously in Canada.
    Includes bibliographical references and index.
    ISBN-13: 978-0-471-78353-4 (cloth)
    ISBN-10: 0-471-78353-6 (cloth)
1. Income tax deductions for charitable contributions–United States.
2. Charities–Taxation–United States. 3. Inheritance and transfer tax–Deductions–Law and legislation–United States. 4. Gifts–Taxation–Deductions–Law and legislation–United States. 5. Charitable uses, trusts, and foundations–United States. 6. Charitable giving.
I. Title.
    KF6388.H62 2007
    343.7305'268–dc22   2006030747

Printed in the United States of America

10   9   8   7   6   5   4   3   2   1

Contents

Preface

This book came into existence principally because of its companion, *Nonprofit Law Made Easy*. In format, style, and length, it parallels its sibling. The hope is that these two books, in tandem, will be of assistance in guiding nonlawyers through the maze of law concerning nonprofit, tax-exempt organizations and charitable giving.

This book also, however, blatantly mimics still another Wiley book (the one that started it all), *Not-for-Profit Accounting Made Easy*. Lawyers and accountants in the nonprofit realm populate overlapping universes, so these two companion volumes about the law are a natural fit with the accounting book.

As was noted in the preface to *Nonprofit Law Made Easy*, I have never discussed this accounting book with its author, Warren Ruppel. I cannot imagine, however, that he extracted as much enjoyment from the process of writing the law books as I did. After years of writing technical and long books about various aspects of nonprofit law, writing the nonprofit organization and charitable giving books with this approach was pure pleasure. The biggest challenge, not surprisingly, was what to include and (the painful part) what to leave out. This book thus reflects my take on what constitutes the fundamentals of the law of charitable giving.

In any event, I had an easier time of it than Mr. Ruppel did. He had to *create* his book; I had merely to *imitate* it. The substance obviously is different but the format is unabashedly copied. Consequently, both of the law books are about the same length as his, there also are a dozen chapters, each chapter opens with an inventory of what is coming, and ends with a chapter summary, and there are no footnotes (another painful part). The three books share a similar dust jacket. So Mr. Ruppel and Wiley designed the original vessel; I poured my descriptions of the law into it.

Back to this matter of what to include and what to exclude. I included in this book the absolute basics (such as the definition of a charitable gift, the percentage limitations, rules as to gifts of prop-

erty, planned giving, and the substantiation and appraisal requirements). Other all-time favorites in here are the deduction reduction rules, the twice-basis deductions, uses of life insurance, and
international charitable giving. I wanted to include more, so I toyed
with some emerging concepts; thus, there are law summaries concerning donor-advised funds, contributions of vehicles and intellectual property, and the corporate sponsorship rules. Even
stripping this field of law to its basics, there is a need to discuss a
dollop of antitrust and securities law, the alternative minimum tax,
and the foreign tax credit.

Nonprofit law is as dynamic as law can get; capturing what appears to be the "basics" at a point in time can be elusive. For example, as this book went to press, Congress (the 109th, meeting
2005–2006) enacted major charitable giving legislation, the IRS has
ambitious regulations and rulings projects, and the courts are certain to contribute their share of new law. I have tried to inject references to the prospects of this and other coming law among the
summaries of the basics.

As a nonaccountant in the nonprofit field, I am glad to have
Not-for-Profit Accounting Made Easy as a guide to the basics of the accounting principles and rules. I have tried to emulate Mr. Ruppel's
work, to provide an equally valuable volume for the nonlawyer who
wants a grounding in charitable giving law.

I extend my thanks to Dexter Gasque, senior production editor, and to Susan McDermott senior editor, for their support and
assistance in creating this book.

Bruce R. Hopkins

November, 2006

ABOUT THE AUTHOR

BRUCE R. HOPKINS is the country's leading authority on tax-exempt organizations and is a senior partner with the firm Polsinelli Shalton Welte Suelthaus PC. He is also the author of 19 books, including *The Law of Tax-Exempt Organizations, 9th Edition*; *Planning Guide for the Law of Tax-Exempt Organizations*; *Nonprofit Law Made Easy*; *650 Essential Nonprofit Law Questions Answered*; *The Law of Fundraising, 3rd Edition*; *Private Foundations: Tax Law and Compliance, 2nd Edition*; *The Tax Law of Charitable Giving, 3rd Edition*; *The Law of Intermediate Sanctions*; and *The Law of Tax-Exempt Healthcare Organizations, 2nd Edition,* as well as the newsletter *Bruce R. Hopkins' Nonprofit Counsel,* all published by John Wiley & Sons.

CHAPTER 1

Charitable Giving Law: Basic Concepts

The purpose of this chapter is to provide basic information about the law concerning contributions (usually deductible ones) to charitable organizations. This information will serve as a basis for understanding much of the law summarized in the subsequent chapters. Specifically, this chapter will:

- Describe organizations that are considered *charitable* entities for these purposes
- Define the term *charitable contribution*
- Explore some unique aspects of charitable giving
- Provide an introduction to the charitable contribution deduction
- Explain the differences between *public charities* and *private foundations*
- Discuss the elements affecting the deductibility of charitable contributions
- Explain the *grantor trust* rules
- Summarize the law as to donor-advised funds
- Review certain subtleties in connection with charitable giving
- Discuss the matter of charitable pledges
- Examine the public policy doctrine

CHARITABLE ORGANIZATIONS

Organizations that attract deductible charitable gifts are termed *qualified donees*. Generically, these entities are known, for this purpose, as *charitable organizations*. More technically, qualified donees are charitable organizations (including educational, religious, and scientific entities), certain fraternal organizations, certain cemetery companies, and most veterans' organizations. Contributions to both private and public charities are deductible, but the law favors gifts to public charities.

Federal, state, and local governmental bodies are charitable donees. State or local law, however, may preclude a governmental entity from accepting charitable gifts. In most jurisdictions, a charitable organization can be established to solicit deductible contributions for and make grants to governmental bodies. This is a common technique for public schools, colleges, universities, and hospitals.

An otherwise nonqualifying organization may be allowed to receive a deductible charitable gift, where the gift property is used for charitable purposes or received by an agent for a charitable organization (see Chapter 8). An example of the former is a gift to a trade association that is earmarked for a charitable fund within the association. Examples of an agent for a charity is a title-holding company that holds a property for charitable purposes and a for-profit company that acquires and disposes of vehicles as part of a charity's used vehicle donation program.

CHARITABLE CONTRIBUTIONS

A fundamental requirement of the charitable contribution deduction law is that the cash or property transferred to a charitable organization must be transferred in the form of a *gift*. That is, before there can be a charitable gift, the underlying transaction must constitute a gift. Merely because money is paid or property is transferred to a charity does not necessarily mean that the payment or transfer is a gift. When a tax-exempt university's tuition, an exempt hospital's healthcare fee, or an exempt association's dues are paid, there is no gift, despite the fact that the recipient is charitable, and thus there is no charitable deduction for the payment.

The terms *contribution*, *gift*, and *donation* are essentially synonymous. Each term is used in the charitable giving context, although the larger the amount or value of the transfer, the lesser is the likelihood that the term *donation* is used. Thus, for example, a contribution to a charity of used clothing is likely to be termed a donation but not a gift to a charity of a large parcel of real estate, which is usually thought of as a contribution. The term *gift* is employed when the donee is not a charitable entity (most often, an individual) (see Chapter 5).

Basically, a gift has two elements: It involves a transfer that is *voluntary* and is motivated by something other than *consideration* (value received in return for a payment or transfer). Where payments are made to receive something in exchange (education, health care, etc.), the transaction is a *purchase*; there is no gift. (As discussed in Chapter 12, however, a transaction can be both a contribution and a purchase.)

The law places more emphasis on what is received by the payor than on the mere existence of a payment or transfer. The federal income tax regulations state that a transfer is not a contribution when it is made "with a reasonable expectation of financial return commensurate with the amount of the donation." Instead, this type of a payment is a purchase of a product or a service. Thus, the IRS stated that a contribution is a "voluntary transfer of money or property that is made with no expectation of procuring financial benefit commensurate with the amount of the transfer." When a single transaction is partially a gift and partially a purchase, and when a charity is the payee, only the gift portion is deductible.

The U.S. Supreme Court, in an oft-quoted pronouncement, observed that a gift is a transfer motivated by "detached or disinterested generosity." The Court also characterized a gift as a payment stimulated "out of affection, respect, admiration, charity, or like impulses." Thus, the focus in this area for the most part has been an objective analysis, comparing what the "donee" parted with and what (if anything) the "donor" received net in exchange.

Another factor, that of *donative intent*, is sometimes taken into consideration. The federal tax regulations state that, for any part of a payment made in the context of a charity auction (see Chapter 7) to be deductible as a charitable gift, the patron must have donative intent. More broadly, a congressional committee report contains the observation that the term *gift* is "generally interpreted to mean a voluntary transfer of money or other property without receipt of adequate consideration and with donative intent." This statement added that, if a taxpayer receives or expects to receive a quid pro quo in exchange for a transfer to charity, the

taxpayer "may be able to deduct the excess of the amount transferred over the fair market value of any benefit received in return
provided the excess payment is made with the intention of making
a gift."

A federal court of appeals described the matter as to what is a
gift this way: It is a "particularly confused issue of federal taxation."
The statutory law on the subject, said this court, is "cryptic," and
"neither Congress nor the courts have offered any very satisfactory
definitions" of the terms *gift* and *contribution*.

INTRODUCTION TO CHARITABLE DEDUCTIONS

The basic concept of the federal income tax deduction for a charitable contribution is this: Corporations and individuals who itemize their deductions can deduct on their annual tax return, within
certain limits, an amount equivalent to the amount contributed
(money) or to the value of a contribution (property) to a qualified
donee. A charitable contribution often gives rise to a deduction for
state income tax purposes; a local tax deduction may also be
available.

Deductions for charitable gifts are also allowed under the federal gift tax and estate tax laws (see Chapter 5). Donors and the
charitable organizations they support commonly expect gifts to be
in the form of outright transfers of money or property. For both
parties (donor and donee), a gift is usually a unilateral transaction,
in a financial sense: The donor parts with the contributed item; the
charity acquires it.

The advantages to the donor, from the making of a charitable
gift, generally are the resulting charitable deduction and the grat-
ification derived from the giving. Planned giving (see Chapter 9)
provides additional financial and tax advantages to the donor.
Overall, these are the economic advantages that can result from a
charitable gift:

- A federal, state, and/or local tax deduction
- Avoidance of capital gains taxation
- Creation of or an increase in cash flow
- Improved tax treatment of income
- Free professional tax and investment management services
- Opportunity to transfer property between the generations
  of a family
- Receipt of benefits from the charitable donee

PRIVATE FOUNDATIONS

Tax-exempt charitable organizations (charitable donees) are of two types: public charities and private foundations. The federal tax law does not (other than by implication) define the term *private foundation*. This is the case although a section of the Internal Revenue Code is captioned "Private Foundation Defined." This section should be titled "Public Charity Defined" because that is what it really does. That is, the section defines what a private foundation is not. Another perspective on the point is that, technically, a private foundation is any tax-exempt charitable entity that is not a public charity.

Nonetheless, a private foundation generally is an organization that has these four characteristics:

1. It is, as noted, a tax-exempt, charitable, educational, scientific, or like organization (and is thus subject to the rules applicable to charitable organizations generally).
2. It is funded (often on only one occasion) from a single source (such as an individual, a family, or a business).
3. Its ongoing revenue is income from investment assets (so that a foundation operates much like an endowment fund).
4. It does not have its own program but rather makes grants in furtherance of the charitable ends of other organizations (and sometimes individuals).

It is because of this second characteristic that an organization is considered to be *private*. (That term does not pertain to an organization's board, although a board can be private in the sense that it consists of representatives of a single corporation or a single family. Nonetheless, a public charity can likewise have a private board.)

Every tax-exempt, charitable organization is presumed to be a private foundation. A showing that the organization is a form of public charity rebuts this presumption.

PUBLIC CHARITIES

There are three fundamental types of public charities:

1. Institutions
2. Publicly supported charities
3. Supporting organizations (so classified because of their nexus to one or more other tax-exempt organizations)

Institutions

The *institutions* are not private foundations because of their functions. They are churches (including synagogues and mosques) and certain other religious organizations; colleges, universities, and schools; hospitals and other providers of health care; medical research organizations; and governmental units.

Publicly Supported Charities

A *publicly supported charity* is the antithesis of a private foundation. While, as noted, a private foundation is a charity that is privately funded, a publicly supported charity is a charitable organization that receives financial support on an ongoing basis from the public. Thus, this public charity status is dependent on the nature of the funding of the organizations. Most of the elements of the definition of the term *publicly supported charity* focus on the meaning, in the appropriate context, of the term *public.*

    There are two types of publicly supported charities:

1. The *donative* type
2. The *service-provider* type

Donative Publicly Supported Charity

A donative publicly supported charity is an organization that *normally* receives a *substantial part* of its financial support from direct or indirect contributions from the *public* and/or from one or more governmental units in the form of grants. (The statute uses the term *general public,* but that is a redundancy.)

    Most donative publicly supported charities must derive at least one-third of their financial support (the *support ratio*) from eligible governmental and/or public sources. Except for new entities, the normal time span for measuring the organization's support is its most recent four tax years (the *support computation period*).

    Public support can come from individuals, corporations, trusts, other charitable organizations, or other legal entities. The total amount of contributions or grants from any one donor or grantor during the support computation period generally is not public support to the extent that the amount exceeds 2 percent of the organization's allowable total support received during that period. The 2 percent limitation, however, does not apply to support in the form of grants from other donative publicly supported organizations or from governmental units. All grant support from these two sources is public support.

Donors who have certain relationships with one another (such as spouses or individuals and controlled businesses) must share a single 2 percent limitation. Multiple contributions or grants from any one source are aggregated over the support computation period and treated as a single gift or grant.

In the computation of its support ratio, a donative publicly supported organization cannot include amounts received from the exercise or performance of its tax-exempt functions (*program service revenue*). An organization cannot, however, meet this *public support test* if it receives almost all of its support from its related activities and only an insignificant amount of support from the public and/or governmental units in the form of grants.

For example, charity X has been in existence several years. X reports for financial purposes on the calendar-year basis. X is and is striving to remain a donative-type publicly supported charity. Assessing X's status in 2007, during 2003 to 2006, X received $10 million in charitable contributions and grants. The 2 percent threshold thus is $200,000. The target minimum numerator of the public support fraction thus is $3,334,000. Over that four-year period, X received $3.5 million in public support. Its public support ratio, therefore, is 35 percent. Consequently, as of 2007, X is a donative-type publicly supported charity.

Service-Provider Publicly Supported Charity

A service-provider publicly supported charitable organization normally must receive more than one-third of its financial support in the form of gifts and grants, membership fees, and/or gross receipts in the form of program service revenue. Amounts that are eligible as public support are those derived from *permitted sources.* These sources are governmental agencies, the other types of institutions, donative publicly supported charities, and persons who are not *disqualified persons* with respect to the organization.

Like the law concerning donative publicly supported charitable organization, the service-provider organization rules take into account financial support received over the organization's most recent four tax years (the meaning of the word *normally*) and utilize a one-third support fraction.

Exempt function revenue can count as public support for the service-provider organization, but only to the extent that the revenue from any one source does not exceed the greater of $5,000 or 1 percent of the organization's support during the support computation period involved. Also, support of this nature, to constitute public support, cannot come from disqualified persons.

Thus, these rules place limits on qualifying gifts and grants to service-provider publicly supported charitable organizations. As noted, public support cannot come from *disqualified persons.* These persons are an organization's directors (or trustees), officers, members of their families, persons controlled by disqualified persons (such as businesses, trusts, and estates), and substantial contributors. A *substantial contributor* is a person who contributes or bequeaths an aggregate amount of more than $5,000 to a charitable organization, where that amount is more than 2 percent of the contributions and bequests received by the organization over the totality of its existence.

To qualify as a service-provider publicly supported charitable organization, the entity may not receive more than one-third of its financial support in the form of investment income.

For example, charity Y has been in existence several years. Y reports for financial purposes on the calendar-year basis. Y is striving to remain a service-provider publicly supported charity. Assessing Y's status in 2007, during 2003 to 2006, Y received $10 million in charitable contributions and grants. The target minimum numerator of the public support fraction thus is $3,334,000. Over that four-year period, Y received $3.5 million in contributions, grants, and exempt function income from sources other than disqualified persons (public support). Its public support ratio, therefore, is 35 percent. Consequently, as of 2007, Y is a service-provider publicly supported charity.

Supporting Organizations

The third category of charitable organization that is not a private foundation is the *supporting organization.* A supporting organization is an entity that is related, structurally or operationally, to one or more institutions and/or publicly supported organizations (or, in some instances, other organizations). A supporting organization must be organized, and at all times operated, in an active relationship with one or more eligible supported organizations.

This relationship must be one of three types, with the inter-action between the organizations different for each type:

1. *Operated, supervised, or controlled by one or more eligible sup-ported organization(s)*. This is a parent-subsidiary relation-ship, where the parent maintains a significant degree of direction over the policies, programs, and other activities of the supporting organization. This type of entity is infor-mally known as a *Type I* supporting organization.
2. *Supervised or controlled in connection with one or more eligible supported organization(s)*. This is a brother-sister relation-ship, where there is common supervision or control by the persons heading both the supporting and supported or-ganizations. This type of entity is informally known as a *Type II* supporting organization.
3. *Operated in connection with one or more eligible supported organi-zation(s)*. This means that the supporting organization is re-sponsive to and significantly involved in the operation of one or more supported organizations. This type of entity is in-formally known as a *Type III* supporting organization.

Most supported organizations are charitable, educational, re-ligious, and like entities. Nonetheless, it is possible to structure a relationship where the supported organization is a tax-exempt so-cial welfare, agricultural, horticultural, labor, or trade, business, or professional association. The basic requirement is that this type of supported organization must satisfy the public support test appli-cable to service-provider publicly supported organizations.

There is no limitation as to the number of organizations that can be supported by a supporting organization. Moreover, there is no limitation as to the number of supporting organizations a sup-ported organization may have. Disqualified persons with respect to a supporting organization may not control, directly or indirectly, the supporting organization.

A supporting organization may be established by the organi-zation or organizations that it is to support. Also, one or more donors may form a supporting organization. In this sense, a sup-porting organization is an alternative, from a prospective donor's viewpoint, to a private foundation. The fundamental difference be-tween these choices is the control element: A donor to a private foundation can retain control over the foundation's resources; a donor to a supporting organization cannot.

WHAT DIFFERENCE DOES IT MAKE?

As noted, a tax-exempt charitable organization is either a public charity or a private foundation. From a law perspective, it is usually important for the organization to qualify as a public charity. That is, there is no law advantage to private foundation status.

Here are the disadvantages to classification as a private foundation:

- The need to comply with a battery of onerous rules, namely, prohibitions on self-dealing, insufficient grants for charitable purposes, excess business holdings, jeopardizing investments, and certain types of grants and other expenditures
- A tax on net investment income
- Extensive record-keeping and reporting responsibilities
- Narrow limitations on gift deductibility
- The reality that private foundations are highly unlikely to make grants to other private foundations

The biggest advantage to the use of a private foundation is that the donor or donors can retain control over the funds and property they have contributed (and taken a deduction for) to the organization.

TYPES OF DONORS

A *donor* is a person who makes a gift. A donor thus can be a person who makes a contribution to a charitable organization. A donor may or may not obtain a charitable contribution deduction as the result of a charitable gift. Many factors operate to determine this outcome, as will be described.

There are several types of donors, that is, several categories of persons who can make contributions to charitable organizations:

- Individuals
- C (or regular) corporations
- S (or small business) corporations
- Partnerships
- Limited liability companies
- Trusts
- Estates (where the gifts are termed *bequests* [in instances of transfers of money or personal property] or *devises* [in instances of transfers of real property]) (see Chapter 5)

Some of these organizations are classified for tax law purposes as *pass-through entities*, which means that they are not subject to federal income taxation. (Rather, the taxation is of the shareholders or members.) Pass-through entities are S corporations, partnerships, and limited liability companies. When a pass-through entity makes a charitable contribution, each shareholder or member takes into account his, her, or its distributive share of the resulting deduction (see Chapter 3).

FACTORS AFFECTING DEDUCTIBILITY OF CONTRIBUTIONS

Several factors affect the deductibility (or the extent of deductibility) of charitable contributions, including these:

- The transaction must, in fact, be a gift.
- The recipient of the gift must be an eligible charitable organization.
- The nature of the donor.
- The *acceptance* by the charitable organization of the money or property that was the subject of the ostensible gift.
- When the donor is an individual, whether the donor itemizes deductions.
- The year of the gift (see Chapter 3).
- The subject of the gift, whether money or property (see Chapter 2).
- If the gift is of property, the nature of the property that is contributed, such as:
  - Long-term capital gain property;
  - Short-term capital gain property;
  - Ordinary income property;
  - Inventory (see Chapter 6).
- If the gift is of property, the value of the property.
- The public charity/private foundation status of the charitable recipient.
- The nature of the gift recipient if it is an organization other than a public charity or private foundation.
- The use to which the contributed property is put, such as the unrelated use of tangible personal property (see Chapter 8).
- The nature of the interest in the money or property contributed, that is, whether the gift is of an outright interest or a partial interest (see Chapters 7 and 9).
- Compliance with record-keeping, reporting, appraisal, and other substantiation requirements (see Chapter 12).

GRANTOR TRUST RULES

The *grantor trust rules* apply with respect to grantors and others who are treated, for tax law purposes, as substantial owners of property held in a trust—that is, those persons who have retained substantial domination and control over a trust. These rules tax to the grantor the income of the grantor trust; technically, the income of the trust, along with appropriate tax deductions (including the charitable contribution deduction) and tax credits, is attributed to the grantor. A *grantor* is a person who transfers property to a trust.

There are five circumstances in which a grantor is regarded as an owner of some portion of a trust and thus is taxed on the income of the trust. A grantor is treated as the owner of any portion of a trust:

1. In which he or she has a reversionary interest in either the corpus of or the income from the trust if, as of the inception of that portion of the trust, the value of the interest exceeds 5 percent of the value of the portion
2. In respect of which the beneficial enjoyment of the corpus or the income from it is subject to a power of disposition, exercisable by the grantor or a nonadverse party, or both, without the approval or consent of any adverse party
3. When certain administrative powers over the trust exist and the grantor can or does benefit by reason of these powers
4. If the grantor or a nonadverse party has a power to revoke the trust or return the corpus to the grantor
5. If the grantor or a nonadverse party has the power to distribute income to or for the benefit of the grantor or his or her spouse

In some instances, a person other than a grantor is treated as a substantial owner of a portion of a trust. These rules also may apply with respect to foreign trusts having one or more U.S. beneficiaries.

DONOR-ADVISED FUNDS

An alternative to a private foundation or a supporting organization is the *donor-advised fund*. Although this term is not formally defined in the law, in this circumstance, a donor makes a gift to a public charity where the donee, instead of placing the gift property in its general treasury, deposits the gift item in a discrete fund (segregated account) within the charity (with the fund usually bearing the name of the donor). By contract, the donor is provided the opportunity to thereafter advise the charity as to dispositions from the fund, such as grants to other charitable organizations. The charitable deduction is likely to be defeated, however, where the arrangement amounts to a *donor-directed fund*, which provides a donor with the contractual right to direct (rather than merely advise as to) the subsequent distributions of the gifted money or property.

The IRS approved an arrangement where a donor made a gift of property to a charitable organization, yet retained the right to manage the investment of the property placed into a designated account. There were several conditions and restrictions attached to this right, with the charity empowered (by an agreement) to terminate the relationship at any time for any reason. This authority to manage investments usually terminates after a set number of years from the date of the gift.

Note: This ability to manage the investment of charitable assets appeals only to those individuals who enjoy financial management and/or who believe they can do a better job of investing than the charity. The governing board of a charitable organization, however, has certain fiduciary responsibilities. One of them is prudent stewardship of the organization's income and assets. It may be questioned whether turning asset management over to a person solely because that person is a donor to the entity comports with the requirements as to appropriate governance of a charitable organization.

The grantor trust rules (described earlier) can be invoked in this context. These rules can be used to evaluate whether a grantor (donor) retained rights with respect to property transferred to a charity that would cause the transaction to be regarded as less than an outright gift. The rules look to determine whether the grantor has, despite the transaction, retained significant ownership interests.

Donor-advised funds are controversial. Some contend that the maintenance of these funds is not a charitable activity. An extension of this assertion is that an organization that has maintenance of these funds as its primary or sole activity cannot qualify for tax exemption as a charitable organization. Critics argue that the process is akin to establishing and maintaining a commercial bank account holding deposits for the private benefit of a customer. (This is not the case; with a bank account, the customer can withdraw the deposited funds, while a transfer to a donor-advised fund is an irrevocable gift.) The courts are rejecting these arguments.

Another contention is that these transfers are not *gifts* in the first instance (and thus are not payments giving rise to a charitable deduction). The ostensible reason: The *donor* has not, by reason of the agreement with the charity, parted with all of his, her, or its right, title, and interest in and to the gift money or property. To assess this, the IRS applies a set of *material restrictions* rules that were promulgated in the private foundation setting to test whether a private foundation has properly terminated its status when granting its assets to one or more public charities.

Still another issue is whether the charitable organizations that maintain donor-advised funds are publicly supported charities. The gifts (assuming that is what they are) to the charity (assuming that is what it is) are forms of public support for purposes of both the donative publicly supported charity and the service-provider public charity. Almost always, however, these entities are the donative type. Then, when a grant is made from an account within a public charity to another charity, it can be public support for the grantee. Some in the IRS and elsewhere are uncomfortable with the view that a gift (or a portion of it) can constitute public support for two charities. That is, nonetheless, the case.

The ultimate criticism of donor-advised funds is that they constitute a way to avoid the private foundation restrictions. That is, as a matter of literal fact, true. They are, however, a *lawful* way to sidestep the private foundation rules. Congress is likely to legislate limitations and requirements regarding contributions to and operations of donor-advised funds.

CHARITABLE GIVING SUBTLETIES

There is far more to the law of charitable giving than a simple transfer of money or property from a donor to a donee. A sample of subtleties in charitable giving circumstances, some involving deductible gifts and some not, follows.

Incidental Benefit

As a general rule, a donor is entitled to a charitable deduction for a contribution of money or property to a charitable organization where the donor has given all of his, her, or its full title, rights, and interest in the property. That is, if the "donor" receives from the charity, in exchange, value approximately equal to the "gift" amount, there is, in fact, no gift-and thus no charitable deduction. (In some circumstances, there can be a charitable gift element when benefits are provided to the donor that have value less than that of the money or property transferred [see Chapter 12].)

When, however, a benefit provided to a donor by a donee is *incidental*, the charitable contribution deduction is not defeated. Token items provided in exchange for a charitable gift—such as address labels, key chains, and pins—are often lawfully disregarded when ascertaining a charitable deduction. Another illustration of an incidental benefit arising out of a charitable gift is the *naming opportunity*; a person can, for example, make a charitable gift and have a building or other facility (such as a stadium or room) named in honor of him or her and still receive a full charitable deduction. A donor can contribute land to a charitable organization and obtain a charitable deduction for its fair value, even though land owned by the donor that is adjacent to the gifted property is enhanced in value. In two of many IRS and court rulings on this point:

- An organization made a deductible contribution to a police department to assist the department in offering rewards for information leading to the conviction of individuals engaging in criminal activity in the community in which the donor organization was located.
- An individual made a deductible contribution to a charitable organization of a tract of land and retained the right during his lifetime to train his hunting dogs on the trails extending throughout the tract.

Absence of Value Transferred

A charitable contribution deduction can be denied because nothing of substance or value was transferred to a charitable organization. For example, a charitable deduction for the transfer by a corporation to a charitable entity of a "film library" was denied by a court on the ground that what was conveyed (negatives) had little value. (The donor claimed a deduction of more than $10 million.) Likewise, a corporation that believed it was making a gift of property to a state for use as a park had its claim for a charitable deduction rejected, with a court ruling that the state already owned the property by virtue of the doctrine of adverse possession. Another illustration of this rule is the *circular gift*, where persons contrive to pass money from one entity to another so as to generate a charitable deduction, when in fact the organizations are an "integrated whole" and therefore nothing of economic substance occurred.

Perhaps the best example of all of this point was provided in the case of two individuals who were granted a permit by the federal government to graze livestock on a parcel of government-owned land in a national forest adjacent to their ranch. The ranch was later sold; the grazing permit reverted to the government. These individuals nonetheless claimed a charitable contribution deduction for the alleged value of the permit. A court concluded that, because the federal government already held all right, title, and interest in the property, it did not receive any value when the permit was waived back to it. As this court sagely observed, "[o]ne cannot donate something one does not own or possess."

Anticipatory Income Assignments

A transaction may appear superficially to be a charitable gift of property but, in actuality, be an anticipatory assignment of the income from the property that would otherwise have flowed directly to the transferor. In other words, the "donor" is endeavoring to avoid paying income tax by trying to divert the income to another person (in these instances, a charity). An anticipatory assignment of income occurs in the charitable giving setting when a person has certain rights in the contributed property that have so matured that the person has the right to the proceeds from the property at the time the transfer is made. If the transaction is an assignment of income, there may not be a charitable contribution deduction for the fair market value of the property transferred; the transferor may be taxable on the proceeds diverted to the charitable organization and the charitable deduction (if any) may be determined as if the gift were of the after-tax income.

Note: This doctrine is similar to the step transaction doctrine (see Chapter 2).

The distinction between a gift of property and an assignment of the property's income is rarely easy to make. These rules are applied on a case-by-case basis. A major factor in the court cases is the extent of the "donor's" control over the timing of the generation of the income. One court applied the doctrine because the "realities and substance" rather than the "hypothetical possibilities" of the matter showed that the donor knew that the likelihood that property would not soon be yielding income (taxable to the "donor") was remote. By contrast, another court held that the donor did not know with "virtual certainty" that income returns were imminent; the donor merely had knowledge that the creation of the income was a "reasonable probability."

Mandatory Gifts

The concept of the *mandatory gift* has an oxymoronic ring to it, and for good reason: As mentioned, deductible charitable contributions are required to be *voluntary*. The Supreme Court ruled that a payment to a charitable organization proceeding from the "constraining force of a moral or legal duty" is not a charitable gift. There are transfers to charitable organizations that are mandated by statute, regulation, court order, contract, or even the charitable entity itself.

An individual was precluded, by a court, from deducting a sum paid to fill a gully in a city street, inasmuch as the payment was made in compliance with an order issued by the city. A national environmental organization was chastised, in 2005, by a congressional committee for selling parcels of land that became subject to conservation easements to private parties at a reduced price, then requiring the purchasers to make ostensible charitable contributions to the charity (often at closing), the amount of which just happened to be the difference between the discounted sales price and the fair value of the property. The IRS is ruling that so-called down payment assistance organizations are serving private purposes and are "encouraging the avoidance of federal income tax" when they require sellers of the homes to make "voluntary contributions" to the charity, the amount of which is determined by the financial assistance provided by the charity to the purchasers of the homes; the agency is ruling that the payments by the sellers are "fees received in exchange for the sale of a program-related service."

CHARITABLE PLEDGES

The making of a charitable pledge—a promise to make a charitable contribution—does not give rise to an income tax charitable contribution deduction. Any deduction that is occasioned by the pledge, such as it may be, is determined at the time the pledge is satisfied.

The enforceability of a charitable pledge is a matter of state law. Some states require the existence of consideration as a prerequisite to the existence of an enforceable pledge. Other states will enforce a charitable pledge on broader, social grounds, such as reliance. A typical circumstance concerning the latter approach arises where a person pledges a significant gift to a charity for a building and the charity commences construction of it in reliance on the forthcoming gift.

Usually, a pledge is made by a potential donor in the form of a written statement—a promise to the potential charitable donee of one or more contributions to be made sometime in the future. Pursuant to a *funding agreement,* a person may commit in writing to make multiple contributions to a charitable organization over a stated period for purposes such as general operations or endowment; the charitable contribution (and resulting deduction) arises in each year of actual payment. A variation on this approach is a pledge to charity of a stock option; the pledge produces an income tax charitable deduction in the year in which the charitable donee, having acquired the option, exercises it.

PUBLIC POLICY CONSIDERATIONS

A doctrine in the law of nonprofit organizations states that an entity cannot be tax-exempt as a charitable one if it engages in an activity that is contrary to public policy. For example, the U.S. Supreme Court held that it is contrary to federal public policy for a private school to engage in racially discriminatory practices as to its student body and faculty; this type of discrimination was found to bar tax exemption of the school as a charitable or educational organization. This doctrine is infrequently applied in the charitable giving setting.

In one case, an individual contributed certain Native American artifacts to a museum; a portion of the collection consisted of items covered by eagle and migratory bird protection laws. The IRS contended that there should not be any charitable deduction for these gifts, on the ground that acquisition of the items was contrary to public policy. Nonetheless, a court held that these donors had a sufficient ownership interest in these items to contribute them to the museum, even though the donors may have violated federal law when they acquired the items.

There are other aspects of the public policy doctrine; one concerns the efficacy of the imposition of certain conditions subsequent on the terms and conditions of a gift. In the principal case, an individual transferred certain property interests to a trust benefiting his children. The instrument making the gift provided that, should there be a final determination that any part of the transfer was subject to gift tax, all the parties agreed that the excess property decreed to be subject to the tax would automatically be deemed not included in the conveyance and be the sole property of the individual, free of trust.

The court held that this provision was a condition subsequent that was void because it was contrary to public policy. It wrote that "[w]e do not think that the gift tax can be avoided by any such device as this." A contrary holding, wrote the court, would mean that, "upon a decision that the gift was subject to tax, the court making such decision must hold it not a gift and therefore not subject to tax." This holding would be made in the context of litigation to which the donees of the property were not parties, so the decision would not be binding on them and they would be able to enforce the gift notwithstanding the court's decision. Wrote the court: "It is manifest that a condition which involves this sort of trifling with the judicial process cannot be sustained."

This condition subsequently was found to be contrary to public policy for three reasons. First, "it has a tendency to discourage the collection of the [gift] tax by the public officials charged with its collection, since the only effect of an attempt to enforce the tax would be to defeat the gift."

Second, the "effect of the condition would be to obstruct the administration of justice by requiring the courts to pass upon a moot case." That is, if the condition "were valid and the gift were held subject to tax, the only effect of the holding would be to defeat the gift so that it would not be subject to tax." The consequence would be that the donor "would thus secure the opinion of the court as to the taxability of the gift, when there would be before the court no controversy whatever with the taxing authorities which the court could decide, the only possible controversy being as to the validity of the gift and being between the donor and persons not before the court."

Third, the condition "is to the effect that the final judgment of a court is to be held for naught because of the provision of an indenture necessarily before the court when the judgment is rendered." The court noted that gift tax liability cannot be the subject of a federal court declaratory judgment. The condition thus "could not be given the effect of invalidating a judgment which had been rendered when the instrument containing the condition was before the court, since all matters are merged in the judgment." The court rephrased its distress with the voided condition: The condition "is not to become operative until there has been a judgment; but after the judgment has been rendered it cannot become operative because the matter involved is concluded by the judgment."

In a similar case, a husband and wife transferred shares of stock to their three children. At the time of the gifts, these individuals executed a gift adjustment agreement that was intended to ensure that the parents' gift tax liability for the stock transfers would not exceed the unified credit against tax to which they were entitled at the time. This agreement stated that, if it should be finally determined for federal gift tax purposes that the fair market value of the transferred stock either was less than or greater than $2,000 per share, an adjustment would be made to the number of shares conveyed, so that each donor would have transferred $50,000 worth of stock to each donee.

The court in this case declined to give effect to the gift adjustment agreement, inasmuch as honoring the agreement would run counter to public policy concerns. It wrote that a "condition that causes a part of a gift to lapse if it is determined for Federal gift tax purposes that the value of the gift exceeds a given amount, so as to avoid a gift tax deficiency," involves a "trifling with the judicial process." If valid, this type of condition would "compel" the court to "issue, in effect, a declaratory judgment as to the stock's value, while rendering the case moot as a consequence." Yet there was "no assurance that the [parents] will actually reclaim a portion of the stock previously conveyed to their sons, and our decision on the question of valuation in a gift tax suit is not binding upon the sons, who are not parties to this action." The sons, the court added, "may yet enforce the gifts."

There is another line of law, captured by this quotation: "The purpose of Congress in providing deductions for charitable gifts was to encourage gifts for charitable purposes; and in order to make such purposes effective, there must be a reasonable probability that the charity actually will receive the use and benefit of the gift, for which the deduction is claimed." A dissenting opinion in a court case stitched these aspects of the case law together in an attempt to defeat charitable contributions that the dissenter viewed as caused by an increase in value of property facilitated by the court majority. The dissent concluded that the "possibility of an increased charitable deduction serves to discourage [the IRS] from collecting tax on the transaction because any attempt to enforce the tax due on the transaction is of no advantage to the fisc." It argued that the charity involved would never be able to benefit from the gifts, and characterized the charitable deduction as "against public policy" and "plainly wrong."

In perhaps the best application of the public policy doctrine in the charitable giving setting occurred when the IRS issued regulations concerning charitable lead trusts (see Chapter 9) in an effort to stop the practice of using the lives of seriously ill individuals to measure the income interest period, so as to move income and assets away from charitable beneficiaries prematurely and to private beneficiaries instead. The IRS observed that, "similar to the vulture, the promoters of this form of charitable lead trust circle in on mortally ill people," thus giving rise to the term *vulture* or *ghoul* charitable lead trust. The agency stated: "Marketing schemes that exploit the misfortunes of some for the benefit of others are contrary to public policy."

SOME STATISTICS

Annual charitable giving in the United States is nearing $300 billion. (In 2005, the precise amount was $260.28 billion.) About 75 percent of this giving is from living individuals. Other gifts (or grants) are derived from business corporations, private foundations, and estates (bequests and devises). Approximately one-third of annual charitable giving is to religious entities. The other donees, in descending order of amounts received, are educational institutions, health care organizations, arts and humanities entities, public-society benefit organizations, environmental groups, and international organizations.

There are about 1 million charitable organizations registered with the Internal Revenue Service; that number continues to grow.

Hundreds of thousands of other charitable organizations exist. Overall, the U.S. nonprofit sector is edging close to accounting for about 10 percent of the nation's economy. The sector employs more people than any of these industries: agriculture, mining, construction, transportation, communications, other public utilities, finance, insurance, and real estate. The nonprofit component of the United States generates revenue that exceeds the gross domestic product of all but six foreign countries (China, France, Germany, Italy, Japan, and the United Kingdom).

SUMMARY

This chapter provided basic information about the laws that pertain to charitable giving. The discussion started with an analysis of the fundamentals, including the meaning of the terms *charitable organization* and *charitable contribution*. The chapter also offered an introduction to the charitable deduction, summarized the differences between the terms *public charity* and *private foundation*, identified the various types of donors, and inventoried the factors affecting the deductibility of gifts. It discussed some of today's subtle charitable gift situations and summarized the law concerning charitable pledges. The law as to grantor trusts and donor-advised funds was explained. The chapter concluded with a look at applicability of the public policy doctrine, and statistics pertaining to charitable giving and the charitable sector generally. These topics provide the reader with the fundamentals of the law of charitable giving. The balance of the book is devoted to an examination of specific law subjects and issues. This frame, coupled with the information provided in the remainder of the book, provide the nonlawyer with a usable understanding of charitable giving law.

CHAPTER 2

Contributions of Money and Property

The purpose of this chapter is to summarize the fundamental federal tax law rules concerning charitable contributions of money and other property. The calculation of the charitable contribution deduction must be made under these rules before application of the general percentage limitations (see Chapter 4). Contributions of money or property, where the donor is creating an interest in the item being transferred, are subject to other rules (see Chapters 7 and 9). Determining the charitable deduction arising from a gift of property can be more complex than many individuals realize. Specifically, this chapter will:

- Describe the rules concerning charitable contributions of money
- Explain the tax law distinctions as to types of property
- Summarize the factors underlying a charitable deduction for a gift of property
- Introduce the deduction reduction rules
- Explain the rules concerning gifts of property for unrelated use
- Summarize the step transaction doctrine
- Review the law as to valuation of contributed property

CONTRIBUTIONS OF MONEY

An individual or other donor may make a contribution of money— usually U.S. currency—to a charitable organization. The resulting charitable deduction is based on the amount of funds transferred.

A gift of money in the form of currency of a country other than the United States (such as a contribution of a coin collection) may be treated as a gift of property other than money; that is, the amount of the deduction may be based on the inherent value of the currency rather than its face amount.

When a contribution is made in the form of U.S. funds, there is, of course, no issue as to valuation, as there can be in connection with contributions of other property (see the following section). Gifts of money nonetheless can be subject to substantiation requirements (see Chapter 12).

NATURE OF PROPERTY

Aside from the eligibility of the gift recipient (see Chapter 1), the other basic element in determining whether a charitable contribution is deductible is the nature of the property given. Basically, the distinctions are between outright giving and planned giving (see Chapter 9) and between gifts of cash and gifts of property. In many instances, the tax law differentiates between personal property and real property and between tangible property and intangible property (securities).

The federal income tax treatment of gifts of property is dependent on whether the property is capital gain property. The tax law makes a distinction between *long-term capital gain* and *short-term capital gain*. Property that is not capital gain property is *ordinary income property*. These three terms are based on the tax classification of the type of revenue that would be generated on sale of the property. Short-term capital gain property is generally treated the same as ordinary income property. Therefore, the actual distinction is between capital gain property (really long-term capital gain property) and ordinary income property.

Capital gain property is a capital asset that has appreciated in value and, if sold, would give rise to long-term capital gain. To result in long-term capital gain, property must be held for at least 12 months. Most forms of capital gain property are securities and real estate.

The charitable deduction for capital gain property is often equal to its fair market value or at least is computed using that value. Gifts of ordinary income property generally produce a deduction equivalent to the donor's cost basis in the property. The law provides exceptions to this basis-only rule; an example is a gift by a corporation out of its inventory (see Chapter 6). A charitable deduction based on the full fair market value of an item of appreciated property (with no recognition of the built-in capital gain) is a critical feature of the federal tax law incentives for charitable giving.

CONTRIBUTIONS OF PROPERTY IN GENERAL

The law of charitable giving becomes more complex in the case of a donor who makes a contribution of property rather than a contribution of money. At the outset, a determination must be made as to the value of the property. This value is known as the *fair market value* of the property.

In many instances, the federal income tax charitable contribution deduction for contributions of property is based on the fair market value of that property. There are instances, however, when that value must be reduced for purposes of computing the charitable deduction. Generally, when this reduction in the deduction is required, the amount that is deductible is the amount equal to the donor's basis in the property.

Because the deduction for a gift of property is often based on the fair market value of the property, a donor can benefit when the property has increased in value since the date on which the donor acquired the property. The property is said to have *appreciated* in value; property in this circumstance is known as *appreciated property*. When certain requirements are satisfied, a donor is entitled to a charitable deduction based on the full fair market value of the property.

This rule—allowance of the charitable deduction based on the full value of an item of property—is one of the rules in the tax law that is most beneficial to donors. It is particularly so when one considers that the donor in this circumstance is not required to recognize any gain on the transfer. The gain is the amount that would have been recognized had the donor sold the property; it is sometimes referred to as the *appreciation element*.

The donor's ability to have a charitable deduction based on the fair market value of the property and not recognize gain on the appreciation element in the property is viewed by some as an unwarranted benefit to donors and a violation of tax policy. Indeed, in some instances, such as a bargain sale (see Chapter 7), recognition of gain is required.

Likewise, a loss is not recognized when an item of property is contributed to a charity. In this circumstance, the donor should sell the property, experience the loss, and contribute the sales proceeds to charity. By contrast, the donor of appreciated property is usually best advised to contribute the property to a charitable organization rather than sell the property and donate the after-tax proceeds to the charity.

The donor's ability to take a charitable deduction for a contribution of property, based on the fair market value of the property, depends on several factors. Chief among these are the:

- Nature of the property contributed
- Tax classification of the charitable donee
- Use to which the charitable donee puts the property

As to the first of these factors, the federal tax law categorizes items of property in three ways:

1. Long-term capital gain property
2. Short-term capital gain property
3. Ordinary income property

As to the second of these factors, the federal tax law classifies entities as to which deductible charitable contributions can be made regarding:

- Public charitable organizations
- Private foundations
- Governmental bodies
- Other types of tax-exempt organizations (such as veteran's organizations) (see Chapter 1)

As to the third of these factors, the federal law divides the use to which a charitable organization puts donated property as:

- A use that is related to the donee organization's tax-exempt purpose (*related use*)
- A use that is not related to the donee organization's tax-exempt purpose (*unrelated use*)

The extent to which a contribution of property is deductible for federal income tax purposes is dependent on the interplay of these factors, plus:

- The value of the property
- The percentage limitations (see Chapter 4)
- Compliance with the substantiation rules (see Chapter 12)

CONTRIBUTIONS OF LONG-TERM CAPITAL GAIN PROPERTY IN GENERAL

When a donor makes a contribution of *long-term capital gain property* to a public charitable organization, the charitable deduction is generally based on the full fair market value of the property. There generally is no need for the donor to recognize the capital gain element. This rule is also generally applicable when the donee is a governmental entity.

For example, an individual made a contribution of 10 shares of publicly traded securities to a public charitable organization. This stock, which constituted long-term capital gain property in the hands of this individual, had a total fair market value of $3,000. Consequently, this individual was entitled to a federal income tax charitable contribution deduction based on the $3,000 amount for the year of the gift.

The rule often is not applicable when the donee is a charitable organization other than a public charitable organization. In that instance, the charitable deduction generally is confined to the donor's basis in the property.

CONTRIBUTIONS OF ORDINARY INCOME PROPERTY

The federal tax law places limitations on the deductibility of property that, if sold, would give rise to gain that is not long-term capital gain. This type of property, which is termed *ordinary income property*, includes *short-term capital gain property*.

Federal tax law provides a rule requiring the modification of what would otherwise be the charitable deduction for a contribution of property that is ordinary income property.

Ordinary Income Property Defined

The categories of property for charitable giving purposes have been discussed. Again, ordinary income property is property that has appreciated in value, any portion of the gain on which would give rise to ordinary income (or short-term capital gain) if the property had been sold by the donor at its fair market value at the time of the charitable gift. Ordinary income is income that is not long-term capital gain. For these purposes, ordinary income and short-term capital gain are regarded as the same. Thus, ordinary income property is property that, if sold at its fair market value by the donor at the time of its contribution to a charitable organization, would generate a gain that is not long-term capital gain.

Examples of ordinary income property are:

- Property held by the donor primarily for sale to customers in the ordinary course of a trade or business (inventory)
- A capital asset held for a period of time that is less than the period required to cause the property to become long-term capital gain property (short-term capital gain property)
- A work of art created by the donor
- A manuscript created by the donor
- Letters and memoranda prepared by or for the donor
- Stock acquired in a nontaxable transaction that, if sold, would generate ordinary income
- Stock in a collapsible corporation that, if sold, would generate ordinary income
- Stock in certain foreign corporations that, if sold, would generate ordinary income
- Property used in a trade or business, treated as a capital asset, if gain would have been recognized, on sale of the property by the donor at its fair market value at the time of the contribution, as ordinary income by reason of the application of recapture rules

The term *ordinary income property* does not include an income interest in respect of which a federal income tax charitable contribution deduction is allowed.

It is the position of the IRS that, when individuals purchase items with the intent of retaining them for the requisite capital gain holding period and thereafter donating them to a charitable organization for the purpose of generating a charitable contribution deduction (in an amount greater than the acquisition price), the individuals are engaged in a *charitable donation venture*. The consequence of this view is that the properties held for contribution purposes are items of inventory of the venture and thus are forms of ordinary income property. This position, however, is being rejected in the courts.

In one instance, the IRS ruled that an individual who purchased books at a volume discount from a company located in a country where the retail price was fixed by law and then imported them into the United States, warehoused the books for a period just beyond the capital gain holding period, and then donated them to charitable organizations was engaged in an activity tantamount to the activities of a book dealer, so that the books were held to be ordinary income property. In another case, the IRS ruled that an individual who raised ornamental plants as a hobby and each year donated a large number of them to various charitable organizations was engaged in activities substantially equivalent to those of commercial dealers, so that the contributed property was held to be ordinary income property. The agency also so ruled in an instance involving an individual, not an art dealer, who purchased a substantial part of the total limited edition of a particular lithograph print and contributed the prints to various art museums.

Deduction Reduction Rule

Often, as noted, the rule for the deduction arising from a gift of property to a charitable organization is that the amount of the deduction is equal to the fair market value of the property at the time of the gift. In the case of a charitable gift of ordinary income property, however, the amount of the charitable contribution for the gift of the property must be reduced by the amount of gain that would have been recognized as gain, which is not long-term capital gain, if the property had been sold by the donor at its fair market value determined at the time of the contribution to the charitable organization. The amount of gain that is taken into account in making this reduction is sometimes termed the *ordinary income element.*

Consequently, this deduction reduction rule basically means that a donor's deduction for a contribution of an item of ordinary income property to a charitable organization is confined to the donor's basis in the property. The amount that is deductible is the fair market value of the property, reduced by the amount that is equal to the ordinary income element. In one case, a company that contributed its film library to a charitable organization was advised by the IRS that its charitable contribution deduction was zero, in that the library was akin to letters and memoranda and thus not a capital asset. Because the costs associated with establishing the library were expensed as incurred, the basis in the property was zero. The value of the property contributed had to be reduced by its full amount.

This rule applies:

- Irrespective of whether the donor is an individual or a corporation

- Irrespective of the tax classification of the charitable organization that is the donee (e.g., public or private charity [see Chapter 1])
- Irrespective of whether the charitable contribution is made to or for the use of a charitable organization (see Chapter 8)
- To a gift of ordinary income property prior to application of the appropriate percentage limitation(s) (see Chapter 4)

As an illustration, an individual on June 15 contributed to a charitable organization shares of stock having a fair market value of $5,000. This individual acquired the stock on the immediately previous March 1 for $3,000. The resulting charitable deduction was $3,000 (the amount equal to the donor's basis in the stock). Technically, this donor was required to reduce the potential charitable deduction ($5,000) by the ordinary income element inherent in the property ($2,000). This result occurred because this individual did not hold the stock long enough for the shares to become long-term capital gain property.

Special Rules of Inapplicability

This deduction reduction rule does not apply to reduce the amount of the charitable contribution when, by reason of the transfer of the contributed property, ordinary income or capital gain is recognized by the donor in the same tax year in which the contribution is made. Thus, if recognition of the income or gain occurs in the same tax year in which the contribution is made, this rule is inapplicable when income or gain is recognized on:

- The transfer of an installment obligation to a charitable organization
- The transfer of an obligation issued at a discount to a charitable organization
- The assignment of income to a charitable organization

Also, this deduction rule does not apply to a charitable contribution by a nonresident alien individual or a foreign corporation of property, the sale or other disposition of which within the United States would have resulted in gain that is not effectively connected with the conduct of a trade or business in the United States.

CERTAIN CONTRIBUTIONS OF CAPITAL GAIN PROPERTY

In general, contributions of long-term capital gain property to public charitable organizations are deductible, with the federal income tax charitable contribution deduction computed on the basis of the fair market value of the property.

When contributions are made to a charitable organization that is not a public charitable organization, however, a deduction reduction rule applies. Nonetheless, this rule does not apply with respect to gifts to:

- Private operating foundations
- Pass-through foundations
- Common fund foundations

General Deduction Reduction Rule

The general deduction reduction rule is: When a charitable gift of capital gain property is made, the amount of the charitable deduction that would otherwise be determined must be reduced by the amount of gain that would have been long-term capital gain if the property contributed had been sold by the donor at its fair market value, determined at the time of the contribution, when the gift is to or for the use of a private foundation (with the three exceptions just listed).

In these circumstances, if the contributed property is capital gain property, the charitable deduction that would otherwise be determined must be reduced by the amount of the unrealized appreciation in value. The charitable deduction under these rules is confined to the basis in the property.

As an illustration, an individual owned a painting that she purchased for $25,000 and had a value of $50,000. The property was long-term capital gain property. She contributed this painting to a standard (nonoperating) private foundation. The resulting charitable contribution deduction was $25,000. If the painting had been contributed to a private operating foundation or a public charity, however, the resulting charitable deduction (to the extent of this rule) would have been $50,000.

This rule applies:

- Irrespective of whether the donor is an individual or a corporation

- Irrespective of whether the charitable contribution is made to or for the use of a charitable organization (see Chapter 8)
- To a gift of property prior to application of the appropriate percentage limitation(s) (see Chapter 4)

Qualified Appreciated Stock

An exception to the deduction reduction rule is that it does not apply in the case of a contribution of qualified appreciated stock. That is, when this exception is applicable, the charitable deduction for a contribution of stock to a private foundation is based on the fair market value of the stock at the time of the gift.

Basically, the term *qualified appreciated stock* means any stock for which (as of the date of the contribution) market quotations are readily available on an established securities market, and that is capital gain property.

In the sole court case on the point, it was held that stock contributed to a private foundation did not give rise to a charitable deduction based on its fair market value, because the stock did not constitute qualified appreciated stock. The stock involved was that of a bank holding company. The shares were not listed on the New York Stock Exchange, the American Stock Exchange, or any city or regional stock exchange, nor were the shares regularly traded in the national or any regional over-the-counter market for which published quotations are available. The shares were not those of a mutual fund. A brokerage firm occasionally provided a suggested share price based on the new asset value of the bank. The procedure for someone wishing to purchase or sell shares of the corporation was to contact an officer of the bank or a local stock brokerage firm specializing in the shares. An attempt would be made to match a potential seller with a potential buyer; the shares were not frequently sold. The court held that the stock could not constitute qualified appreciated stock because the market quotations requirement had not been satisfied.

The term *qualified appreciated stock* does not include any stock of a corporation contributed by a donor to a private foundation to the extent that the amount of stock contributed (including prior gifts of the stock by the donor) exceeds 10 percent (in value) of all of the outstanding stock of the corporation. In making this calculation, an individual must take into account all contributions made by any member of his or her family.

CONTRIBUTIONS OF PROPERTY FOR UNRELATED USE

Another special rule concerning calculation of the charitable deduction potentially applies when a donor makes a contribution of tangible personal property to a charitable organization.

General Rule

The special rule is: When a charitable gift of tangible personal property is made, the amount of the charitable deduction that would otherwise be determined must be reduced by the amount of gain that would have been long-term capital gain if the property contributed had been sold by the donor at its fair market value, determined at the time of the contribution, when the use by the donee is unrelated to the donee's tax-exempt purpose. This rule also applies when the donee is a governmental unit, if the use to which the contributed property is put is for a purpose other than an exclusively public purpose.

In these circumstances, when the contributed property is capital gain property, the charitable deduction that would otherwise be determined must be reduced by the amount of the unrealized appreciation in value.

This rule applies:

- Irrespective of whether the donor is an individual or a corporation
- Irrespective of the tax classification of the charitable organization that is the donee (e.g., public or private charity [see Chapter 1])
- Irrespective of whether the charitable contribution is made to or for the use of a charitable organization (see Chapter 8)
- To a gift of tangible personal property prior to application of the appropriate percentage limitation(s) (see Chapter 4)

When tangible personal property is put to a related use by the recipient charitable organization, the charitable deduction is based on the fair market value of the property (i.e., there is no deduction for the capital gain element).

Unrelated Use

The term *unrelated use* means a use of an item of contributed property by a charitable organization that is not related to the purpose or function constituting the basis of the tax exemption for the charitable organization, or by a governmental unit that is for a purpose other than an exclusively public purpose.

As an example, an individual owned a painting that he purchased for $25,000 and that had a value of $50,000. In his hands, the property was long-term capital gain property. This individual contributed the painting to a tax-exempt educational institution, which used the painting for educational purposes by placing it in its library for display and study by art students. Because this use of the painting was a related use, the resulting charitable contribution deduction computed under this rule was $50,000.

If a charitable donee sells an item of tangible personal property donated to it, this deduction reduction rule is triggered, because sale of the property is not a related use of the property. Thus, donors of tangible personal property should exercise caution when contemplating a gift of the property, particularly when the donor knows the property is going to be promptly sold (such as a gift to support an auction).

As an illustration, assume the facts of the prior example, except the educational institution decided to promptly sell the painting and use the proceeds of the sale for educational purposes. This use of the property was an unrelated use; the donor's charitable deduction computed under this rule was $25,000 ($50,000 reduced by the long-term capital gain element of $25,000). This is the tax law outcome even though the proceeds of the sale were put to a related use.

If furnishings contributed to a charitable organization are used by it in its offices and buildings in the course of carrying out its exempt functions, the use of the property is not an unrelated use. If a set or collection of items of tangible personal property is contributed to a charitable organization or governmental unit, the use of the set or collection is not an unrelated use if the donee sells or otherwise disposes of only an insubstantial portion of the set or collection. The use by a trust of tangible personal property contributed to it for the benefit of a charitable organization is an unrelated use if the use by the trust is one that would have been unrelated if used directly by the charitable organization. This last rule is of particular importance in the context of planned giving, where property contributed is often given to a trust, such as a charitable remainder trust (see Chapter 9).

A donor who makes a charitable contribution of tangible personal property to or for the use of a charitable organization or governmental unit may treat the property as not being put to an unrelated use by the donee if the donor establishes that the property is not in fact put to an unrelated use by the donee, or at the time of the contribution or at the time the contribution is treated as made, it is reasonable to anticipate that the property will not be put to an unrelated use by the donee.

In the case of a contribution of tangible personal property to or for the use of a museum, if the object donated is of a general type normally retained by the museum or other museums for museum purposes, it is considered reasonable for the donor to anticipate, unless the donor has actual knowledge to the contrary, that the object will not be put to an unrelated use by the donee, whether the object is later sold or exchanged by the donee or not.

STEP TRANSACTION DOCTRINE

As a general rule, a contribution of appreciated capital gain property to a public charitable organization is deductible on the basis of the fair market value of the property and the capital gain element is not taxable to the donor. There is, however, a huge trap in this context, one that has snared many unwitting donors.

It is all too easy for a donor and donee to succumb to these temptations. The charitable donee often does not want to hold the gift property and thus is delighted that a prospective buyer is present. The donor may see the prearranged sale as a favor to the charity, saving the charity the need to pursue purchasers of the property. The step transaction doctrine is of no consequence in law to the charitable donee (absent fraud); the donor, however, can have what looks like a large appreciated property charitable deduction undone.

General Principles

If the donee charitable organization sells the property soon after the contribution is made, the donor may be placed in the position of having to recognize, for federal income tax purposes, the capital gain element. This can happen when, under the facts and circumstances surrounding the gift, the donee was legally obligated to sell the gift property to a purchaser that was prearranged by the donor. In this situation, the law regards the transaction as a sale of the property by the "donor" to the third-party purchaser and a gift of the after-tax sales proceeds to the charitable organization.

This is the *step transaction doctrine*, under which two or more ostensibly independent transactions (here, the gift to and subsequent sale by the donee) are consolidated and treated as a single transaction for federal tax purposes. The key to avoiding this tax-adverse outcome is to be certain that the charitable organization was not legally bound at the time of the gift to sell the property to the prospective purchaser.

This sidestep of the step transaction doctrine has its origins in a famous court case, where a gift of stock in a closely held corporation was made to a charitable organization, followed by a pre-arranged redemption. The transaction was not recharacterized as a redemption between the donor and the redeeming corporation and a later gift of the redemption proceeds to the charity. This was the outcome, although the donor held voting control over both the corporation and the charitable organization. The IRS lost this case because the charity was not legally bound to redeem the stock, nor was the corporation in a position to compel the redemption.

Illustrative Litigation

The step transaction rule has been and continues to be the subject of considerable litigation. Several court opinions illustrate the nature of this controversy. In one instance, a court ruled that a gift to a charitable organization of the long-term capital gains in certain commodity futures contracts gave rise to a charitable contribution deduction and that the gifts and subsequent sales of the contracts were not step transactions within a unified plan.

This case concerned an individual who formed a private operating foundation in the early 1970s and had been president of it since it was established. From time to time, he contributed futures contracts to the foundation and claimed charitable contribution deductions for these gifts. In 1974 he obtained a private letter ruling from the IRS that the charitable contributions deductions were proper and that no gain need be recognized when the foundation sold the contracts.

In 1981, however, the federal tax law was changed. Beginning that year, all commodities futures contracts acquired and positions established had to be marked to market at year-end and the gains (or losses) had to be characterized as being 60 percent long-term capital gains (or losses) and 40 percent short-term gains (or losses), regardless of how long the contracts had been held. This revision in the law posed a problem for this individual because the charitable deduction for a gift of short-term capital gain property is confined to the donor's basis in the property; there is no deduction for the full fair market value of the property (as there is for most gifts of long-term capital gain property). He solved the dilemma by donating only the long-term gain portion of the futures contracts.

In 1982 this individual entered into an agreement under which he contributed the long-term capital gains of selected futures contracts from his personal accounts at a brokerage house and retained for himself the short-term capital gains. For the most part, the selected contracts were sold on the same day the gift was made, and the portions of the proceeds representing the long-term capital gains were transferred to an account of the foundation at the same brokerage house. The donor chose the futures contracts to be donated according to the funding needs of the foundation and the amount of unrealized long-term capital gains inherent in the contracts. Once the contracts were transferred to a special account, they were to be immediately sold, pursuant to a standing instruction. On audit for 1982, the IRS took the position that the full amount of the capital gains on the sales of these contracts was includable in this individual's taxable income; the IRS also disallowed the charitable deductions for that year and prior years. The IRS's position rested on two arguments: (1) the transfers of a portion of the gain to the foundation were a taxable anticipatory assignment of income; and (2) the step transaction doctrine should apply, thereby collapsing separate interrelated transactions into a single transaction for tax purposes.

The step transaction doctrine was inapplicable in this instance, the individual argued, because no prearrangements were made with respect to the gifts. He maintained that he donated all of his interest in the long-term capital gain portions of the futures contracts, free and clear. The IRS, by contrast, contended that the gift transfers should be treated together with the later future sales and division of proceeds as a single transaction. The government argued that this individual's plan was to meet the foundation's operating needs by selling selected futures contracts with unrealized appreciation of equal amounts. Rather than donating cash, this argument went, he tried to donate the futures contracts with a restriction that he would keep the short-term capital gains on their sale.

The court said that the question in the case was "[h]ow related were the decisions to sell the futures to their donation?" The court looked to the matter of control and found that the donation agreements and powers of attorney executed by the individual supported his position that the trustees of the foundation had control over the sale of the futures contracts once they were transferred into the broker's special account. Thus, the court concluded that the issue of the donor's control over the sale of the contracts "was not such that the donations and sales could be viewed as step transactions encompassed within a unified plan."

As this case illustrated, the question posed by the step transaction doctrine involves the relationship among various seemingly independent transactions. In this case, the question was: How related were the decisions to sell the futures contracts to the contributions of them? Had some prearrangement existed by which the individual donated selected contracts to cover the charitable organization's operating expenses, and had he received in return short-term gains without having to pay taxes on the full amount of the futures contracts, the transfers could have been viewed as a step transaction within a larger plan. In this connection, one court held that "if, by means of restrictions on a gift to a charitable donee, either explicitly formulated or implied or understood, the donor so restricts the discretion of the donee that all that remains to be done is to carry out the donor's prearranged plan for designation of the stock, the donor had effectively realized the gain inherent in the appreciated property."

As to this case, the individual claimed that the sales were not prearranged but rather were the prudent acts of the trustees of a charitable organization in need of operating funds. The IRS argued that the standing instruction reflected a prearranged plan to use the charity to sell the futures contracts, cover its needs with the long-term gains, and enable the individual to keep the short-term gains without having to pay taxes on the entire proceeds of the sale. The court held, however, that there was no evidence to suggest that the individual was the source of the standing instruction, and thus that his control over the sale of the contracts was not such that the contributions and sales could be viewed as step transactions encompassed within a unified plan.

In a similar case, a court held that contribution of appreciated futures contracts to a charitable organization controlled by an individual did not result in income to the individual when the contracts were sold shortly after they had been donated. The court dismissed the importance of control between the business and the recipient charitable organization and the fact that everyone involved anticipated that the gifted property would be sold or otherwise liquidated. Wrote the court: "Only through such a step could the purpose of the charitable contribution be achieved."

In another instance, an individual made annual gifts, for 10 consecutive years, to a university of closely held stock in a corporation of which he was the majority shareholder, an officer, and a director. He retained a life interest in the gift property and confined his charitable contribution deduction to the value of the remainder interest (see Chapter 9). Each year the university tendered stock to the corporation for redemption; each year the corporation redeemed it. There was no contract evidencing this cycle of events. The university invested the redemption proceeds in income-producing securities and made quarterly disbursements to the donor.

The IRS asserted that the donor employed the university as a tax-free conduit for withdrawing funds from the corporation and that the redemption payments by the corporation to the university were in reality constructive dividend payments to the donor. The court on appeal nicely framed the dispute: "Our aim is to determine whether [the donor's] gifts of the [c]orporation's shares [to the university] prior to redemption should be given independent significance or whether they should be regarded as meaningless intervening steps in a single, integrated transaction designed to avoid tax liability by the use of mere formalisms."

The IRS wanted the court to "infer from the systematic nature of the gift-redemption cycle" that the donor and donee had "reached a mutually beneficial understanding." But the court declined to find any informal agreement between the parties; it also refused to base tax liability on a "fictional one" created by the IRS. The court so held even though the donor was the majority shareholder of the corporation, so that his vote alone was sufficient to ensure redemption of the university's shares. The court wrote that "foresight and planning do not transform a non-taxable event into one that is taxable."

In still another instance, an individual donated promissory notes issued by a company he controlled to three charitable foundations several weeks prior to redemption of the notes. A court held that he did not realize income in connection with these gifts or the subsequent redemption of the notes by the company. The court observed: "A gift of appreciated property does not result in income to the donor so long as he gives the property away absolutely and parts with title thereto before the property gives rise to income by way of a sale."

In one more instance involving facts of this nature, a court took note of the fact that the concept of a charitable organization originated before and independently of the sale, the deed of trust for the property contributed was executed before and independent of the sale, and at the time the deed of trust was executed, "no mutual understanding or meeting of the minds or contract existed between the parties."

There are cases to the contrary, however, holding that the transfer of the property to a charitable organization "served no business purpose other than an attempt at tax avoidance."

In the end, perhaps the matter of the step transaction doctrine comes down to this observation by a court: "Useful as the step transaction doctrine may be in the interpretation of equivocal contracts and ambiguous events, it cannot generate events which never took place just so an additional tax liability might be asserted."

IRS Rulings

The step transaction doctrine occasionally appears in IRS private letter rulings as well. In one instance, an individual planned to fund a charitable remainder trust (see Chapter 9) with a significant block of stock of a corporation. It was anticipated that the trust would sell most, if not all, of this stock in order to diversify its assets. The stock first had to be offered to the corporation, under a right of first refusal, which allowed the corporation to redeem the stock for its fair market value. The donor was the sole initial trustee of the trust.

The IRS focused, in this instance, on whether the trust would be legally bound to redeem the stock. Although it did not answer that question, the agency assumed that to be the case and also assumed that the trust could not be compelled by the corporation to redeem the stock. Thus, the IRS held that the transfer of the stock by the donor to the trust, followed by the redemption, would not be recharacterized for federal income tax purposes as a redemption of the stock by the corporation followed by a contribution of the redemption proceeds to the trust. The IRS also held that the same principles would apply if the stock were sold rather than redeemed. This holding assumed that the donor had not prearranged a sale of the stock before contributing it to the trust under circumstances in which the trust would be obligated to complete the sales transaction.

In another situation, an individual planned to contribute a musical instrument to a charitable remainder trust. The instrument was used in the donor's profession; the donor was not a dealer in this type of instrument, nor was the instrument depreciated for tax purposes. Again, the issue was presented: If the trust subsequently sold the instrument for a gain, would that gain have to be recognized by the donor? The IRS presumed that there was no prearranged sales contract legally requiring the trust to sell the instrument following the gift. With this presumption, the IRS was able to hold that any later gain on a sale of the instrument would not be taxable to the donor.

VALUATION OF PROPERTY

The valuation of property contributed to charitable organizations is one of the largest problems facing the charitable sector, lawmakers, regulators, and the courts. The criteria for property valuation is vague, there have been considerable abuses in this area (resulting in inflated charitable deductions), and the penalty system devised at the federal level (see Chapter 8) is not effective. Because Congress has been unable to resolve the dilemma as to how to legislate compliance with valuation principles, another approach is being taken: confining the charitable deduction to the amount of funds a charity actually receives from the disposition or holding of the gift property. Two recent manifestations of this attack on the valuation problem are the rules concerning gifts of vehicles and intellectual property (see Chapter 6).

The determination of an income tax deduction for a contribution of property to a charitable organization is likely to require valuation of the property. (Valuation is not always needed; an example of this is ascertainment of the value of publicly traded securities solely on the basis of the daily reported stock exchange information.) There are appraisal requirements for larger charitable contributions (see Chapter 12). The value of gift property is an integral part of the charitable gift substantiation requirements and the quid pro quo contribution rules.

Too frequently, the valuation of property is not restricted to good faith estimates by charitable organizations or the work of appraisers. There can be controversy in this area between contributors and the IRS, with the matter forced into court for resolution. In this type of litigation, a court is called on to decide the value of one or more items of gift property. Valuation is an issue of fact, not law. A typical case in this regard will entail expert witnesses for one or both sides in an attempt to convince the court of the merits of a particular value. A court may rely on the expertise of one or more of these witnesses or may disregard them; a court may establish a value on the basis of its own interpretation of the facts. (In an illustration of a court dismissing the testimony of an expert witness, a court rejected the testimony of an expert appraiser, finding his values to be "financial fantasies.")

The pertinent value in this context is the fair market value of the property. As a general rule, the *fair market value* of an item of property is, according to the tax regulations, the price at which the property would change hands between a willing buyer and a willing seller, neither being under any compulsion to buy or sell and both having reasonable knowledge of relevant facts. The valuation standard for charitable contribution deduction purposes generally is the same as that used in the estate and gift context.

The rules in that setting provide that the fair market value of an item of property is to be determined in the market in which the property is "most commonly sold to the public." Normally, a sale to the public refers to a sale to the "retail customer who is the ultimate consumer of the property." The ultimate consumer is deemed to be a customer who does not hold the property for resale. The determination of the appropriate market for valuation purposes is a question of fact. A court may conclude that the wholesale market for a property is the appropriate market to utilize in this regard. Once the appropriate market is identified, the fair market value of the property involved is determined by the amount that consumers would pay, in that market, for the property on the date of its contribution for charitable purposes.

The amount of a charitable contribution, determined for deduction purposes, can be affected by a restriction placed by the donor on the use of the donated property. Such a restriction may preclude valuation of the property on the basis of the "highest and best" use of it, which usually is reflected in the largest value for the property. The IRS said that the value of property contributed to a charitable organization is the "price that a reasonably knowledgeable willing buyer would pay a reasonably knowledgeable willing seller for the property subject to any restrictions imposed at the time of the contribution." The agency added that "[p]roperty otherwise intrinsically more valuable[,] that is encumbered by some restriction or condition limiting its marketability or use, must be valued in light of such limitation."

Often it is difficult to understand how a court arrived at a valuation amount, other than it was set between the donor's claimed deduction amount and the amount asserted by the IRS. In one instance, the donor's amount was $201,000, the IRS's amount was $20,500, and the court's amount was $75,000. In another instance, the donor's amount was $350,000, the IRS's amount was $70,000, and the court's amount was $130,000. In a third example, the donor's amount was $667,420, the IRS's amount was $138,000, and the court's amount was $534,144. There can be quite a swing in these figures; in a case, the donor's claimed deduction was $1.89 million and the value decided by the court was $67,500. In another case, the donor claimed a charitable deduction for $2.75 million; in placing the value of the property at $38,000, the court wrote that the donor had to have known that his appraiser's "estimate was hooey, the sort of number ginned up to put one over on the revenooers."

There can also be humor (as court opinions go) in these cases. In one, a court decided to value a parcel of land as one tract rather than on its basis for division into 24 lots. This court wrote (in 1986) that, in ascertaining the value of the land, the "appropriate question is what a hypothetical Malcolm Forbes would have paid for it as one tract, rather than what two dozen hypothetical yuppies would have paid for it" as separate lots. Then the court termed the difference between the two valuations as being "rather like the difference between the worth of a gravid or potentially gravid sow and the postpartum worth of sow-cum-shoats."

If the value of a property is determined by a trial court and the case is appealed, the appellate court will likely expect some explanation from the lower court as to the basis for its factual conclusions. The court of appeals will not want to have to speculate as to how the lower court arrived at its view of the value. Certainly, finding a valuation figure that has as its only virtue the fact that it is within the ranges of value suggested by the litigants' expert witnesses will not suffice. As one appellate court stated, it is not sufficient for the lower court to provide the "pieces of the puzzle"; the court of appeals undoubtedly will want the lower court to divulge "how it put them together."

Another court of appeals wrote that it was not prepared to permit the court below, "whenever it disagrees with the valuations offered by both sides, simply to shut its eyes and pick at random any number that happens to lie somewhere between the [IRS's] valuation and the taxpayer's." This court continued with the observation that "[o]nly by happenstance will such a blind choice avoid a valuation that is either unacceptably low or unacceptably high." This analysis ended with the court's pronouncement that the "random walk approach, which leaves no trail for the appellate court to follow, may be a sensible way to pick stocks, but it is not an appropriate way to determine the value of a charitable donation."

Yet, in a rare valuation case where a court found the testimony of both sides' expert witnesses credible, it openly concluded that the value of the gift property is "most accurately reflected by a figure between those advocated by plaintiff and the government." Explaining that the property appraisal process is "more an art than a science," the court said that it was "thus compelled to apply its own artistic brush to establish a reasonable value for the land that accurately reflects all of the evidence presented in this proceeding." (In other words, rather than base property valuation on the testimony of a credible expert, the court chose to invoke some other amount!)

SUMMARY

This chapter provided a summary of the different ways property is characterized for federal tax purposes. The chapter then summarized the rules concerning charitable contributions of money and other forms of property. Although gifts of property often give rise to charitable deductions that are based on the fair market value of the property, this chapter explained the rules by which some charitable deductions must be reduced by the amount of an element of gain. The chapter offered a warning about the tax law trap into which an unwitting donor may fall, occasioned by application of the step transaction doctrine, and explored the law concerning the valuation of gift property.

CHAPTER 3

Timing of Charitable Deductions

The purpose of this chapter is to summarize the federal tax law rules that pertain to the timing of charitable deductions, that is, the determination of the year of gifts to charity. As a general rule, a federal income tax charitable contribution deduction arises at the time of, and for the year in which, the contribution is actually made. A significant exception to this rule is the body of law concerning the tax deductibility of contributions carried over to a year subsequent to the one in which the gift was made; in this situation, the contribution is made in one year but the allowable charitable deduction arises in, and is treated for tax purposes as paid in, another year. The mere making of a pledge to a charitable organization does not result in an income tax charitable deduction (see Chapter 1). Specifically, this chapter will summarize the concepts of title to and delivery of property, explain the rules where the timing of a charitable deduction is dictated by statute, and explain the rules concerning:

- The making of charitable gifts by check
- The making of charitable gifts by credit or debit card
- The making of charitable gifts by telephone
- Charitable gifts of securities
- Charitable gifts of copyright interests
- Charitable gifts by means of notes
- Charitable gifts by means of letters of credit
- Charitable gifts of property subject to an option
- Charitable gifts of credit card rebates

- Charitable gifts of tangible personal property
- Charitable gifts of real property
- Charitable gifts by corporations
- Charitable gifts by partnerships
- Charitable gifts made by means of the Internet

OVERVIEW

The matter of timing of a federal income tax charitable contribution deduction concerns the tax year for which the gift is deductible. To determine this year, the federal tax law follows the concept of *title*; that is, the contribution is for the year in which title to the item that is the subject of the gift passes from the donor to the donee. Title to property generally passes when all of the rights to and interests in the property have been properly and completely transferred.

The element that is critical to the passage of title to an item of property is *delivery*, inasmuch as delivery is the way title in property is actually transferred from one person to another. In an instance of the transfer of title to real estate, for example, title is transferred on the date that a deed of conveyance was executed, not on a previous date when the parties signed a contract for the sale of the property. Consequently, a charitable contribution deduction generally comes into being on the date the gift property is delivered by the donor to the charitable donee. This general rule assumes a number of elements, including:

- The absence of a condition (that may occur either before or after the transfer) that defeats, or will defeat, the clear passage of title to the donee (see Chapter 8), unless
  - The condition is so remote as to be negligible.
  - The condition is one that entails a legitimate restriction on the donee's use of the gift property (such as a confining of the use of the gift for scholarships or for the acquisition of a building for use by the charitable donee in its charitable activities).
- Compliance with the substantiation requirements (see Chapter 12).

When the mail is used, the U.S. Postal Service is considered the agent of the recipient. Thus, when a contribution is mailed, the date of gift is usually the date the item is placed in the U.S. mail system.

The concept of delivery, however, does not necessarily mean that the donee must take actual physical possession of the property before a gift of the property becomes deductible. Title may pass when the charitable donee has the right or entitlement to possession of the property. Thus, a court wrote that the "donee simply must have the right to interrupt the donor's possession and the right to have physical possession of the property during each year following the donation." This can involve forms of *constructive delivery*, but the donor must give up custody, control, and management of the property; otherwise, the gift transaction is not complete.

CONTRIBUTIONS OF MONEY IN GENERAL

A charitable contribution of U.S. currency is deductible for the year in which the money is mailed or otherwise delivered to the charitable donee. This rule pertains to situations in which the gift is made in cash rather than by check. Of course, the title to the money passes at the time the ownership of the currency changes hands. Actions indicating intent to make a gift of money, such as instructions to a bookkeeper, are insufficient; the deduction arises in the year of actual payment.

CONTRIBUTIONS OF MONEY BY CHECK

A gift of money may be made to a charitable organization by means of a check; in this context, the general rules just cited apply. That is, title to the funds passes, and thus a charitable gift is made, at the time the check is mailed or otherwise delivered to the charitable donee. This rule also applies when the gift is made using a third-party check. In addition to these assumptions, however, this rule presumes that the check evidencing the contribution clears the bank involved in due course. Thus, a "gift" of a bad check is no gift at all.

Therefore, charitable gifts by check made at year-end may be deductible for the year in which the check was written, even though the check evidencing the gift does not clear the account involved until early in the subsequent year. This rule is reflected in the *relation-back doctrine*.

Nonetheless, the general rules concerning gifts apply. Thus, the IRS declared that a gift "is not consummated by the mere delivery of the donor's own check or note" and that the gift by means of a check "does not become complete until it is paid, certified, or accepted by the drawee, or is negotiated for the value to a third person." For example, in one instance, when checks were written immediately prior to an individual's death, there were inadequate funds in the account, and the checks were not presented for payment until approximately eight months after death, the value of the gift of the checks was held by the IRS to be includible in the decedent's estate.

A charitable gift involving a postdated check becomes deductible as of the date of the check, assuming that all other requirements are satisfied. A check involving a charitable gift that has not cleared the bank prior to the death of the donor gives rise to a federal income tax charitable contribution deduction as of the time the check was delivered to the donee.

A postdated check is essentially a promissory note. A court stated that a postdated check "is not a promise to pay presently and does not mature until the day of its date, after which it is payable on demand the same as if it had not been issued until that date although it is, as in the case of a promissory note, a negotiable instrument from the time issued." The rules concerning gifts by promissory notes are discussed in the next section.

CONTRIBUTIONS BY DEBIT OR CREDIT CARD

An income tax charitable contribution can be made, and be deductible, by means of a debit or credit card. When a gift is made using a bank-based card, the contribution is deductible for the year the donor charges the gift on the account (rather than for the year when the account including the charged amount is paid). In reaching this conclusion, the IRS concluded that the cardholder, by using the card to make the contribution, became immediately indebted to a third party (the bank) in such a way that the cardholder could not thereafter prevent the charitable organization from receiving payment. This is because the card draft received by the charitable organization from the credit cardholder is immediately creditable by the bank to the organization's account as if it were a check.

In this regard, the IRS analogized this situation to that in which a charitable contribution is made using borrowed funds. The IRS reasoned: "Since the cardholder's use of the credit card creates the cardholder's own debt to a third party, the use of a bank credit card to make a charitable contribution is equivalent to the use of borrowed funds to make a contribution." The general rule is that, when a deductible payment is made with borrowed money, the deduction is not postponed until the year in which the borrowed money is repaid. These expenses must be deducted in the year they are paid and not when the loans are repaid.

Gifts by means of a bank card need to be distinguished from gifts by means of a promissory note and the like. The issuance of a promissory note (or debenture bond) represents a mere promise to pay at some future date, and delivery of the note (or bond) to a charitable organization is not a requisite "payment."

CONTRIBUTIONS OF MONEY BY TELEPHONE

A deductible income tax charitable contribution can be made by means of the telephone. This can occur through use of a pay-by-phone account maintained at a financial institution. When the gift is made by transfer from this type of account, which the donor has initiated by telephone, the deduction arises on the date the financial institution makes the payment to the charitable organization. In this instance, the financial institution is acting as the agent of the donor (see Chapter 8).

CONTRIBUTIONS OF SECURITIES

The law has constructed a formal system for the transfer of title for some items of property. This is the case in connection with stocks, bonds, and other securities (which are forms of intangible personal property). A security usually is evidenced by a certificate; title to the underlying security can be transferred by an endorsement on the certificate, indicating transfer of the security from one person to another. Transfers of securities are usually effected by brokers.

Thus, a person may make a contribution of a security to a charitable organization, and create a federal income tax contribution deduction, when the properly endorsed certificate evidencing the security is delivered to the charitable organization. This type of a transfer to an agent of the charitable donee can also accomplish delivery.

When the properly endorsed certificate is mailed to a charitable organization or an agent of the organization, the deduction arises as of the date on which the certificate was mailed. When the certificate is unconditionally delivered to the corporation that issued the security or to a broker acting on behalf of the donor, for purposes of arranging for transfer of title to the security to the charitable donee, the charitable deduction comes into being on the date the transfer of the security is formally recorded by the issuing corporation. When the certificate is delivered to a broker representing the charitable donee, however, the deduction arises as of the date of delivery. Mere notation on the records of the transferee charitable organization of a contribution of securities is not sufficient to cause effective transfer of title.

Court cases illustrate the intricacies of these rules. In one instance, an individual decided to contribute stock to several charities, wanting to make these gifts before a payment of money for some of the shares pursuant to a tender offer and before accrual of the right to dividend income from these shares. The donor sent a letter to a trust company withdrawing the stock from a trust and requesting delivery of the stock to a bank. On the same day, the donor wrote to the bank identifying the charitable donees. Further, on the same day, the donees were sent a memorandum directing them to instruct the bank as to the disposition of the stock (i.e., whether the donees wanted to accept the tender offer or retain the stock). The final offer was made about one week later, with the actual transfer of the shares on the corporation's books made approximately one month following the sending of the letters and memorandum by the donor. In the interim, dividends were declared; they were sent to the charities by the bank. The donor claimed a charitable deduction for the gifts of the securities and did not report the dividends as income.

The IRS concluded, in this instance, that the donor had control of the stock when it was sold and therefore attributed the capital gain on the sale of the securities to the donor. The dividend income was also found to be gross income to the donor. The issues were litigated, with the donor prevailing. The court found that the donor had established a voluntary trust for the donees, using an independent part (the bank) as trustee. This, said the court, effectively removed any potential for the exercise of control by the donor "despite the failure to accomplish titular transfer [of the stock] on the corporate books." The federal income tax regulation on the point was held to be inapplicable, inasmuch as delivery was neither to the donor's agent nor to the issuing corporation or its agent. Thus, delivery was held to be effected on tender of the stock by the bank to the offeror, which was prior to the stock sale dates and the dividend declaration date. The consequence of all this was that the donor was held to have the charitable deduction for the gifts of the stock and not to have any capital gain or dividend income tax liability.

By contrast, in another case, capital gain in property was ruled by a court to be taxable to the donors of appreciated securities to charitable organizations. This was because, by the date the gifts were completed, the securities had ripened from interests in a viable corporation into a fixed right to receive money, by means of an ongoing tender offer or a pending merger agreement. Therefore, despite the gifts, the gain in the stock was taxable to the donors.

The donors in this case owned 18 percent of a privately held corporation, as to which they served as several of its officers and directors. These securities were obtained in 1985. On July 28, 1988, the corporation entered into a merger agreement. The transaction was planned and negotiated by one of the donors. The resulting tender offer was the subject of a letter sent to all shareholders on August 3, 1988. The stock price set for the offer embodied a 24 percent premium over the market price for a share of the corporation's stock as of July 1988.

The tender offer (and thus the merger agreement) was conditioned on the acquisition of at least 85 percent of the outstanding shares of the corporation by the expiration date of the tender offer, originally set for August 30, 1988. This minimum tender condition was waivable at the discretion of the acquiring entity. Certain of the donors were expected to continue to have extensive involvement in managing the business, including being executive committee and board members. The tender offer started August 3, 1988, and was successfully completed on September 9, 1988. By August 31, 1988, more than 50 percent of the stock had been tendered. On September 12, 1988, acquisition of more than 95 percent of the stock was announced.

During the course of this tender offer, the donors transferred some of their stock in the corporation to three charities. Two of them were family foundations created on August 26, 1988. Various letters to the stockbroker authorizing the transfers were ostensibly executed in August 1988. The date the broker formally transferred title to the securities to the charities was September 8, 1988. Final letters of authorization were signed the next day.

The donors in this case contended that the date of delivery of the stock directly to the charities was September 8, 1988—the date the broker prepared the documentation formally transferring title to the securities. They also contended, however, that the stockbroker was acting as agent for the charities, so that the dates of delivery of the stock were in August 1988. The court rejected both arguments. The gift completion date was found to be September 9,

1988, with no transfer that was legally binding and irrevocable until then; it was also held that the stockbroker did not function as agent for the charities before that date.

The court determined that the stock in this case had ripened from an interest in a viable corporation to a fixed right to receive cash by August 31, 1988—the date by which more than one-half of the stock had been tendered. That is, by that date, the court held, it was practically certain that the tender offer and the merger would be successfully completed. The donors argued, unsuccessfully, that the stock did not ripen until September 12, 1988, because the tender offer and the merger could have been derailed. The likelihood of that happening was viewed by the courts as remote and hypothetical at best. Thus, because the fixed right to receive money ripened as of August 31, 1988, and the gifts did not formally become effective until September 9, 1988, the gain was taxable to the donors.

CONTRIBUTIONS OF COPYRIGHT INTERESTS

Another item of intangible personal property that, to be transferred, must be passed in a formal manner is a copyright interest. State law essentially governs as to whether a properly completed transfer of a copyright interest occurred, but only after certain federal law restrictions are satisfied. The federal requirements involve a written transfer instrument signed by the donor as owner. A copyright certificate is issued; however, possession of the certificate does not constitute ownership of the copyright itself.

In one instance, an individual physically presented a copyright certificate, for a book that was generating royalties, to a charitable organization in an attempt to make a charitable gift. There was no executed written transfer instrument and no formal action was taken by the recipient organization to formally transfer the copyright to itself. A court held that, "[t]herefore, standing alone, . . . [the individual's] physical presentation of the copyright certificate to . . . [the charitable organization], although accomplished with much ceremony, was insufficient to transfer a legal interest in the copyright" to the charity; "[t]his invalid transfer," the court continued, "does not begin to qualify as a deductible charitable contribution."

CONTRIBUTIONS BY MEANS OF NOTES

The making of a note promising to pay money and/or transfer property to a charitable organization, and delivery of the note to the charity, does not create a charitable contribution deduction. This is because a mere promise to pay does not affect transfer of title to the property. Of course, when the money and/or property is actually transferred to the charitable donee, in satisfaction of the requirements of the note, an income tax charitable contribution deduction results. (A promissory note is an item of intangible personal property.)

These distinctions are based on the rule that a charitable deduction is available only for the year the contribution is actually paid. Delivery of a note is not payment of the amount it represents.

A note in these circumstances may bear interest, or purport to bear interest. The tax consequences of payment of the interest depend on the enforceability of the note. If the note is enforceable, the payment of interest on the note is not likely to be deductible as an interest expense; if the note is not enforceable, the additional amounts paid are not interest for tax purposes but are deductible as charitable contributions.

CONTRIBUTIONS BY LETTERS OF CREDIT

A charitable contribution made by means of an irrevocable banker's letter of credit is the basis of a charitable deduction as of the date the letter of credit was established. This is because an irrevocable letter of credit from a bank is the equivalent of money.

In one instance, an individual established an irrevocable banker's letter of credit in favor of a charitable organization. The letter of credit was for $150,000, payable by drafts drawn by the charity. The $150,000 was distributed to the charitable organization in four amounts, one in the year the letter of credit was established and the other three in the subsequent year. The IRS ruled that the entire $150,000 was deductible by this individual for the year in which the letter of credit was established, because the full amount was made available without restriction to the charitable organization. The fact that the charity withdrew only a portion of the amount available during the first year was held to be immaterial, because the charitable organization could have withdrawn the entire amount.

CONTRIBUTIONS OF PROPERTY SUBJECT TO OPTION

A person may own an item of property and create an option by which another person may purchase the property at a certain price at or during a certain time. An option may be created for or transferred to a charitable organization. There is no federal income tax charitable contribution deduction, however, for the transfer of property subject to an option to a charitable organization. Rather, the general rule is that the charitable deduction arises at the time the option is exercised by the charitable donee.

Thus, the transfer to a charitable organization of property subject to an option by the option writer is similar to the transfer of a note or pledge by the maker. In the note situation, there is a promise to pay money at a future date; in the pledge situation, there is a promise to pay money or transfer some other property, or to do both, at a future date. In the option situation, there is a promise to sell property at a future date.

For-profit corporations may pledge stock options to charitable organizations. These transactions can generate tax law issues, particularly if the donee is a disqualified person with respect to the donor, such as by being a substantial contributor (see Chapter 1). These issues of law include the timing of the resulting charitable contribution deduction.

In one instance, a for-profit publicly traded corporation established a private foundation as its charitable giving vehicle. This corporation, being a substantial contributor to the foundation, was a disqualified person with respect to it. The corporation proposed to pledge to the foundation stock options for the purchase of shares of common stock of the corporation; the corporation did not receive any consideration for this pledge. The business purpose underlying the pledge was to further the charitable purpose of the foundation and other charitable organizations.

These options will be exercisable at a price specified in a stock option pledge agreement. This private foundation will not directly exercise the options because payment of the purchase price to the corporation would be an act of self-dealing. Rather, the foundation will either transfer the options to one or more unrelated public charitable organizations or engage in a cashless "net exercise" transaction with the corporation. Pursuant to this net exercise procedure, the holder of options would elect to receive shares of the corporation's stock in an amount equal to the net value of the options being exercised on the date of exercise. This net value of the options is calculated by subtracting the exercise price for the number of the options being exercised from the value of the shares that the holder would have received as the result of a direct exercise. If the holder were to elect the net exercise procedure, the holder would notify the corporation of the number of options being exercised, along with written notice of its direction to use the procedure, and the corporation would issue to the holder the number of shares of the corporation's stock computed using a formula specified in the option pledge agreement.

The foundation may sell the stock options to an unrelated charity for a fair market value price, with the value of the option affected by the terms in the option pledge agreement. Alternatively, the foundation may grant options to an unrelated charity, with the grantee expected to exercise the options prior to their expiration.

The IRS ruled that the pledge of the stock options by the corporation to the foundation did not constitute self-dealing because of the absence of consideration and the charitable purposes to be served. The pledges are not extensions of credit. The net exercise procedure does not entail a sale or exchange, the IRS concluded, so there would not be self-dealing for that reason. The sale of an option by the foundation to an unrelated charity would not be self-dealing inasmuch as the cancellation of the enforceable pledge would be for consideration paid by a nondisqualified person or an entity not controlled by a disqualified person. The exercise of a stock option by an unrelated charity also would not constitute self-dealing.

Stock options are not assets susceptible of use to produce interest, dividends, rents, or royalties. Thus, the proceeds received by the foundation from the sale of stock options to an unrelated charity would be excluded from the computation of the foundation's net investment income for tax purposes. The IRS ruled that the gain on the sale of stock options would be excluded from the computation of the foundation's unrelated business income.

The IRS ruled that, if the foundation transfers the options to an unrelated charitable organization and that charity engages in a cash exercise of the options, the corporation will be entitled to a federal income tax charitable deduction only on the exercise of the options by the unrelated charity. Moreover, the agency held that this deduction will be for an amount equal to the difference between the exercise price and the fair market value of the corporation's stock transferred to the foundation on the exercise. The IRS further ruled that, if the foundation transfers the options to an unrelated charity and that charity engages in a net exercise of the options, the corporation will be entitled to a charitable deduction only at the time of the net exercise. This deduction will be for an amount equal to the fair market value of the corporation's stock transferred to the charitable organization on the net exercise.

A charitable deduction can also arise when the option expires. In one instance, a small business (an S) corporation executed a deed, contributing a tract of land to a charitable organization; the corporation retained an option to repurchase the land for a nominal amount. The IRS concluded that there was more than a remote possibility that the option would be exercised. The gift was made in 1993; the option was set to expire in 1995. For 1993, each of the shareholders of the corporation claimed a charitable contribution deduction for their share of the fair market value of the property. The IRS, however, determined that, because of the option, there could not be charitable deductions for 1993, but that the deductions could be taken with respect to 1995.

CONTRIBUTIONS OF CREDIT CARD REBATES

A deductible charitable contribution can arise when the user of a credit card causes a percentage of the price of an item purchased with the card at a participating retailer to be transferred, by the company sponsoring the card, to a charitable organization selected by the cardholder.

A cardholder may claim the deduction for the tax year in which the company made payments to one or more charitable organizations on the cardholder's behalf. The company is not functioning as an agent for the donee charities. Instead, the company serves as agent for the cardholders with respect to the rebate amounts it holds. Thus, although the rebates are held by the company, the cardholders retain control over them.

For a charitable gift to be deductible, there must be the requisite delivery. It is not enough that there is to be delivery to a party for subsequent delivery to a charitable organization. Accordingly, there is no delivery of a charitable contribution when the company receives the rebate amounts, nor when cardholders fail to claim rebates for their personal use. Rather, delivery occurs when the company transfers the rebate funds to the designated charities. (If the company served as the agent of the charities, the charitable deduction would arise at the time the company received the rebate amounts.) This type of program is designed to allow individuals to have the charitable deduction in the year of the rebate by enabling the company to transfer the rebates to charity before the close of the tax year.

CONTRIBUTIONS OF TANGIBLE PERSONAL PROPERTY

A person may make deductible gifts of tangible personal property to a charitable organization. Items of tangible personal property include works of art, furniture, automobiles, and clothing.

Usually there is no formal system in law for the recording and transfer of an item of tangible personal property. (The obvious exception, of course, is the title requirements involving motor vehicles.) In appropriate circumstances, however, the execution of a deed of gift can evidence transfer of title in tangible personal property to a charitable organization.

CONTRIBUTIONS OF REAL PROPERTY

A person may make a contribution of real property to a charitable organization and receive an income tax charitable deduction. There is, of course, a formal system in law for the recording and transfer of title to parcels of real estate; transfers of real property are generally affected by means of deeds.

As to the timing of the deduction, the contribution of a gift of real property generally occurs on the date the donor delivers a deed to the property to the charitable donee. Recording of the deed is not necessary to make the transfer complete.

A court denied a charitable contribution deduction for a transfer of mortgaged land to a charitable organization by a partnership because the property was subject to a special warranty deed. Under state law, the donor partnership remained liable on the outstanding mortgage. The deed imposed an obligation on the grantor to protect the grantee against adverse claims that might impair the grantee's title to the land. Thus, the court held that the warranty was merely a promise to make payments in the future, with a charitable deduction available when the payments were actually made.

TIMING SET BY STATUTE

Occasionally the timing of a charitable contribution deduction is established by statute. The most notable (and recent) example of this type of legislation concerns the charitable deduction(s) that may arise because of a gift to charity of intellectual property (see Chapter 6).

Contributions of most types of intellectual property initially give rise to a charitable contribution deduction that is confined to the donor's basis in the property, although there may be one or more subsequent charitable deductions. This basis-only deduction is available in the year of the gift. In that year and/or subsequent years, there may be a charitable deduction equal to a percentage of net income that flows to the charitable donee as the consequence of the gift of the property.

That is, a portion of this income to the charity is allocated to a tax year of the donor, although this income allocation process is inapplicable to income received by or accrued to the donee after 10 years from the date of the gift. The process is also inapplicable to donee income received by or accrued to the donee after the expiration of the legal life of the property.

A table of sliding-scale percentages that appears in the Internal Revenue Code (and is reproduced in Chapter 6) determines the amount of donee income that materializes into a charitable deduction, for one or more years. Thus, if, following a contribution of this nature, the charitable donee receives income from the property in the year of the gift, and/or in the subsequent tax year of the donor, that amount becomes, in full, a charitable contribution deduction for the donor (subject to the percentage limitations [see Chapter 4]). If, for example, income from the property is received by the charitable donee eight years after the gift, the donor receives a charitable deduction equal to 40 percent of the donee income. As the table indicates, the opportunity for an intellectual property charitable deduction terminates after the twelfth year of the donor ending after the date of the gift.

CONTRIBUTIONS BY CORPORATIONS

The foregoing rules apply with respect to gifts by both individual and corporate donors. Thus, the general rule that a federal income tax charitable contribution deduction arises at the time of, and for the year in which, the contribution is made is equally applicable to individual and corporate donors.

A corporation that reports its taxable income using the accrual method of accounting may, however, at its election, deduct charitable contributions paid within $2\frac{1}{2}$ months after the close of its tax year, as long as: (1) the board of directors of the corporation authorized the making of a charitable contribution during the tax year, and (2) the charitable contribution is made after the close of the tax year of the corporation and within the $2^{1}/_{2}$-month period. (This rule was created because corporations intending to make the maximum charitable contribution allowable as a deduction experienced difficulty in determining, before the end of the tax year, what their net income would be.) This election must be made at the time the return for the tax year is filed, by reporting the contribution on the return. There must be, attached to the return, a written declaration that the resolution authorizing the contribution was adopted by the board of directors during the tax year involved, and the declaration must be verified by a statement signed by an officer authorized to sign the return that it is made under penalties of perjury. A copy of the resolution of the board of directors authorizing the contribution must also be attached to the return. To satisfy this rule, contributions of property need not be segregated by year; there is no requirement that the donees be identified at the time the resolution is adopted.

This rule applies only to regular (or C) corporations; deductions under this rule are not available to small business (or S) corporations, which are treated the same as partnerships for tax purposes. (Each shareholder of an S corporation takes into account the shareholder's pro rata share of the corporation's items of income, loss, deduction, or credit.) Rather, a small business corporation must report the charitable contribution on its tax return for the year in which the contribution was actually made. This is because this type of corporation generally computes its taxable income in the same manner as an individual. Certain deductions are not allowable to these corporations, including the charitable contribution deduction.

CONTRIBUTIONS BY PARTNERSHIPS

The taxable income of a partnership generally is computed in the same manner as is the case for individuals; however, the charitable contribution deduction is not allowed to the partnership. Rather, each partner separately takes into account the partner's distributive share of the partnership's charitable contributions.

A partner's distributive share of charitable contributions made by a partnership during a tax year of the partnership is allowed as a charitable deduction on the partner's tax return for the partner's tax year within which the tax year of the partnership ends. The aggregate of the partner's share of the partnership contributions and the partner's own (directly made) contributions are subject to the various percentage limitations on annual deductibility (see Chapter 4).

Moreover, when a partnership makes a charitable contribution of property, the basis of each partner's interest in the partnership is decreased (but not below zero) by the amount of the partner's share of the partnership's basis in the property contributed.

The adjusted basis of a partner's interest in a partnership must be increased by the sum of the partner's distributive share for the tax year and prior tax years of the taxable income of the partnership, the income of the partnership that is exempt from tax, and the excess of the deductions for depletion over the basis of the property subject to depletion. The adjusted basis of a partner's interest in a partnership must be decreased (but not below zero) by distributions by the partnership as well as by the sum of the partner's distributive share for the tax year and prior tax years of the losses of the partnership and expenditures of the partnership that are not deductible in computing taxable income and not properly chargeable to a capital account.

The adjustments to the basis of a partner's interest in a partnership are necessary to prevent inappropriate or unintended benefits or detriments to the partners. Generally, the basis of a partner's interest in a partnership is adjusted to reflect the tax allocations of the partnership to that partner. This adjustment ensures that the partners take into account the income and loss of the partnership only once. Also, adjustments must be made to reflect certain nontaxable events in the partnership. For example, a partner's share of nontaxable income (such as exempt income) is added to the basis of the partner's interest because, absent a basis adjustment, the partner could recognize gain with respect to the tax-exempt income (such as on a sale or redemption of the partner's interest) and the benefit of the tax-exempt income would be lost to the partner. Likewise, a partner's share of nondeductible expenditures must be deducted from the partner's basis to prevent that amount from giving rise to a loss to the partner on a sale or redemption of the partner's interest in the partnership.

In determining whether a transaction results in exempt income or a nondeductible noncapital expenditure, the inquiry must be whether the transaction has a permanent effect on the partnership's basis in its assets, without a corresponding current or future effect on its taxable income.

An example may clarify these points. A and B each contribute an equal amount of money to form a general partnership. Under the partnership agreement, each item of income, gain, loss, and deduction of the partnership is allocated 50 percent to A and 50 percent to B. This partnership has unencumbered property, having a basis of $60,000 and a fair market value of $100,000. The partnership contributes the property to a charitable organization. (This property is not of the type that requires reduction of the charitable deduction by elements of ordinary income or capital gain [see Chapter 2].)

As discussed, the contribution of this property by this partnership is not taken into account in computing the partnership's taxable income. Consequently, the contribution results in a permanent decrease in the aggregate basis of the assets of the partnership that is not taken into account by the partnership in determining its taxable income and is not taken into account for federal income tax purposes in any other manner. Therefore, the contribution of the property, and the resulting permanent decrease in partnership basis, is an expenditure of the partnership that is not deductible in computing its taxable income and is not properly chargeable to a capital account.

Reducing the partners' bases in their partnership interests by their respective shares of the permanent decrease in the partnership's basis in its assets preserves the intended benefit of providing a deduction for the fair market value of appreciated property without recognition of the appreciation. By contrast, reducing the partners' bases in their partnership interests by the fair market value of the contributed property would subsequently cause the partners to recognize gain (or a reduced loss), such as on a disposition of their partnership interests, attributable to the unrecognized appreciation in this contributed property at the time of the contribution.

In this example, under the partnership agreement, partnership items are allocated equally between A and B. Accordingly, the basis of A's and B's interests in the partnership is reduced by $30,000 each.

CONTRIBUTIONS BY MEANS OF THE INTERNET

One of the many issues that have arisen out of the utilization of the Internet as a medium to obtain charitable contributions is the tax consequences of the use of for-profit entities by charitable organizations to collect the payments. These entities may deduct a donation service fee and remit the balance to the charity involved.

If the gift is considered made to the for-profit organization, the charitable contribution deduction may be defeated. Otherwise, the matter turns on principles of the law as to principal and agent. If the for-profit intermediary is functioning as an agent for the charitable organization, the full amount of the contribution is deductible (not just the amount contributed net of the service fee). If, however, the for-profit intermediary is serving as the agent of the donor, the charitable contribution deduction will not come into being until the intermediary delivers the gift money (or perhaps other property) to the charitable organization.

Because of delays in processing the gift, a donor may be placed in the position of initiating the transaction late in a year, then find that the charitable deduction is not available until the subsequent year.

SUMMARY

This chapter provided a summary of the basic concepts of title to and delivery of property to charitable organizations. Then the chapter explained the various issues of timing of charitable deductions, in situations such as gifts by means of credit card, notes, and letters of credit. The chapter explained the rules concerning gifts of property subject to an option, gifts of copyright interests, gifts of securities, gifts of credit card rebates, gifts of tangible personal property, and gifts of real property. The chapter concluded with a summary of rules unique to charitable giving by corporations and partnerships.

CHAPTER 4

Percentage Limitations on Charitable Deductions

The purpose of this chapter is to summarize the law pertaining to one of the most important—and complex—aspects of the federal tax law of charitable giving: the various percentage limitations on otherwise allowable charitable contribution deductions. Specifically, this chapter will:

- Detail the law concerning the various percentage limitations on the charitable contribution deductions for individuals
- Summarize the various ways in which these percentage limitations may interrelate
- Explain the charitable deduction carryover rules for individuals
- Describe how these rules apply in varying circumstances involving spouses
- Summarize the law as to individuals' net operating loss carryovers and carrybacks
- Outline the rules regarding what information about charitable gifts must be submitted to the IRS
- Explain the percentage limitation, carryover rules, and net operating loss carryover and carryback rules for corporations

INTRODUCTION

One of the elements in determining the extent of deductibility of a charitable gift is the nature of the item contributed.

Nature of Gift

It must be reiterated that the federal income tax law basically distinguishes between gifts of money and gifts of property (see Chapter 2). As to the latter, the law differentiates between these categories of property:

- Long-term capital gain property
- Ordinary income property
- Short-term capital gain property

These terms describe categories of property on the basis of the tax categorization of the revenue that would result on sale of the property. For example, *long-term capital gain property* is property that, if sold, would generate long-term capital gain. Because these terms use the word *gain,* it is usually understood that these properties have appreciated in value (*appreciated property*) and thus would produce a gain at sale. Long-term capital gain property is often referred to as *capital gain property.*

For charitable deduction purposes , contributions of ordinary income property and short-term capital gain property are generally treated the same as gifts of money. Thus, the tax rules that reference the deductibility of gifts of money are generally also applicable to gifts of property that, if sold, would give rise to ordinary income or to short-term capital gain.

Tax Law Classification of Donee

Another element affecting the deductibility of a charitable contribution is the federal tax law classification of the charitable donee. (This factor is applicable only in the case of giving by individuals.) That is, the law in this context basically differentiates between gifts to public charitable organizations and gifts to private foundations and certain other tax-exempt organizations (see Chapter 1). The term *public charitable organization* is used to refer to a charitable organization that is not a private foundation. The principal types of public charitable organizations are churches, schools, colleges, universities, hospitals, a variety of publicly supported charitable organizations, and supporting organizations.

The deductibility of gifts by individuals involves several sets, and sometimes combinations, of percentage limitations. The percentages that are applicable to individuals are applied to an individual donor's contribution base.

Here are the key points of this chapter:

- An individual's contribution base essentially is the same as his or her adjusted gross income.
- An individual's federal income tax charitable contribution deduction for a tax year is subject to limitations of 50, 30, and/or 20 percent of the individual's contribution base.
- The maximum federal income tax charitable contribution deduction for a tax year for an individual is 50 percent of his or her contribution base.
- An individual's federal income tax charitable contribution deduction for a tax year cannot exceed an amount equal to 50 percent of his or her contribution base when the gift (or gifts) is of money (and/or ordinary income property and/or short-term capital gain property) and the charitable recipient is a public charitable organization.
- In general, an individual's federal income tax charitable contribution deduction for a tax year cannot exceed an amount equal to 30 percent of his or her contribution base when the gift is of capital gain property that has appreciated in value and the charitable recipient is a public charitable organization.
- An individual donor can elect to have a 50 percent limitation apply, when the gift is of capital gain property that has appreciated in value and the charitable recipient is a public charitable organization, by reducing the deduction by the amount of the appreciation element.
- An individual's federal income tax charitable contribution deduction for a tax year cannot exceed an amount equal to 30 percent of his or her contribution base when the gift (or gifts) is of money and the charitable recipient is an entity other than a public charitable organization.
- An individual's federal income tax charitable contribution deduction for a tax year cannot exceed an amount equal to 20 percent of his or her contribution base when the gift is of capital gain property that has appreciated in value and the charitable recipient is an entity other than a public charitable organization.
- These limitations are blended when an individual donor contributes more than one type of item (money or property) in a tax year and/or gives to more than one type of charitable organization in a tax year.

- Each of these percentage limitation rules allows for contributions in excess of the limitation to be carried forward and deducted over the subsequent five years, in order of time.
- If a husband and wife file a joint return, the deduction for charitable contributions is the aggregate of the contributions made by the spouses, and the percentage limitations are based on the aggregate contribution base of the spouses.
- The charitable contribution deduction for a corporation for a tax year is subject to a limitation of 10 percent of the corporation's pretax net income.
- No percentage limitations apply in the estate tax or gift tax charitable contribution deduction context (see Chapter 5).

Other Limitation Rules

Two other limitation rules are discussed in Chapter 8 but warrant mention at this point so that they can be correlated with the information in this chapter.

1. If an individual contributes an item of tangible personal property that has appreciated in value to a public charitable organization, but the public charity does not use the property for a purpose that is related to its tax-exempt purposes, the donor must reduce the deduction by the entirety of the capital gain element.
2. When an individual makes a contribution of an item of appreciated property to a charitable organization that is not a public charitable organization, the donor must reduce the deduction by all of the capital gain element.

INDIVIDUALS' CONTRIBUTION BASE

The percentage limitations used in ascertaining the deductibility of charitable gifts are applied, in the case of individuals, to an amount equal to the donor's contribution base. The term *contribution base* means the individual's adjusted gross income, computed without regard to any net operating loss carryback to the tax year. For most individuals, the amounts constituting the contribution base and adjusted gross income are the same.

CORPORATIONS' TAXABLE INCOME

The concept of a contribution base is not applicable to contributions by corporations. Rather, the percentage limitation is applicable to a corporation's taxable income. *Taxable income* is gross income less expenses, determined without regard to the charitable contribution deduction rules, rules providing special deductions for corporations, any net operating loss carryback to the tax year, and any capital loss carryback to the tax year.

A corporation on the accrual method of accounting can elect to treat a contribution as having been made in a tax year if it is actually donated during the first $2^1/_2$ months of the following year. Corporate gifts of property are generally subject to the deduction reduction rules (see Chapter 8).

A business organization that is a *flow-through entity* generates a different tax result when it comes to charitable deductions. (These organizations are partnerships, other joint ventures, small business (S) corporations, and limited liability companies.) Entities of this nature, even though they may make charitable gifts, do not claim charitable contribution deductions. Instead, the deduction is passed through to the partners, members, or other owners on an allocable basis, and they claim their share of the deduction on their tax return.

OVERVIEW OF PERCENTAGE LIMITATIONS

Because of the intricacies of these percentage limitation rules, an overview of them is appropriate. The percentage limitations are applied in connection with the contribution year or years involved. In the context of the tax rules concerning charitable giving, a tax year in which a gift is made is termed a *contribution year*.

General Rules

An individual's federal income tax charitable contribution deduction for a tax year is subject to limitations of 50, 30, and/or 20 percent of the individual's contribution base. The limitation or limitations that are applicable depend on the tax classification of the charitable organization that is the donee and the nature of the item (money or property) that is contributed. Irrespective of the combination of charities and gifts, however, an individual's income tax charitable deduction for a tax year cannot exceed an amount equal to 50 percent of his or her contribution base. If a husband and wife file a joint return, the deduction for charitable contributions is the aggregate of the contributions made by the spouses; the percentage limitations are based on the aggregate contribution of the spouses.

Contributions of money to public charitable organizations, in a tax year, are deductible in an amount not in excess of 50 percent of the individual donor's contribution base for that year. This 50 percent limitation also applies with respect to gifts of tangible personal property that have been reduced by the capital gain element because the property was put to an unrelated use by the donee charitable organization.

A 30 percent limitation is applicable when the contribution (or contributions) is to one or more public charitable organizations and the gift or gifts are of capital gain property. This rule applies with respect to gifts that do not have to be reduced by the amount of the appreciation element inherent in the property. When a special election is made, contributions of capital gain property may be subject to the 50 percent limitation rather than the 30 percent limitation.

In general, contributions of money to private foundations (and/or certain other donees, such as veterans' organizations and fraternal organizations) in a tax year are deductible in an amount not in excess of 30 percent of the individual donor's contribution base for that year. If the contributions are less, however, the limitation is an amount equal to the excess of 50 percent of the donor's contribution base for the year over the amount of charitable contributions allowable under the 50 percent limitation.

Contributions of capital gain property to private foundations and certain other donee organizations are usually subject to a 20 percent limitation.

Contributions by a corporation are deductible for a tax year in an amount not to exceed 10 percent of the corporation's taxable income, computed with certain adjustments.

Carryover Rules

Donors of gifts that exceed the applicable percentage limitation are entitled to carry the excess amounts forward, for purposes of deduction over the succeeding five years, in order of time. The carryover rules apply to:

- Individuals, in relation to the 50 percent limitation
- Individuals, in relation to the 30 percent limitation, concerning gifts of capital gain property
- Individuals, in relation to the general 30 percent limitation
- Individuals, in relation to the 20 percent limitation
- Corporations

The carryover rules apply with respect to contributions made during a tax year in excess of the applicable percentage limitation, even when the donor elects to use the standard deduction for that year instead of itemizing the deductions allowable in computing taxable income for that year.

The carryover provisions do not apply to contributions made out of an estate. Nor do the provisions apply to a trust unless the trust is a private foundation that is allowed a charitable deduction subject to the provisions applicable to individuals.

50 PERCENT LIMITATION

The maximum federal income tax charitable contribution deduction for a tax year for an individual is 50 percent of the individual's contribution base.

General Rules

An individual's charitable contributions made during a tax year to one or more public charitable organizations, when the gifts are of money, are deductible to the extent that the contributions in the aggregate do not exceed 50 percent of the individual's contribution base for the tax year.

This limitation applies with respect to gifts to public and publicly supported charitable organizations, private operating foundations, governmental units, and certain types of foundations. A contribution to a charitable organization that is not a public charitable organization does not qualify for the 50 percent limitation, notwithstanding the fact that the organization makes the contribution available to a public charitable organization.

When an individual makes a contribution of an item of tangible personal property that has appreciated in value to a public charitable organization, but the public charity does not use the property for a purpose that is related to its tax-exempt purposes, the donor must reduce the deduction by all of the capital gain element (see

Chapter 8). (The *capital gain element* is the portion of the proceeds that would have been long-term capital gain had the property been sold.) Once the (potentially) deductible amount is determined under this rule, the amount is then subjected, for purposes of determining the actual charitable contribution deduction, to the 50 percent limitation.

There are, then, five instances in which a charitable contribution deduction may be limited by the 50 percent limitation:

1. Gifts of money
2. Gifts of ordinary income property (property the sale of which would produce ordinary income)
3. Gifts of short-term capital gain property (property the sale of which would produce short-term capital gain)
4. Gifts of capital gain property for which the charitable deduction was reduced by the amount of the capital gain element because the charitable donee put the property to an unrelated use
5. Gifts of capital gain property as to which a special election is made

Carryover Rules

In general, the excess of:

The amount of the charitable contribution or contributions
of money made by an individual in a contribution year
to one or more public charitable organizations
divided by
50 percent of the individual's contribution base
for the contribution year

is treated as a charitable contribution paid by the individual to a public charitable organization, subject to the 50 percent limitation, in each of the five tax years immediately succeeding the contribution year, in order of time. Thus, for federal income tax purposes, an amount paid to a charitable organization in one year is, when the carryover rules are applied, treated as paid to a charitable organization in a subsequent year.

In applying these rules, the amount of the excess contributions that are to be treated as paid to a public charitable organization in any one of the five tax years immediately succeeding the contribution year may not exceed the lesser of these three amounts:

1. The amount by which 50 percent of the donor's contribution base for the succeeding tax year involved exceeds the sum of:

   The charitable contributions actually made (computed without regard to the carryover rules) by the donor in the year to public charitable organizations, and

   The charitable contributions, other than contributions of capital gain property to which the 30 percent limitation applies, made to public charitable organizations in years preceding the contribution year which, pursuant to the carryover rules, are treated as having been paid to a public charitable organization in the succeeding tax year involved

2. In the case of the first tax year succeeding the contribution year, the amount of the excess charitable contribution in the contribution year

3. For the second, third, fourth, and fifth tax years succeeding the contribution year, the portion of the excess charitable contribution in the contribution year that has not been treated as paid to a public charitable organization in a year intervening between the contribution year and the succeeding year involved

If a donor, in any one of the five tax years succeeding a contribution year, elects to utilize the standard deduction instead of itemizing deductions allowable in computing taxable income, the lesser of these three amounts must be treated as paid (but not allowable as a deduction) for the year of the election. This rule applies because the standard deduction is deemed to include the charitable contribution deduction (for the individual who does not itemize his or her tax deductions); absent this rule, an individual in this situation would, in effect, receive a double deduction for a charitable contribution.

30 PERCENT LIMITATION FOR GIFTS OF CERTAIN PROPERTY

A 30 percent limitation applies with respect to charitable contributions of certain property that has appreciated in value since the donor acquired the property, when the recipient is a public charitable organization. Thus, even though the donee is a public charitable organization, the percentage limitation in this context is 30 percent, not 50 percent.

General Rules

To be subject to treatment under this 30 percent limitation, an item of property must satisfy three requirements:

1. The property must be a capital asset.
2. If the property was sold by the donor at its fair market value at the time of the contribution, the sale would result in the recognition of gain, all or any portion of which would be long-term capital gain.
3. The circumstances are not such that the amount of the contribution needs to be reduced by the appreciation element inherent in the capital gain property.

Property that qualifies for this 30 percent limitation is, as noted, referred to throughout as *capital gain property.*

The fair market value of an item of capital gain property is used in calculating the value of the deduction, although the actual deduction for a contribution year may be less as the result of this (or other) limitation.

In general, then, an individual may deduct charitable contributions of capital gain property made during a tax year to any public charitable organization to the extent that the contributions in the aggregate do not exceed 30 percent of the donor's contribution base.

The full 30 percent limitation may not always apply, however; that is to say, the allowable amount for a contribution year may be less. This is because contributions of money to public charitable organizations, and the applicable percentage limitations, have to be taken into account first. In this process, the value of the capital gain property contributed to public charitable organizations that must be used is the full fair market value, not the amount limited by the 30 percent rule.

The federal income tax law thus establishes an order of priority for categories of gifts to public charitable organizations, which can determine the deductibility of charitable gifts. The federal income tax law favors the giving of money, rather than property, to public charitable organizations. Therefore, when computing current or carried-forward charitable deductions, contributions of money to public charitable organizations are considered first.

When a donor makes a gift of an undivided fractional interest in an item of property that is qualified capital gain property, the donee is a public charity, and the electable 50 percent limitation is not elected, the amount of the gift is determined under this 30 percent limitation. The amount of the gift will equal the product of (1) the fraction times (2) the fair market value of the entire item of property at the time of the gift of the fractional interest.

Carryover Rules

Subject to certain conditions and limitations, the excess of:

> The amount of the charitable contributions of capital gain
> property subject to the 30 percent limitation made
> by an individual in a contribution year
> to public charitable organizations
> divided by
> 30 percent of the individual's contribution base
> for the contribution year

is treated as a charitable contribution of capital gain property, subject to this 30 percent limitation, paid by the individual to a public charitable organization in each of the five tax years immediately succeeding the contribution year, in order of time. Also, any charitable contribution of capital gain property subject to the 30 percent limitation that is carried over to these years under the general carryover rules is treated as if it were a carryover of capital gain property under the special carryover rules concerning this type of property.

In applying these rules, the amount of the excess contributions that are to be treated as paid to a public charitable organization in any one of the five tax years immediately succeeding the contribution year may not exceed the lesser of these four amounts:

1. The amount by which 30 percent of the donor's contribution base for the succeeding tax year involved exceeds the sum of:

   The charitable contributions of capital gain property made (computed without regard to the carryover rules) by the donor in the year to public charitable organizations, and

   The charitable contributions of capital gain property made to public charitable organizations in years preceding the contribution year that, pursuant to the contribution rules, are treated as having been paid to a public charitable organization in the succeeding tax year involved

2. The amount by which 50 percent of the donor's contribution base for the succeeding tax year involved exceeds the sum of:

    The charitable contributions made (computed without regard to the carryover rules) to public charitable organizations by the donor in the year,

    The charitable contributions of capital gain property made to public charitable organizations in years preceding the contribution year that, pursuant to the carryover rules, are treated as having been paid to a public charitable organization in the succeeding year involved, and

    The charitable contributions made to public charitable organizations, other than contributions of capital gain property, that, pursuant to the general carryover rules, are treated as having been paid to a public charitable organization in the succeeding year

3. In the case of the first tax year succeeding the contribution year, the amount of the excess charitable contribution of capital gain property in the contribution year

4. In the case of the second, third, fourth, and fifth tax years succeeding the contribution year, the portion of the excess charitable contribution of capital gain property in the contribution year that has not been treated as paid to a public charitable organization in a year intervening between the contribution year and the succeeding tax year involved.

For purposes of applying the first and second of these amounts, the amount of charitable contributions of capital gain property actually made in a year succeeding the contribution year is determined by first applying the 30 percent limitation.

If a donor, in any one of the four tax years succeeding a contribution year, elects to utilize the standard deduction instead of itemizing the deductions allowable in computing taxable income, the return in such a year must be treated as paid (but not allowable as a deduction), in the year the standard deduction is used, the lesser of the above four amounts.

ELECTABLE 50 PERCENT LIMITATION

Individual donors have an opportunity to elect application of the 50 percent limitation where the 30 percent limitation would otherwise apply.

General Rules

An individual donor may elect, for any tax year, to reduce his or her potential federal income tax charitable contribution deduction, occasioned by the gift or gifts of capital gain property to charity made during the tax year, by the amount of what would have been long-term capital gain had the property been sold, in exchange for use of the 50 percent limitation. This election may be made with respect to contributions of capital gain property carried over to the year involved even though the donor has not made any contribution of capital gain property in the year. If this election is made, the 30 percent limitation and the carryover rules with respect to it are inapplicable to the contributions made during the year. This means that the 50 percent limitation applies.

In deciding whether to make this election, an individual must determine whether the 50 percent limitation or the 30 percent limitation is most suitable for him or her (or them) under the circumstances. A principal factor is usually the extent to which the property has appreciated in value; this election can be preferable when the property value appreciation is slight. Another factor is whether the donor is seeking the maximum charitable contribution deduction for a contribution year. Because capital gain property generally is deductible using the fair market value of the property, the 30 percent limitation can operate to reduce what would otherwise be a larger charitable contribution deduction if the 50 percent limitation applied. This election enables a donor to calculate the deduction by using the fair market value of the property rather than simply the basis in the property.

If there are carryovers to a year of charitable contributions of capital gain property made in preceding, qualifying years (subject to the 30 percent limitation), the amount of the contributions in each preceding year must be revised as if this deduction reduction rule had applied to them in the preceding year and must be carried over to the year and succeeding years as contributions of property other than capital gain property. The percentage limitations for the preceding year and for any year intervening between that year and the year of the election are not redetermined; likewise, the amount of any charitable deduction allowed for the years with respect to the charitable contributions of capital gain property in the preceding year is not redetermined. The amount of the charitable deduction so allowed in the preceding tax year must, however, be subtracted from the reduced amount of the charitable contributions made in that year (i.e., the capital gain element must be subtracted) to determine the excess amount carried over from that year. If the amount of the deduction so allowed in the preceding tax year equals or exceeds the reduced amount of the charitable contributions, there may not be any carryover from that year to the year of the election.

This election may be made for each year in which a charitable contribution of capital gain property is made or to which the charitable deduction is carried over under the rules of the 30 percent limitation. If there are also carryovers, under the general rules concerning carryovers of excess contributions, to the year of the election by reason of this election for a previous tax year, these carryovers may not be redetermined by reason of the subsequent election. When the election is made, however, it must apply with respect to all contributions of capital gain property made to public charitable organizations during the contribution year.

If a husband and wife file a joint federal income tax return for a year in which a charitable contribution is made, and one of the spouses makes this election in a later year when he or she files a separate return, or if a spouse dies after a contribution year for which a joint return is filed, any excess contribution of capital gain property that is carried over to the election year from the contribution year must be allocated between the husband and wife, as provided under the rules concerning carryovers of excess contributions. If a husband and wife file separate returns in a contribution year, any election in a later year when a joint return is filed applies to any excess contributions of capital gain property of either individual carried over from the contribution year to the election year. This is also the case when two individuals marry and file a joint return. A remarried individual who filed a joint return with his or her former spouse for a contribution year and thereafter filed a joint return with his or her present spouse must treat the carryover to the election year as provided under the rules concerning carryovers of excess contributions.

When this election is made, the charitable contribution deduction must be reduced by application of the deduction reduction rule (see Chapter 8). If the property that is the subject of the gift is tangible personal property, the charitable deduction that would otherwise be determined must be reduced as provided for in the deduction reduction rule applicable to gifts of this type of property that are put to an unrelated use. This second rule applies (1) even though the gift of property is in fact clearly put to a related use and (2) irrespective of whether the gift is an outright gift or a conveyance of an undivided fractional interest in the property.

Moreover, when this election is made (and the deduction reduction rule is triggered), and the charitable contribution is of less than the donor's entire interest in the contributed property, the donor's adjusted basis in the property must be allocated between the interest contributed and any interest not contributed. An example of this situation is presented in an IRS private letter ruling for a donor who contributed undivided fractional interests in works of art to a museum; the IRS pointed out that if the 50 percent limitation was elected, the deduction reduction rule and the basis allocation rule would apply. The IRS ruled that, in this instance, the amount of the income tax charitable contribution attributable to any gift would equal the product of (1) this fraction times (2) another fraction, the numerator of which is the donor's adjusted basis in her interest in the work immediately preceding the gift of the fractional interest, and the denominator of which is the fraction representing the portion of her ownership in the entire work immediately preceding the gift of the fractional interest.

This election is made by attaching to the federal income tax return for the year of the election a statement indicating that the election is being made. Preferably, the statement will refer to the appropriate sections of the Internal Revenue Code and, ideally, of the regulations. If there is a carryover to the year of any charitable contributions of capital gain property from a previous year or years, the statement must show the recomputation of the carryover, setting forth sufficient information with respect to the previous year or any intervening year to show the basis of the recomputation. The statement must indicate the IRS location where the return for the previous year or years was filed, the name or names in which the return or returns were filed, and whether each of the returns was a joint return or a separate return.

Timing of Election

This election cannot be made retroactively. In the principal case on the point, the donors calculated their charitable deduction for a significant gift of property (which was highly appreciated in value) by making this election. This act produced a charitable deduction for the year of the gift and for two subsequent years. Two years later the donors recalculated their charitable deduction stemming from the gift and filed amended returns using the 30 percent limitation. This approach gave them a smaller deduction in the year of the gift and the two following years, but it produced a charitable contribution in each of the next three tax years. Litigation was launched when the IRS disallowed the deductions for the most recent three years.

One of the arguments advanced by the donors was that they had never made a valid election to use the 50 percent limitation, so they were not bound by that initial decision. The court held, however, that the election was valid, noting that no particular words are required and that adequate notice as to the election had been provided to the IRS.

The other argument was that the election is revocable. Persuaded by the government's argument that irrevocability is required to avoid burdensome uncertainties in administration of the revenue laws, the court held that the donors were bound by their election in the year of the gift. The court observed that "where . . . the taxpayer's initial election later becomes, through hindsight, less financially advantageous than some other option, the improvident election does not enable the taxpayers to revoke that election."

GENERAL 30 PERCENT LIMITATION

A 30 percent limitation generally applies in instances of contributions of money to charitable organizations other than public charities.

General Rules

Normally, an individual's charitable contributions made during a year, to one or more charitable organizations other than public charitable organizations, when the subject of the gift is money, are deductible to the extent that these contributions in the aggregate do not exceed 30 percent of the individual's contribution base for the year. Separate rules apply when the property is long-term capital gain property and is contributed to charitable organizations other than public charitable organizations. This limitation applies to donees such as private foundations, veterans' organizations, fraternal organizations, and certain cemetery companies.

In some instances, however, the actual annual limitation on deductible gifts of this nature is less than the 30 percent limitation.

This occurs when gifts of money and/or capital gain property to public charitable organizations are also made in the same contribution year. Thus, if the amount is less, the limitation will be an amount equal to the excess of 50 percent of the donor's contribution base for the year over the amount of deductible charitable contributions that are allowable under the 50 percent limitation. This rule is discussed more fully in the next section.

Carryover Rules

In general, the excess of:

The amount of the charitable contribution or contributions of capital gain property made by an individual in a contribution year to one or more public charitable organizations

divided by

30 percent of the individual's contribution base for the contribution year

is treated as a charitable contribution paid by the individual to a public charitable organization, subject to the 30 percent limitation, in each of the five years immediately succeeding the contribution year. As noted previously, for federal income tax purposes, when the carryover rules are applied, an amount paid to a charitable organization in one year is treated as paid to the charitable organization in a subsequent year.

INTERPLAY OF 50 PERCENT/SPECIAL 30 PERCENT LIMITATIONS

In computing the charitable contribution deduction, contributions of money to public charitable organizations are taken into account before contributions of capital gain property to public charitable organizations.

INTERPLAY OF 50 PERCENT/GENERAL 30 PERCENT LIMITATIONS

When an individual donor makes, in the same year, gifts of money and/or capital gain property to one or more public charitable organizations and gifts of money in circumstances involving the general 30 percent limitation, the charitable contribution deduction is computed by first taking into consideration the gift or gifts to one or more public charitable organizations. The contributions subject to the 30 percent limitation are deductible, in whole or in part, only to the extent that (1) these gifts do not exceed the 30 percent limitation, or (2) the gift or gifts to one or more public charitable organizations do not, in the aggregate, exceed the amount allowable by the 50 percent limitation.

The actual deductible amount is the lesser of these two items. That is, the maximum amount deductible in any one year for gifts subject to the 30 percent limitation in these circumstances is the lesser of the amount capped by the 30 percent limitation or the amount (if any) represented by the "gap" between the amount contributed to one or more public charitable organizations during the year and the maximum amount allowable under the 50 percent limitation for the year.

INTERPLAY OF SPECIAL 30 PERCENT/GENERAL 30 PERCENT LIMITATIONS

The federal income tax law favors gifts of capital gain property to public charitable organizations over gifts of money to charitable organizations that are not public charitable organizations. Thus, a gift of money to, for example, a private foundation may not be fully deductible under the general 30 percent limitation because of a gift of capital gain property in the same year to a public charitable organization.

20 PERCENT LIMITATION

In general, contributions of capital gain property by individuals to charitable organizations that are not public charitable organizations are subject to a 20 percent limitation. This limitation is a percentage of the donor's contribution base for the contribution year.

General Rules

In some instances, however, the actual annual limitation on deductible gifts of this nature is less than the 20 percent limitation. This occurs when gifts of capital gain property to public charitable organizations are also made in the same contribution year. Thus, the charitable deduction for this type of gift is confined to the lesser of:

- The amount allowable under the 20 percent limitation
- An amount equal to the excess of 30 percent of the donor's contribution base for the year over the amount of charitable contributions of capital gain property to public charitable organizations that are allowable under the 30 percent limitation

This 20 percent limitation applies to contributions of property when the amount of the gift, for deduction purposes, was reduced under the deduction reduction rules (see Chapter 8).

Carryover Rules

In general, the excess of:

The amount of the charitable contribution or contributions of capital gain property made by an individual in a contribution year to one or more charitable organizations that are not public charitable organizations

divided by

20 percent of the individual's contribution base for the contribution year

is treated as a charitable contribution paid by the individual to a nonpublic charitable organization, subject to the 20 percent limitation, in each of the five years immediately succeeding the contribution year.

CONTRIBUTIONS FOR USE OF CHARITY

The federal income tax law provides for a charitable contribution deduction for gifts to or for the use of one or more qualified charitable donees. Charitable contributions discussed in other sections of this chapter are gifts *to* a charitable organization. Contributions *for the use* of a charitable organization are discussed in Chapter 8.

Contributions for the use of a charitable organization are subject to the general 30 percent limitation.

BLENDING PERCENTAGE LIMITATIONS

A donor who is an individual may make gifts of various types to charitable organizations of various tax classifications in a single year. These gifts may be partly of money and partly of property. The property may or may not be capital gain property. The charitable donees may be public charities, private foundations, veterans' organizations, or other charitable recipients. The law provides for application of the various percentage limitations in situations in which differing types of gifts are made and/or differing categories of charitable organizations are recipients of the gifts.

When an individual contributes cash to public and private charities in the same year, an inevitable interplay between the 50 percent limitation and the 30 percent limitation results. When an individual contributes money and capital gain property to one or more public charities in the same year, there likewise is an interplay between the 50 percent limitation and the special 30 percent limitation. Also, there can be an interplay between percentage limitations when capital gain property is contributed in the same year to both or one or more public charities and one or more charitable organizations that are not public ones. In some (complicated) instances, all of the percentage limitations are applicable.

No matter what the mix of gift subjects and gift recipients may be, the maximum amount that may be deducted by an individual in any one year, as the result of one or more charitable gifts, is an amount equal to 50 percent of the donor's contribution base. Contributions of money to public charitable organizations are considered before contributions of money to charitable organizations that are not public charitable organizations. Contributions of money are taken into account before contributions of capital gain property. Contributions of capital gain property to public charitable organizations are taken into account before contributions of this type of property to nonpublic charitable organizations.

When the documentation is not precise, the charitable contribution deduction is likely to default to the 20 percent limitation. For example, the IRS, having ruled that two trusts qualified as charitable remainder unitrusts (see Chapter 9), pointed out that the power of certain individuals to name charitable beneficiaries was not confined to the naming of public charities. Therefore, because of the possibility that a private foundation might be designated as a beneficiary, the IRS ruled that charitable contributions to the trust were limited, for deduction purposes, to the 20 percent limitation.

Charitable gift amounts that exceed these various limitations can be, as discussed, carried forward and be potentially deductible in subsequent years. Just as there can be an interplay of gifts and money in the same year, however, there can be an interplay of two or more years in conjunction with a single gift (because of one or more carryovers). In computing allowable deductions for that year, a charitable contribution in a current year is considered before taking into account contribution deductions based on carryovers.

INDIVIDUALS' NET OPERATING LOSS CARRYOVERS AND CARRYBACKS

An individual having a net operating loss carryover from a prior year, which is available as a deduction in a contribution year, must apply a special rule for net operating loss carryovers in computing the excess charitable contributions for the contribution year.

Carryover Rules

In determining the amount of excess charitable contributions that must be treated as paid in each of the five years succeeding the contribution year, the excess charitable contributions described must be reduced by the amount by which the excess reduces taxable income (for purposes of determining the portion of a net operating loss that must be carried to tax years succeeding the contribution year under the general rule concerning net operating loss carryovers). This increases the net operating loss carried to a succeeding year. In reducing taxable income under these rules, an individual who has made charitable contributions in the contribution year to public organizations and to other charitable organizations must first deduct the contributions made to public charitable organizations from his or her adjusted gross income, computed without regard to his or her net operating loss deduction, before any of the contributions made to other charitable organizations may be deducted form adjusted gross income. Thus, if the excess of the contributions made in the contribution year to public charitable organizations over the amount deductible in the contribution year is utilized to reduce taxable income (under the general rules concerning net operating loss carryovers) for the year, thereby serving to increase the amount of the net operating loss carryover to a succeeding year or years, no part of the excess charitable contributions made in the contribution year may be treated as paid in any of the five immediately succeeding tax years. If only a portion of the excess charitable contributions is so used, the excess charitable contributions need to be reduced only to that extent.

Carryback Rules

The amount of the excess charitable contribution for a contribution year may not be increased because a net operating loss carryback is available as a deduction in the contribution year.

The amount of the charitable contribution from a preceding year that is treated as paid in a current tax year (the *deduction year*) may not be reduced because a net operating loss carryback is available as a deduction in the deduction year. Additionally, in determining the amount of the net operating loss, for any year subsequent to the deduction year, which is a carryback or carryover to years succeeding the deduction year, the amount of contributions made to public charitable organizations in the deduction year must be limited to the amount of the contributions that were actually made in the deduction year and those that were treated as paid in that year. Moreover, these contributions may not exceed the 50 percent limitation or, in the case of capital gain property, the 30 percent limitation, computed without regard to any of the net operating loss deduction modifications for the deduction year.

RULES FOR SPOUSES

If a husband and wife:

- File a joint return for a contribution year,
- Compute an excess charitable contribution for that year, and
- File separate returns for one or more of the five years immediately succeeding the contribution year,

any excess charitable contribution for the contribution year that is unused at the beginning of the first of these five years for which separate returns are filed must be allocated between the husband and the wife. For purposes of this allocation, a computation must be made of the amount of any excess charitable contribution that each spouse would have computed if separate returns had been filed for the contribution year.

The portion of the total unused excess charitable contribution for the contribution year allocated to each spouse must be an amount that bears the same ratio to the unused excess charitable contribution as the spouse's excess contribution, based on the separate return computation, bears to the total excess contributions of both spouses, based on the separate return computation. To the extent that a portion of the amount allocated to either spouse is not treated as a charitable contribution to a public charitable organization in the year in which separate returns are filed, each spouse must treat his or her respective unused portion as the available charitable contribution carryover to the next succeeding year in which the joint excess charitable contribution may be treated as paid. If a husband and wife file a joint return for one of the five years immediately succeeding the contribution year with respect to which a joint excess charitable contribution is computed, and following the first year for which the husband and wife filed separate returns, the amounts allocated to each spouse for this first year must be aggregated for purposes of determining the amount of the available charitable contribution carryover to the succeeding year. The amounts allocated must be reduced by the portion of the amounts treated as paid to a public charitable organization in this first year and in any year intervening between this first year and the succeeding year in which the joint return is filed.

In the case of a husband and wife, when:

- Either or both of the spouses filed a separate income tax return for a contribution year,
- They computed an excess charitable contribution for the year under these rules, and
- They filed a joint income tax return for one or more of the years succeeding the contribution year,

their excess charitable contribution for the contribution year that was unused at the beginning of the first year for which a tax return was filed must be aggregated for purposes of determining the portion of the unused charitable contribution that must be treated (in determining the amount considered as paid in years succeeding a contribution year) as a charitable contribution paid to a public charitable organization. This rule also applies in the case of two single individuals who are subsequently married and file a joint return. A remarried individual who filed a joint return with a former spouse in a contribution year with respect to which an excess charitable contribution was computed, and who in any one of the five years succeeding the contribution year filed a joint return with his or her present spouse, must treat the unused portion of the excess charitable contribution allocated to him or her in the same manner as the unused portion of an excess charitable contribution computed in a contribution year in which he or she filed a separate return, for purposes of determining the amount considered as paid in years succeeding a contribution year to a public charitable organization in the succeeding year.

When one spouse dies, any unused portion of an excess charitable contribution allowable to that spouse is not treated as paid in the year in which the death occurs, or in any subsequent year, except on a separate return made for the deceased spouse by a fiduciary for the year that ends with the date of death or on a joint return for the year in which the death occurs.

INFORMATION REQUIREMENTS

If, in a year, a deduction is claimed in respect of an excess charitable contribution that, in accordance with the rules for determining an amount considered as paid in years succeeding a contribution year, is treated (in whole or in part) as paid in the year, the donor must attach to his or her return a statement showing:

- The contribution year (or years) in which the excess charitable contributions were made
- The excess charitable contributions made in each contribution year and the amount of the excess charitable contributions consisting of capital gain property
- The portion of the excess, or each of the excess, treated as paid in any year intervening between the contribution year and the year for which the return is filed, and the portion of the excess that consists of capital gain property
- Whether an election has been made under the rules allowing the 50 percent limitation with respect to contributions of capital gain property or not, so as to affect any of the excess contributions of capital gain property
- Whatever other information the tax returns or the instructions accompanying them may reasonably require

PERCENTAGE LIMITATION FOR CORPORATIONS

General Rules

The deduction in a year for charitable contributions by a corporation subject to income taxation is limited to 10 percent of the corporation's taxable income for the year, computed with certain adjustments.

Much of the foregoing law as to the characterization of property is equally applicable to contributions by corporations. For example, the general rule is that a deduction for a charitable gift of a capital asset by a corporation is determined using the fair market value of the property at the time of the gift. A corporation may, however, donate to charity what is known as a *corporate archive*. In one of these instances, the gift was of a newspaper clipping library by a newspaper publisher. In another instance, a broadcasting company contributed a film library, consisting of footage documenting local news stories. These archives were compiled and maintained by employees of the company. The IRS held in these cases that the items were property similar to a letter or memorandum prepared or produced for the donor, and therefore were excluded from the definition of *capital asset* (see Chapter 2). Thus, the amount of the gift had to be confined to the donor's basis in the property.

Carryover Rules

Any charitable contributions made by a corporation in a year (a *contribution year*) in excess of the amount deductible in the contribution year under the 10 percent limitation are deductible in each of the five immediately succeeding years, but only to the extent of the lesser of these amounts:

- The excess of the maximum amount deductible for the succeeding year, under the 10 percent limitation, over the sum of the charitable contributions made in that year, plus the aggregate of the excess contributions made in years before the contribution year that are deductible under these rules in the succeeding year
- In the first year succeeding the contribution year, the amount of the excess charitable contributions

- In the second, third, fourth, and fifth years succeeding the contribution year, the portion of the excess charitable contributions not deductible under these rules for any year intervening between the contribution year and the succeeding year

These rules apply to excess charitable contributions by a corporation, whether the contributions are made to or for the use of the recipient charitable organization or not (see Chapter 8) and whether the donee is a public charitable organization or not.

CORPORATIONS' NET OPERATING LOSS CARRYOVERS AND CARRYBACKS

A corporation having a net operating loss carryover from any year must apply a special rule concerning these carryovers before computing the excess charitable contribution carryover from any year.

Carryover Rules

This special rule is: In determining the amount of excess charitable contributions that may be deducted in years succeeding the contribution year, the excess of the charitable contributions made by a corporation in the contribution year over the amount deductible in that year must be reduced by the amount by which the excess (1) reduces taxable income for purposes of determining the net operating loss carryover under the net operating loss deduction rules and (2) increases a net operating loss carryover to a succeeding year. Thus, if the excess of the contributions made in a year over the amount deductible in a year is utilized to reduce taxable income (under the rules for determining net operating loss carryover) for the year, thereby increasing the amount of the net operating loss carryover to a succeeding year or years, a charitable contribution carryover is not available. If only a portion of the excess charitable contribution is so used, the charitable contribution carryover must be reduced only to that extent.

Carryback Rules

The amount of the excess contribution for a contribution year is not increased because a net operating loss carryback is available as a deduction in the contribution year. In addition, in determining the amount of the net operating loss for any year subsequent to the contribution year, which is a carryback or carryover to years succeeding the contribution year, the amount of any charitable contributions must be limited to the amount of the contributions that did not exceed 10 percent of the donor's taxable income for the contribution year.

Year Contribution Is Made

Contributions made by a corporation in a contribution year include contributions that are considered as paid during the contribution year.

ILLUSTRATIONS

The examples to follow concerning individuals assume a donor with an annual contribution base of $100,000. The first three limitations apply to gifts to public charities and to private operating foundations.

First, there is a percentage limitation of 50 percent of the donor's contribution base for gifts of cash and ordinary income property. A donor with a $100,000 contribution base may, in a year, make deductible gifts of these items up to a total of $50,000. If an individual makes contributions that exceed the 50 percent limitation, the excess generally may be carried forward and deducted in one to five subsequent years. Thus, if this donor gave $60,000 to public charities in year 1 and made no other charitable gifts in that year, he or she would be entitled to a deduction of $50,000 in year 1, and the remaining $10,000 would be available for deductibility in year 2.

The second percentage limitation is 30 percent of the donor's contribution base for gifts of capital gain property. A donor thus may, in a year, contribute up to $30,000 of qualifying stocks, bonds, real estate, and like property, and receive a charitable deduction for that amount. Any excess (more than 30 percent) of the amount of these gifts is subject to the carryforward rule. If a donor gave $50,000 in capital gain property in year 1 and made no other charitable gifts that year, he or she would be entitled to a charitable contribution deduction of $30,000 in year 1, and the $20,000 would be available in year 2.

A donor who makes gifts of cash and capital gain property to public charities (and/or private operating foundations) in any one year generally is limited by a blend of these percentage limitations. For example, if the donor in year 1 gives $50,000 in cash and $30,000 in appreciated capital gain property to a public charity, his or her charitable deduction in year 1 is $30,000 of capital gain property and $20,000 of the cash (to keep the deduction within the overall 50 percent ceiling); the other $30,000 of cash would be carried forward to year 2 (or to years 2 through 5, depending on the donor's circumstances).

The third percentage limitation allows a donor of capital gain property to use the 50 percent limitation, instead of the 30 percent limitation, where the amount of the contribution is reduced by all of the unrealized appreciation in the value of the property. This election is usually made by donors who want a larger deduction in the year of the gift for an item of property that has not appreciated in value to a great extent. Once made, this election is irrevocable.

The fourth and fifth percentage limitations apply to gifts to private foundations and certain other charitable donees (other than public charities and private operating foundations). These donees are generally veterans' and fraternal organizations.

Under the fourth percentage limitation, contributions of cash and ordinary income property to private foundations and other entities may not exceed 30 percent of the individual donor's contribution base. The carryover rules apply to this type of gift. If the donor gives $50,000 in cash to one or more private foundations in year 1, his or her charitable deduction for that year (assuming no other charitable gifts) is $30,000, with the balance of $20,000 carried forward into subsequent years (up to five).

The carryover rules blend with the first three percentage limitations. For example, if in year 1 a donor gave $65,000 to charity, of which $25,000 went to a public charity and $40,000 to a private foundation, his or her charitable deduction for that year would be $50,000: $30,000 for the gift to the private foundation and $20,000 for the gift to the public charity. The remaining $10,000 of the gift to the foundation and the remaining $5,000 of the gift to the public charity would be carried forward into year 2.

The fifth percentage limitation is 20 percent of the contribution base for gifts of capital gain property to private foundations and other charitable donees. There is a carryforward for any excess deduction amount. For example, if a donor gives appreciated securities having a value of $30,000 to a private foundation in year 1, his or her charitable deduction for year 1 (assuming no other charitable gifts) is $20,000; the remaining $10,000 may be carried forward.

Deductible charitable contributions by corporations in any tax year may not exceed 10 percent of pretax net income. Excess amounts may be carried forward and deducted in subsequent years (up to five). For gifts by corporations, the federal tax laws do not differentiate between gifts to public charities and gifts to private foundations. As an illustration, a corporation that grosses $1 million in a year and incurs $900,000 in expenses in that year (not including charitable gifts) may generally contribute to charity and deduct in that year an amount up to $10,000 (10 percent of $100,000); in computing its taxes, this corporation would report taxable income of $90,000. If the corporation contributed $20,000 in that year, the numbers would remain the same, except that the corporation would have a $10,000 charitable contribution carryforward.

SUMMARY

This chapter described the complex body of federal tax law imposing various percentage limitations on charitable contribution deductions of individuals and corporations. Explored were the 50, 30, and 20 percent limitations on deductions for individuals and various interplays of these rules. The 10 percent limitation on corporations' charitable deductions was summarized. Special rules for spouses were described. The deduction carryovers and the rules pertaining to net operating loss carryovers and carrybacks were summarized.

CHAPTER 5

Estate and Gift Tax Considerations

The purpose of this chapter is to summarize the federal estate and gift tax laws as they relate to charitable giving. These laws came into existence in 1916; they have been a continuous and growing (and controversial) component of the federal tax scheme ever since. Unlike federal income tax law, federal estate and gift taxes are excise taxes on the transfer of property of individuals, either during their lives or on their deaths. Specifically, this chapter will:

- Provide an introduction to the estate and gift tax system
- Summarize the gift tax rules
- Summarize the estate tax rules
- Explain the unification of these taxes
- Review basic estate planning principles
- Explain the generation-skipping transfer tax system

INTRODUCTION TO TAXES

The federal estate and gift taxes are combined in a unified transfer tax system comprising two elements: the *gift tax* and the *estate tax*. The tax is *unified* in that both gift and estate transfers are taxed as an integrated whole.

The federal estate tax is a tax on the value of estate property of an individual passing to others on his or her death. This is not the same as state law inheritance taxes, which tax the beneficiary or recipient of property from a decedent. Thus, the estate tax is a tax on the transmission of wealth at death; it is a tax on the right to dispose of property. The federal gift tax is a tax on the value of property that a living individual passes, to one or more other persons, during his or her life when property of lesser value (if any) is received in return-that is, a transfer of property for less than adequate consideration.

Another transfer tax is the tax on *generation-skipping transfers.* The generation-skipping transfer tax is not integrated with the gift and estate transfer tax system; it is a separate tax on transfers. This tax, however, is complementary to, and works in conjunction with, the unified gift and estate tax system. It reaches transfers of wealth that are otherwise missed by the unified transfer tax. As its name implies, it endeavors to tax transferred wealth that skips a generation.

Apart from their function as revenue-generating devices, the federal transfer taxes serve an important social function. These taxes tend to lessen the concentration of wealth, particularly family wealth. Nevertheless, because of the increasing complexity of the estate and gift tax regime, its growing applicability to greater numbers of individuals, the relatively small amount of tax revenue generated by these taxes, and the moral aspects of the estate tax (detractors term it a "death tax"), consideration is periodically given to repeal of this component of federal taxation, particularly the estate tax.

Although the federal estate and gift taxes apply to nearly any transfer, the traditional focus of concern has been on transfers within the family context. More precisely, the focus is on generational transfers of any family wealth to successive generations.

The income tax, as a progressive tax, sets rates that increase as income levels rise. As a tax on income, however, it has little effect on previously accumulated wealth. It may lessen individuals' ability to accumulate wealth, but it has no effect on previously accumulated wealth—typically family wealth—that is passed from generation to generation.

Unlike the federal income tax, the federal estate tax is, fundamentally, a tax on wealth. It is a tax on personal wealth and generally arises whenever that wealth is transferred gratuitously during an individual's life or on transfer at that individual's death.

The estate tax is designed to lessen concentrations of wealth in families through a progressive tax rate structure. The estate and gift tax rates begin at 18 percent on the first $10,000 of taxable transfers and reach 49 percent on taxable transfers up to $2.5 million. For taxable transfers in excess of $2.5 million but not more than $3 million, the estate and gift tax rate is 53 percent. For taxable transfers of more than $3 million, the top estate and gift tax rate is 55 percent. To phase out the benefit of the graduated brackets and the unified credit, the estate and gift tax is increased by 5 percent on cumulative taxable transfers-in excess of $10 million but not in excess of the amount at which the average tax rate is 55 percent.

Families with small concentrations of wealth are given tax relief. Through the availability of a credit known as the *unified credit*, estates of amounts up to certain levels can pass free of federal estate and gift tax (see next section).

Additionally, small amounts of wealth can be transferred annually to other individuals free of gift tax. Through what is known as the *annual* (gift tax) *exclusion*, as much as $11,000 per individual may be transferred each year free of the unified estate and gift tax during a person's lifetime (see next section).

Given the sizable tax liability associated with large estates, and the natural tendency and desire on the part of individuals to pass as much of their family wealth as possible to the next generation, much attention is paid to estate planning. Estate planning has developed as a means of minimizing or eliminating the amount of transfer taxes incurred in passing on family wealth.

FEDERAL GIFT TAX

Federal tax law imposes an excise tax on the value of an individual's lifetime transfers of property. Not all transfers, however, are subject to the tax. Only transfers that constitute gifts fall within the ambit of this tax.

A *gift,* in common parlance, is understood to be a present or donation. Frequently one makes a gift as an act or expression of love, affection, friendship, or respect. The transaction is generally understood to be gratuitous, and not for any remuneration or other consideration. The term *gift* may have a different meaning for federal gift tax purposes, as contrasted with other federal tax contexts.

Definition of *Gift*

The term *gift* is not defined in the federal statutory tax law, although the IRS has construed the term. A *gift* is defined by the agency as a transfer by which property, or property rights, is gratuitously conferred on another person. The essential characteristics of a gift are:

- Transfer of money, property, or property rights sufficient to vest legal or equitable title in the donee
- Relinquishment of dominion and control over the gift property by the donor
- Absence of full and adequate consideration for the transfer
- No disclaimer or renunciation of the gift by the donee
- Competence of the donor to make the gift

The criteria establishing the essential characteristics of a gift do not take into account the objective or subjective gratuitousness in the transfer. Neither intention nor motivation is a governing factor. If any transfer is made for less than full and adequate consideration, it is deemed a gift if all the other criteria are present.

If, however, as of the date of a gift, a transfer for charitable purposes is dependent on the performance of some act or the happening of a precedent event to become effective, a gift tax charitable deduction is not allowable unless the possibility that the charitable transfer will not become effective is so remote as to be negligible. Further, if an interest has passed to, or is vested in, a charitable organization on the date of the gift and the interest would be defeated by the performance of some act or the happening of some event, the possibility of occurrence of which appeared on that date to be so remote as to be negligible, the gift tax charitable deduction is allowable. These rules are the same as those used for determining whether the income tax charitable contribution deduction and the estate tax contribution deduction are allowable under similar circumstances.

Imposition of Gift Tax in General

Under federal gift tax law, a tax is imposed on the transfer of property by gift during the calendar year by any individual. The federal gift tax applies generally to all individuals, whether they are residents or nonresidents of the United States. Special rules apply throughout the gift tax area to nonresidents and nonresidents who are not citizens of the United States. Corporations and other artificial entities are not subject to the tax.

A U.S. citizen who resides in a U.S. possession is considered a citizen. If, however, an individual acquired U.S. citizenship solely by being a citizen of the possession, or birth or residence in the possession, he or she is considered a nonresident and not a citizen of the United States.

Scope of Covered Transfers and Property

Generally, all property is included within the scope of the federal gift tax. The tax applies to real or personal, tangible or intangible property. It applies to property situated inside or outside the United States. Only transfers of property situated within the United States, however, are covered in the case of a nonresident who is not a citizen of the United States.

Transfers of intangible property by a nonresident who is not a citizen of the United States are not included, unless the intangible property is stock in a domestic corporation or debt obligation of the United States, its political subdivisions, or its citizens. There is a special exception in cases of lost U.S. citizenship.

Also, the tax applies to all types of transfers, whether the transfer is in trust or otherwise, and whether the gift is direct or indirect.

Powers of Appointment

Generally, the exercise, release, or lapse of a general power of appointment is considered to be a transfer subject to the gift tax. A *general power of appointment* over property is the power to appoint property to oneself, one's estate, creditors, or the creditors of that estate.

A power to appoint property to any person or group, other than those included in the definition of a general power of appointment, is not a general power of appointment. For example, a power limited by an ascertainable standard, or in conjunction with some other person, is not a general power. Therefore, powers to consume, invade, or appropriate property for the benefit of the possessor, when limited by an ascertainable standard concerning health, education, support, or maintenance, are not general powers. Further, powers exercisable only in conjunction with the person creating the power, or a person with an adverse interest, are not considered general.

Transfers Deemed to Not Be Gifts

Gifts are transfers for less than adequate consideration. Under the federal gift tax law, certain transfers are deemed to be for full and adequate consideration, and hence do not fall within the definition of a gift. These transfers are all made pursuant to a written marital property settlement agreement that meets certain conditions. A divorce must occur within a three-year period that begins one year before the date the agreement was entered into. Further, the transfers must be to the other spouse in settlement of marital or property rights, or to provide for child support during the minority of children born to the marriage.

Taxable Gifts

Gift and estate taxes and unified and aggregated to take account of all gratuitous transfers, whether during life or taking effect at death. Death is not, however, the taxable event for purposes of the gift tax. Taxable gifts are accounted for and taxed on an annual basis during the life of an individual. A *taxable gift* is the total amount of gifts made during the calendar year above the annual exclusion (if applicable), less allowable gift tax deductions.

Exclusions from Taxable Gift

Five transfers are excluded from the definition of a taxable gift.

1. *Tuition.* The federal gift tax law excludes from tax transfers of property (typically, cash payments) made directly to an educational institution for tuition, on behalf of an individual (typically, but not limited to, descendants). The tax law encourages the private funding of education free of potential transfer tax.

2. *Medical care costs.* The federal gift tax law excludes from tax transfers of property (again, typically cash payments) made directly to a medical care provider for medical care services on behalf of an individual (typically, but not limited to, a family member). Recognizing that health care is expensive and can be a significant financial burden, the federal tax law does not impose an additional financial burden on those who come to the aid of others in the payment of medical services.

3. *Waiver of pension rights.* This exclusion from the definition of a taxable gift is for waivers of certain pension survivor benefits or rights to them.

4. *Loans of artworks.* This exclusion from the definition of a taxable gift involves a loan of any work of art that is ar-

chaeological, historic, or creative tangible personal property. The federal tax excludes from the gift tax loans of art works made to a tax-exempt charitable organization (other than a private foundation) and used for the organization's exempt purposes.

5. *Transfers to political organizations.* This exclusion from the definition of a taxable gift is for transfers to political organizations, such as political parties and political action committees.

Annual Exclusion

As noted, taxable gifts are all gifts made during a calendar year after taking into account the annual exclusion, less allowable deductions. The *annual exclusion* is a fixed dollar amount that is allowed as an exclusion from gift tax. Currently, the amount of the exclusion is $11,000.

There are a number of restrictions on the availability or applicability of the annual exclusion. The exclusion is available annually; it may not be carried over to another year if it is unused or underused. The exclusion is available for the first $11,000 of a gift to each recipient, termed a *donee.* There is no limit on the number of donees that may be gifted money or other property covered by the annual exclusion. Only gifts of present interests are considered for purposes of the annual exclusion. Gifts of future interests in property, including reversions and remainder interests, are denied the exclusion.

Certain transfers made for the benefit of minors are not considered to be future interests under the annual exclusion rules. A transfer for the benefit of a minor qualifies for the annual exclusion when:

- The property, and income from it, may be used only by or for the benefit of the minor before he or she reaches the age of 21, and
- Any remaining property and income is distributed to the minor when he or she reaches 21, or, if the minor dies before reaching 21, to his or her estate, or as he or she appoints pursuant to a general power of appointment.

Valuation of Gift Transfers

The federal gift transfer tax applies to the value of the property transferred as of the date of transfer. When the gift is also a direct skip within the meaning of the generation-skipping transfer tax, however, the value of the gift is increased by the amount of the generation-skipping transfer tax imposed. The value of gifts of money is the amount given. A gift of property other than money is valued at its fair market value.

In the case of transfers of property for less than full and adequate consideration, the value of the property transferred for gift tax purposes is the fair market value of the property less the consideration received.

Basis of Gift Property

The basis of gift property in the hands of the recipient is generally the transferor's basis plus the gift tax paid as a result of the transfer. To account for the transferor's investment in property, the federal income tax provides that the basis in gifted property to a transferee (or donee) is the transferor's basis. This is known as a *transferred* or *carryover basis*. The basis of the property in the hands of the giver (the transferor) is transferred with the gift and becomes the basis of the gift/property in the hands of the recipient (the transferee). As noted, the amount of the transferred basis in gifted property is increased by the amount of gift tax paid by the transferor as a result of the gift.

There is an important limitation on carryover of the transferor's basis. The transferee's basis in gifted property is the same as the basis in the hands of the transferor, except that the basis cannot exceed the fair market value of the property at the time of the gift. What this means is that tax wealth can be transferred, but not tax losses. Should loss property (property in which the basis exceeds the fair market value of the asset) be transferred by gift, the transferee will not be able to recognize the transferor's loss on the property.

An example of the basis rule is a *bargain sale* of property, which is a sale for less than fair market value (insufficient consideration). It is also known as a *part gift/part sale transaction,* as the intention of the transferor is to make a gift of a part of the property (see Chapters 7 and 12).

Gift Tax Deductions

The federal gift tax law provides two deductions from taxable gifts: the marital deduction and the charitable contribution deduction.

Marital Deduction

The federal gift tax law provides an unlimited gift tax deduction for transfers between spouses. Spouses generally can make any number of transfers between themselves, in any amount, free of gift tax. The unlimited marital deduction is, however, subject to a number of conditions and limitations.

Generally, life estates and other terminable interests may not qualify for the marital deduction. *Terminable interests* are interests in property that may be terminated. If one spouse makes a transfer to a transferee spouse of an interest that may terminate, the transfer does not qualify for the marital deduction. Thus, the marital deduction, is not available if:

- The transferor spouse retains or gifts to someone other than the other spouse an interest in the property, and such person may enjoy use or possession of the property on a termination, or
- The transferor spouse retains a power of appointment over use or possession of the property on a termination.

There is an exception to the terminable interest rule. *Qualified terminable interest property* (QTIP) will qualify for the marital deduction if certain conditions are met. The spouse must receive income for life, and no other person may have a power of appointment over the property except to appoint to the other spouse during the other spouse's life. An election must be made to take advantage of the QTIP provisions. A charitable remainder trust (see Chapter 9) will not be disqualified from a marital deduction if the other spouse is the only noncharitable beneficiary of the trust.

The deduction is disallowed in its entirety if the other spouse is not a citizen of the United States. In its place is substituted the annual exclusion with a limit of $100,000, subject to adjustment for inflation. Other rules apply in this context.

Charitable Deduction

Like federal income tax law, the federal gift tax law provides a deduction for gifts to charitable organizations (see Chapter 1).

Citizens and residents of the United States are allowed to deduct all gift transfers to or for the use of:

- The United States, any state (including the District of Columbia), and political subdivisions of states for exclusively public purposes
- Organizations organized and operated exclusively for religious, charitable, scientific, literary, or educational purposes; to foster amateur sports competition (but not athletic facilities or equipment); to encourage art; or for the prevention of cruelty to children or animals (where there is no net earnings inuring to private shareholders or individuals, and the organization is not disqualified because of attempts to influence legislation, and there is no participation in political campaigns)
- Fraternal societies for use exclusively for religious, charitable, scientific, literary, or educational purposes, including encouragement of art or the prevention of cruelty to children or animals
- Veterans' organizations organized in the United States or a possession (where there is no impermissible inurement of net earnings)

The charitable deduction is subject to disallowance in certain cases. Transfers to certain charitable organizations subject to the termination tax applicable with respect to private foundations or to charitable organizations that are no longer tax-exempt do not qualify for the charitable contribution deduction. Generally, a transfer of a remainder interest in property to a charity is not entitled to a charitable gift tax deduction when the transferor retains an interest, or transfers his or her retained interest to a donee, for a use other than the appropriate charitable uses.

A charitable deduction is allowed for transfers of remainder interests to charities by these methods:

- Charitable remainder annuity trust
- Charitable remainder unitrust
- Pooled income fund
- Guaranteed annuity
- Annual fixed percentage distribution of fair market value of property

Three other exceptions to this general rule are contributions of a remainder interest in a personal residence or farm, contributions of an undivided portion of a donor's entire interest in a property, and qualified conservation contributions (see Chapter 9).

As to the second of these three exceptions, an income tax charitable contribution deduction is allowable for a gift of property to a charitable organization when the donee organization is given the right, as a tenant in common with the donor, to possession, dominion, and control of the property for a portion of each year appropriate to its interest in the property. This rule regarding possession for only a portion of the year is not in the gift tax regulations; nonetheless, it is the position of the IRS that this rule applies for gift tax purposes.

Liability for Gift Tax

Gift tax is computed on the value of taxable gift transfers. Liability to pay the tax imposed is on the donor-the transferor of the gift property.

Split Gifts between Spouses

The federal gift tax law allows a nontransferor spouse to agree to share equally in gifts made by the transferor spouse. This permits use of the nontransferor spouse's annual exclusion and unified credit. If the annual exclusion is split, a $22,000 gift-tax-free transfer can be made in lieu of the regular $11,000 exclusion per donee.

When both spouses consent to a split gift, each becomes jointly and severally liable for the entire gift tax liability.

Gift splitting is not permitted on transfers where one spouse gives the other spouse a general power of appointment over the property.

Disclaimers

A person who holds an interest in property, including powers with respect to property, may refuse his or her interest without the refusal being treated as a taxable transfer to that person. This refusal is termed a *qualified disclaimer*. To qualify, the disclaimer must be an irrevocable and unqualified refusal to accept a property interest. Furthermore, to be effective, the disclaimer must meet certain other prescribed form and notice requirements.

When property, or an interest in property, passes to another person as a result of a qualified disclaimer, the person disclaiming the gift is not treated as having made a taxable transfer.

FEDERAL ESTATE TAX

The other component of the unified federal transfer tax system is the estate tax. This aspect of the system concerns transfers of property that take place on the death of an individual.

Gross Estate

The first step in determining estate tax liability is determination of the value of the decedent's *gross estate*. The value of the gross estate is defined as including the date-of-death value of all property, real or personal, tangible or intangible, wherever situated. The value of the gross estate also includes the value of all property to the extent of the interest of the decedent in the property at the time of his or her death.

If the federal estate tax or any state inheritance (or succession, legacy, or estate) tax is payable out of charitable bequests, legacies, or devises, the estate tax charitable contribution deduction is confined to the amount of the bequests, legacies, or devises reduced by the amount of the taxes. When this rule applies, an interrelated calculation is required to determine the amount of the allowable deduction. Generally, state law governs regarding the manner in which death taxes are apportioned to the assets that constitute a decedent's gross estate. The law may provide that if a will specifies an estate-tax apportionment method different from the method provided by statute, the method specified in the will controls. In a court case involving this type of a law, the death taxes and other bequests, debts, and expenses of the decedent that were paid by the residuary estate exhausted the estate; thus, there were no probate assets available for allocation to the charitable bequest, so the deduction was significantly reduced.

The gross estate encompasses a broad spectrum of property. It includes within its ambit the probate estate, contractual payments (such as insurance), and jointly titled property. In addition to the broad sweep of the gross estate given by its statutory definition, the federal estate tax law provides for other inclusions in the gross estate:

- Dower or curtesy interests
- Certain transfers within three years of death
- Retained life estates
- Transfers taking effect at death
- Revocable transfers
- Annuities
- Joint interests
- Powers of appointment
- Life insurance
- Transfers for insufficient consideration

Basic policy reasons cause inclusion of these property interests in a decedent's estate. The decedent retains (as a matter of law) significant beneficial interests in property of this type. Therefore, the decedent should be treated as the owner for purposes of imposing the estate transfer tax. When the retained powers and control over property are such that the decedent has the ability to affect the beneficial use and enjoyment of property during life, or on death, particularly with respect to transferring such interests, the decedent can in all fairness be treated as if he or she were the owner of such property. As a deemed owner, the decedent is taxed on such property as if it were a part of his or her transferable estate on death.

Dower or Curtesy Interests

The full value of all property subject to dower, curtesy, or other similar marital estate interests of the surviving spouse in the decedent's estate are included in the gross estate.

Transfers within Three Years of Death

At one time, the federal estate tax law required that transfers in contemplation of death be included in the estate of the decedent. The policy reason for this rule is obvious: An individual, with knowledge that he or she would soon die, could bypass the estate tax burden through deathbed lifetime gifts of most or all of his or her property.

To rectify this matter, transfers in contemplation of death were recaptured and added back to the taxable estate. This provision, however, also generated a great deal of litigation over whether certain transfers were in *contemplation of death*. To forestall deathbed-type transfers, and to avoid litigation over whether certain transfers were in contemplation of death, a bright-line rule was adopted: All transfers within three years of the decedent's death were added back to the estate.

Transfers made within three years of death that are included in the estate are:

- Transfers with retained life interests
- Transfers taking effect at death
- Revocable transfers
- Life insurance proceeds

Certain other gifts made within three years of death are included in the gross estate, but only for special purposes and calculations.

Retained Life Estates

The gross estate includes property in which the decedent retained for life (or a period ascertainable by reference to the decedent's life) the right to (or the right to appoint) the possession, enjoyment, or income from the property.

Transfers Taking Effect at Death

The gross estate includes the value of all property in which the decedent transferred an interest that can be enjoyed only by surviving the decedent, when the decedent retained a reversionary interest that exceeds 5 percent of the value of the property. A *retained interest* includes any interest to the decedent, his or her estate, or subject to a power of appointment in the decedent.

When the value of a retained reversion is 5 percent or less, this type of a reversion may be included back in the estate.

Revocable Transfers

Property ownership amounts to more than mere legal title. Ownership, in its broader sense, includes a bundle of rights in the property. Legal title is but one of these rights. Other rights include beneficial rights, such as the power to control use and enjoyment of property. One may sever legal title to property and yet retain so many other powers and rights that control of the property (through its use and enjoyment) has been retained. In these cases, the person controlling the property is the de facto owner of the property.

The gross estate includes the value of all property over which the decedent had a power to alter, amend, revoke, or terminate an interest in property. Any form of a revocable transfer is includable in a gross estate.

Annuities

An *annuity* is a contractual arrangement by which a stream of income is paid in exchange for a premium payment. An annuity (periodic income payments) is paid to a beneficiary for a stated period of time. These payments are usually of a specified amount (fixed dollar amount), payable at certain intervals (weekly, monthly, yearly), over a certain period of time (number of years or for life).

The gross estate includes the value of any annuity or other payment receivable by any beneficiary by reason of surviving the decedent, under any form of contract or agreement (other than insurance), if any payment was payable to the decedent, or the decedent had a right to receive a payment, alone or with another, for life or a period not ascertainable without reference to the decedent's life. The amount of payments includable in a gross estate is the amount proportionate to the purchase price paid by the decedent.

Joint Interests

Except for spouses, the gross estate includes the value of all property held as joint tenants with rights of survivorship, unless it can be shown that the interest held originally belonged to some other person. Spouses include only one-half of property owned as joint tenants or as tenants by the entireties in the estate. Jointly held property acquired by gift, bequest, devise, or inheritance includes only the decedent's fractional share of the property.

Powers of Appointment

The gross estate includes the value of property over which the decedent had a general power of appointment at the time of death.

Certain lapses are not treated as releases of general powers over property. When property can be appointed annually but does not exceed the greater of $5,000 or 5 percent of the value of the asset, the lapse of such power is not considered to be the release of a general power over the property. This type of qualifying lapse is subjected to imposition of the estate tax.

Life Insurance

The gross estate includes the value of life insurance receivable by the executor on the life of the decedent and insurance receivable by other beneficiaries when the decedent retained any incidents of ownership at the time of death, exercisable alone or in conjunction with another person. A reversionary interest of more than 5 percent of the value of the policy immediately before death is considered an incident of ownership.

Other incidents of ownership include the power to change beneficiaries, revoke an assignment of the policy, pledge the policy for a loan, or cancel, surrender, or transfer the policy.

The amount or value of the insurance policy includable in the owner's estate is the face amount of the policy rather than its cash surrender value.

Transfers for Insufficient Consideration

The gross estate includes this property transferred for less than full and adequate consideration:

- Certain transfers within three years of death
- Retained life estate
- Transfers taking effect at death
- Revocable transfers
- Powers of appointment

Taxable Estate

The *taxable estate* is the value of the gross estate less allowable deductions. These items are deductions allowable from the gross estate to arrive at the taxable estate:

- Funeral expenses
- Administration expenses
- Claims against the estate
- Unpaid indebtedness included in the gross estate

- Losses and other casualties
- Charitable deduction
- Marital deduction

The two most significant deductions are the charitable and marital estate tax deductions.

Charitable Estate Tax Deduction

A charitable estate tax deduction generally is allowed for the value of all estate transfers of the decedent to or for the use of these entities:

- The United States, any state (including the District of Columbia), and political subdivisions of states for exclusively public purposes
- Organizations organized and operated exclusively for religious, charitable, scientific, literary, or educational purposes; to foster amateur sports competition (but not athletic facilities or equipment); to encourage art; or for the prevention of cruelty to children or animals (where there is no impermissible inurement of net earnings, and the organization is not disqualified because of attempts to influence legislation, and there is no participation in political campaigns)
- Fraternal societies for use exclusively for religious, charitable, scientific, literary, or educational purposes, including encouragement of art or the prevention of cruelty to children or animals
- Veterans' organizations organized by act of Congress, or their departments or local chapters or posts (assuming no impermissible inurement of net earnings)

This charitable deduction may be disallowed. Transfers to certain charitable organizations subject to the termination tax applicable with respect to private foundations, or to charitable organizations that are no longer tax-exempt, do not enjoy the charitable contribution deduction. Generally, a transfer of a split interest in property to a charity is not entitled to an estate tax charitable deduction when an interest in the same property is transferred to a person, or for a use, other than the appropriate charitable uses.

Another context in which the estate tax charitable deduction may be disallowed is in connection with amounts paid to a charitable organization pursuant to the settlement of a will. Deductibility of the payments is not determined on the basis of a good faith adversary proceeding. Rather, the appropriate inquiry is whether the interest in issue reaches the charity pursuant to correctly interpreted and applied state law. The charity must have recognizable, enforceable rights, under state law, to at least some portion of the estate. For example, when a charity was named as a beneficiary in a decedent's will, but not in any of six subsequent wills and a codicil, the IRS concluded that there was little likelihood that the first will would be admitted to probate; thus, the estate was not entitled to any charitable deduction for the payment.

A charitable deduction is allowed for these types of split interests in property when the interest (remainder interest) transferred is:

- Charitable remainder annuity trust
- Charitable remainder unitrust
- Pooled income fund
- Guaranteed annuity
- Annual fixed percentage distribution of fair market value of property (see Chapter 9)

Contributions of split interests in copyrighted tangible works of art are not denied a charitable contribution deduction when the artwork is conveyed separately from the copyright in the work. The split interests of the artwork and its copyright are treated as separate properties. The contribution must be made to a qualified organization that will use the property in a manner related to the organization's tax-exempt function. A qualified organization is a charitable organization other than a private foundation (see Chapter 1).

An estate tax charitable contribution deduction is available in respect of any transfer of a qualified real property interest, as long as the interest meets certain requirements. Essentially, this deduction is available for irrevocable transfers of easements in real property.

Marital Estate Tax Deduction

An unlimited marital deduction is allowed to a decedent for the value of any property transferred to his or her surviving spouse. Transfers of terminable interests in property generally do not qualify for the marital deduction. *Terminable interests* are interests that fail after a certain period of time, the occurrence of a contingency, or failure of an event. An interest that is conditional on the continued survival of the surviving spouse is not considered a terminable interest when the condition does not exceed six months.

The portion of a terminable life estate interest in property given to the surviving spouse is eligible for the marital deduction when the spouse is entitled to receive all the income from the portion of the interest at least annually, with power of appointment in the surviving spouse (or the spouse's estate) over that portion of all the property.

Similarly, in the case of proceeds from a life insurance policy, or an annuity, if the proceeds are payable in installments (or held to pay interest thereon) and the installments are payable at least annually (beginning at least 13 months after the decedent's death), such payments qualify for the marital deduction. The payments must be payable only to the surviving spouse. Further, the surviving spouse (or the surviving spouse's estate) must have the power of appointment over the property.

The marital deduction is available, by election, for qualified terminable interest property. Under a QTIP election, a qualified terminable income interest for the life of the surviving spouse is made subject to the marital deduction. The deduction applies when the surviving spouse has a right, for life, to income as to that portion of property for which an election is made, payable at least annually, or has a life usufruct interest in the property. Further, no person may have a power of appointment over the property during the life of the surviving spouse.

Interests passing to the surviving spouse through a qualified charitable remainder trust qualify for the marital deduction. A trust is qualified if it is a charitable remainder annuity trust or a charitable remainder unitrust (see Chapter 9). The only noncharitable beneficiary under this type of a trust must be the surviving spouse.

UNIFICATION OF TAXES

The estate and gift taxes are unified; this unified federal transfer tax is a progressive tax. As discussed, it taxes the value of transferred property in brackets ranging from a low of 18 percent to a high of 55 percent for estates of more than $3 million.

A credit is available to offset the taxes imposed under the unified estate and gift transfer tax. Known as the *unified credit*, it is available to offset, dollar for dollar, taxes imposed on both lifetime gift transfers and transfers by reason of death.

This credit is in the form of an *applicable credit amount*, which is based on a series of *applicable exclusion amounts*. Under the unified credit, tax-free transfers up to the applicable exclusion amount in asset value can be made during an individual's life and/or on that person's death.

Under the unified transfer tax system, other credits are available to offset or reduce tax liability. These include credit for:

- State death taxes
- Foreign death taxes
- Prior transfer
- Death taxes on remainders

ESTATE PLANNING PRINCIPLES

The term *estate planning* applies to lifetime financial and tax planning for an individual (and his or her family) as well as planning for the transfer of accumulated lifetime wealth. Typically, the estate planner focuses on the lifetime financial resources, needs, and desires of an individual. At the same time, the estate planner looks at that individual's needs and desire to provide for others after the individual's death. The estate planner attempts to satisfy and reconcile these needs and desires by utilizing techniques and devices to reduce or eliminate tax consequences to the individual and his or her estate.

A number of principles guide an estate planner in his or her efforts to reduce the federal transfer tax.

Estate Reduction

The first principle of estate planning is minimization of the value of the property constituting the decedent's gross estate. The federal transfer tax ultimately reaches only that property remaining in, or by tax law included in, the decedent's estate. To avoid or minimize tax, one can reduce an estate so that by the time death (and taxes) arrives, little or nothing remains to be taxed.

A number of techniques are available to accomplish this result. The annual gift tax exclusion is one method for removing assets from the estate. An individual can give up to $11,000 annually to any number of individuals without application of the transfer tax. If the donor individual is married, he or she can aggregate the spouse's annual exclusion and give away $22,000 per year.

The annual exclusion can be leveraged to convey assets that will (or can be expected to) appreciate greatly over time. An annual exclusion amount tax-free gift of appreciating property today may, over time, shelter several times the value of the transfer.

Likewise, an individual can take advantage of the unified credit to make lifetime transfers of more than the annual exclusion amount to remove large assets that will (or can be expected to) appreciate over time. Assets in amounts up to the applicable exclusion amount can be transferred without taxation, and with them any appreciation over the life of the donor.

Estate Freezes and Special Valuation Rules

A complementary device for controlling appreciation in the estate is through what is known as an *estate freeze*. Instead of transferring the entire asset that is expected to appreciate over time, the amount of appreciation in the asset can be frozen at its current level and the appreciation potential conveyed at little or no tax cost.

One technique involves the recapitalization of stock on a corporation. All of the original owners of the stock in the corporation could arrange for the delivery of their stock to the corporation in return for the reissuance of two new classes of stock, often called *common* and *preferred* stock. Each class of stock is granted different attributes.

For example, the preferred stock could be designed to have a right to receive a fixed specified rate of return prior to any of the corporation's profit being shared with respect to the common stock. Only after the right to income of the preferred stock was met could the balance be allocated among the shares of common stock. But the value of the preferred stock could not increase as the corporation grew, because the return with respect to the preferred stock is fixed; therefore, the growth of the corporation would be reflected only in the value of the shares of common stock. As a result, at the time of recapitalization, most of the value of the company would be absorbed by the preferred stock, and, until the company's value grew, the common shares would be attributed little value. In this way, the original shareholders could give the common stock to their children and grandchildren at a low value, and therefore a reduced gift tax cost, while retaining preferred rights to the company's profits. Thus, the parents effectively froze the value of the preferred stock to prevent its growth in their estates and diverted appreciation of the company to the common stock that was transferred by gifts to their children.

These estate freeze techniques have been viewed as abusive transactions; rules were enacted to regulate their use with respect to intrafamily transactions. Rules apply to the taxation of intrafamily transfers of equity interest in corporations and partnerships, the effect of intrafamily agreements restricting transfer of these interests (buy-sell agreements), the taxation of transfers in trust, and the effect of lapsing rights. The overall focus of these rules with respect to intrafamily transfers is on determining whether a gift has been made and, if so, the value of that gift. In effect, the law provides a set of special valuation rules for intrafamily transfers under circumstances in which the transferor retains an interest in property with characteristics that differ from the transferred interest in that property. In general, the framework of the special valuation rules for intrafamily transfers is organized so as to ignore, for transfer tax purposes, attributes of transferred property interests that otherwise would reduce the value of those interests. Thus, the special valuation rules do not prohibit transfers; the rules merely govern the valuation of certain statutory transfers that are allowed to escape application of the special valuation rules.

Some examples of the statutory exceptions to the special valuation rules are:

- Equity interests in business entities that provide for *qualified payments* with respect to the parents' retained preferred equity interest
- Transfers in trust for a family member in which the transferor retains a *qualified annuity, unitrust,* or *remainder interest*
- Buy-sell agreements that are recognized as a valid business arrangement pursuant to which transfers are not made for less than adequate consideration to a family member and the terms of which are comparable to similar arrangements entered into by persons in arm's length transactions
- Restrictions that are imposed by federal or state law or that may be exercised or removed only with the consent of a nonfamily member

Deferral

Another fundamental estate planning technique is deferral of estate tax. The principle concerning the time value of money posits that the deferred or delayed enjoyment of one dollar a year from now is worth less than a dollar today. Therefore, the same amount of money today is worth more than the same amount of money in the future. The greater the deferral, the greater the present value of money.

Deferral of transfer taxes can be accomplished in a number of ways. The most significant method is by transfers to a spouse. The marital deduction is unlimited. Except for the exclusion of certain unqualified terminable interests, taxes can be deferred through transfers to a spouse qualifying for the marital deduction.

Another popular deferral device is use of one or more trusts. Assets placed in trust can provide for support of a spouse, with distribution on death to the children. Similarly, a trust can provide for support of children, with a distribution on death to grandchildren. In either event, taxation of the trust assets would be deferred until after they were distributed to the children or grandchildren. The generation-skipping transfer tax must be carefully considered with respect to these types of transactions.

Generation-Skipping Transfers

Like deferral, a traditional estate planning goal is to pass assets down to as many lower generations as possible with little or no tax. Bypass trusts were used for this purpose. A trust could be created to provide for a transferor's children, with the remainder to the grandchildren. The next lower generation would be skipped over free of estate tax at that level.

Today, that device is limited somewhat by the generation-skipping transfer tax. By utilizing the generation-skipping transfer tax exclusion, however, opportunities to skip generations tax free still exist.

Credit-Maximizing Trusts and Transactions

Another estate planning technique is use of available credits to shield assets from tax and thus maximize tax savings. Spouses can, by reason of the marital deduction, transfer assets to the other free of tax. If a spouse transferred assets out of his or her estate to a person other than his or her spouse, when the amount transferred is shielded by the unified credit, the transfer would also be tax free. That person can be a trust. Thus, an individual can transfer assets to a trust, shielded by the credit, and assets to a spouse, shielded by the marital deduction, in such a way as to reduce or perhaps eliminate estate taxation.

Estate Equalization

Because of the progressive nature of the estate tax, larger estates may be taxed to a greater extent than smaller ones. If one or the other spouse ends up with a proportionately larger estate than the other, higher estate taxes may be the result. To take advantage of the tax savings of lower rates, the estate planner will seek to balance the estates of spouses so that they are approximately equal. Reliance on the marital deduction alone may mean that the value and benefit of one spouse's unified credit is lost. Estate equalization is accomplished by means of a blend of use of the marital deduction and the unified credit.

Revocable Living Trusts

Estate planning can entail use of one or more revocable living trusts. This trust is in the nature of a contract that determines how an individual's property is to be managed and distributed during his or her lifetime, and also at death. A trust is a *living trust* when it is established during the lifetime of the individual creating the trust (the *grantor* of the trust), and it is *revocable* when the grantor has reserved the right to amend or revoke the trust during his or her lifetime. Often the grantor of a revocable living trust is the trustee of the trust.

Once this type of trust is established, the grantor transfers property to the trust during his or her lifetime. Thus, instead of owning certain assets in the individual's name, or owning assets jointly with another (such as the individual's spouse), the assets are "owned" by the individual in the capacity of trustee of the trust. Because the trust is revocable and because the grantor is the trustee, the individual has complete control over and access to the assets that are owned by the trust while he or she is living. Should the individual become incapacitated, the person named as the successor trustee (such as the spouse) would begin to serve, managing and utilizing the property for the individual's benefit. This approach avoids the need for a court to appoint a conservator of the property.

The individual may name beneficiaries to receive assets from the trust. At death, any property owned by the trust or any assets transferred to the trust by reason of death (such as life insurance proceeds, if the trust was designated as the beneficiary) are distributed to the beneficiaries in the manner specified in the trust agreement. In this regard, the trust instrument functions in the same fashion as a will.

Another benefit of a revocable trust is that assets owned by the trust at the death of the grantor are not subject to probate. Likewise, assets that are not owned solely in the decedent's name, or that name beneficiaries pursuant to a contract, are not subject to probate at death. These assets include benefits from individual retirement accounts, other retirement plans, life insurance proceeds, and property with a "pay-on-death" or "transfer-on-death" designation under which the death benefits or property are paid or transferred directly to the designated beneficiary on death. In addition, property held in joint tenancy will not be subject to probate on the occasion of the death of the joint tenant who is the first to die. In the event of the simultaneous deaths of the joint tenants, however, or in the event the surviving joint tenant owns property in his or her name at the time of death, the property will be subject to probate.

Disclaimers

When preparing a revocable living trust, the estate planner should include a disclaimer provision giving the surviving spouse the opportunity to reduce or eliminate future estate taxes. (A *disclaimer* is an irrevocable and unqualified refusal to accept a gift of property.) The trust would provide that, on the death of the first of the spouses to die, the designated successor trustee of the deceased spouse's trust will set aside the trust assets for the benefit of the surviving spouse in a separate trust share, for example, Trust A. Any property allocated to Trust A should qualify for the unlimited marital deduction and, therefore, will not be subject to any federal estate tax at the death of the first of the spouses to die.

Trust A would provide that, while the surviving spouse is living, he or she will be entitled to all of the net income of Trust A as well as trustee-approved distributions of principal from Trust A for the surviving spouse's health, education, maintenance, and support. Also, the surviving spouse would have the absolute right to withdraw any or all of the principal of Trust A. Therefore, unless the surviving spouse is incapacitated, in which case the successor trustee will hold the assets for the surviving spouse's benefit, the surviving spouse will have complete control over the assets of Trust A and will most likely withdraw those assets and add them to his or her own trust.

Each trust would, however, also direct a different distribution of property that the surviving spouse disclaims. Under this arrangement, the surviving spouse can elect to refuse to accept any or all of the property that would otherwise pass to him or her from Trust A. The trusts would provide that, in the event the surviving spouse decides to disclaim any of the assets that would otherwise be distributed to him or her, the disclaimed assets will be set aside by the trustee in another trust share, for example, Trust B. Any assets that are disclaimed and added to Trust B will still be held for the benefit of the surviving spouse. The surviving spouse will receive the net income of Trust B and trustee-approved distributions of principal for his or her health, education, maintenance, and support. The surviving spouse will not, however, have the ability to withdraw the assets from Trust B and, therefore, will be more restricted with respect to any assets disclaimed and added to Trust B.

The reason the surviving spouse would disclaim some of the assets and allow them to pass to Trust B is to make certain that the applicable exclusion amount of the first spouse to die is used (not wasted). The surviving spouse's decision to make a disclaimer will depend on the facts and circumstances that exist at the time of the death of the first spouse, the primary one likely being the size of the estate. Again, the balance of the assets transferred can be protected by the marital deduction. Consequently, the disclaimer trust provisions offer the surviving spouse flexibility to determine whether and to what extent Trust B will be funded.

At the death of the surviving spouse, any remaining assets (after payment of taxes and expenses) would be divided into appropriate shares to provide for transfer to any children and/or to others. These shares would be transferred free of trust, except to the extent the trust instrument limits distributions to beneficiaries who are minors.

Last Will

In addition to a trust, a last will and testament should be prepared. One purpose of a will is to provide for distribution of the individual's tangible personal property at death. Usually these items, or at least most of them, will be transferred to the surviving spouse. Otherwise, this property can be distributed by way of a written list, which designates which beneficiaries are to receive which items of tangible personal property.

Another purpose of a will is to provide that, at death, any property (other than tangible personal property) the individual owns in his or her name—that is, that has not been transferred to a trust prior to death or is not owned in joint tenancy or the like—will pour over into the trust after it passes through probate. A *pourover will* ensures that any property that the individual has not placed in a trust during his or her lifetime will ultimately end up in, and be subject to the dispositive provisions of, the trust.

A will also designates the *personal representative* of the estate (also known as the *executor* or *executrix*). This person administers the probate estate and works with the probate court to properly distribute assets to heirs. If probate is avoided, by transferring property to a trust or owning it in joint tenancy or the like, there will be no probate estate and the personal representative will not have any function.

Durable Power of Attorney

An individual should have a *durable power of attorney* document, designating an attorney-in-fact to make economic decisions for the individual and deal with his or her property should the individual become incapacitated. Durable powers of attorney can avoid the necessity of a court-appointed guardian and/or conservator in the case of incapacity.

Another such document is the *durable power of attorney for health care decisions.* This instrument allows an individual to designate an attorney-in-fact to act in the individual's place in the making of medical decisions. Decisions of this nature include signing medical consents and hiring and discharging physicians.

Living Will

A *living will* enables an individual to direct the termination of artificial life support in the event the individual is terminally ill.

Future of Estate Tax

Serious talk and serious efforts to repeal the estate tax have unfolded in recent years. Support does not seem to exist in Congress, however, for complete repeal. Yet a compromise may be struck. The uncertainty as to the future of the estate tax hampers long-term estate planning.

The unknown future of the estate tax is compounded by the fact that the estate and gift taxes are to be reduced between 2002 and 2009, with the estate tax scheduled for restoration in 2010. In 2002 the rates in excess of 50 percent were repealed. Also, in 2002 the unified credit application exclusion amount was increased to $1 million.

The phase-out of the estate tax is to proceed in this way:

1. In 2003 the estate and gift tax rates in excess of 49 percent were repealed.
2. In 2004 the estate and gift tax rates in excess of 48 percent were repealed, and the unified credit exemption amount for estate tax purposes was increased to $1.5 million (leaving the exemption amount for gift tax purposes at $1 million).
3. In 2005 the estate and gift tax rates in excess of 47 percent were repealed.
4. In 2006 the estate and gift tax rates in excess of 46 percent were repealed, and the unified credit exemption amount for estate tax purposes was increased to $2 million.
5. In 2007 the estate and gift tax rates in excess of 45 percent are to be repealed.
6. In 2009 the unified credit exemption amount will increase to $3.5 million.
7. In 2010 the estate tax is to be repealed.

Thereafter, the estate tax is to be reinstated, at the prior levels.

REMAINDER INTERESTS

Outright bequests to charity by will qualify for the estate tax charitable deduction. To qualify for an estate tax charitable deduction, if a remainder interest bequest to charity is made using a split-interest trust, the trust must be a charitable remainder trust or a pooled income fund (see Chapter 9).

In General

In one instance, the estate tax charitable deduction was denied because the recipient of a bequest did not qualify as a charitable entity. The executor of the estate secured from the organization an affidavit certifying that it was a charitable organization. He failed, however, to review the IRS's Cumulative List of Charitable Organizations; the organization had been deleted from the list prior to the transfer from the estate.

In another instance, a charitable deduction for a portion of the residue of a decedent's estate, transferred to a testamentary trust for the benefit of specified charities, was imperiled because of provisions in the trust document that arguably enabled distributions to noncharitable beneficiaries. A federal court interpreted the language to permit distributions for private benefit, although an appellate court construed the evidence in a manner showing that the decedent's intent was to benefit only charitable entities. The court of appeals did not address a point relied on by the lower court, which was that the trust document failed to—as some courts are requiring—restrict the trustees to holding, using, and distributing the trust property exclusively for charitable purposes.

An estate tax charitable deduction is not available for the bequest to charity of a contingent remainder interest in a farm. A decedent bequeathed a farm to a child for life, with the remainder to a charitable organization. The will also provided, however, that if another child survived the first child, the remainder interest in the farm would vest in the second child instead of the charity. Both individuals were 45 years of age as of the death of the decedent. It was this remainder interest that the IRS found to be too contingent to merit a charitable deduction. The law is that, in the case of a charitable transfer subject to a condition, no deduction is available unless the possibility that the charitable transfer will not become effective is so remote as to be negligible (see Chapter 8). The IRS's position is that a charitable deduction is not allowable when the probability exceeds 5 percent that a noncharitable beneficiary will survive the exhaustion of a fund in which the charity has a remainder interest. Under this rule, any probability in excess of 5 percent that such a contingency will occur and defeat the charity's interest is not considered so remote as to be negligible. Because the two children were of equal age, the actuarial possibility that the second child would survive the first (and thus divest the charity of its remainder interest) was 50 percent. Fifty percent being greater than

5 percent, the IRS held that the "possibility that the charitable remainder transfer in this case will not take effect in possession and enjoyment is not so remote as to be negligible." Thus, the IRS concluded that the bequest did not give rise to an estate tax charitable contribution deduction, even though it otherwise complied with the requirements.

Will Contests

The IRS ruled that, in situations involving settlements of bona fide will contests, when the will creates a charitable remainder trust, the IRS will not challenge the deductibility of immediate payments to charitable organizations on the ground that they were made as part of a split-interest arrangement that would not support an allowable estate tax charitable contribution deduction.

For example, consider the situation in which someone dies, leaving a charitable bequest in the form of a gift to a trust, with income payable to an individual and the remainder interest to a charitable organization. The trust fails to qualify as a charitable remainder trust or pooled income fund, so there is no estate tax charitable deduction. There is a will contest, resulting in a settlement, pursuant to which the estate makes a single payment to the income beneficiary and a distribution to the charitable organization. The IRS's original position in this regard was that an estate tax charitable deduction was not available in these circumstances because the accelerated payment to the charity under the settlement is, in effect, a postmortem modification of a will that did not satisfy the statutory requirements. The courts held, however, that these requirements are not applicable, on the ground that the settlements do not create split interests; the interests passing to the charitable and noncharitable beneficiaries are not interests in the same property. Despite this change in position, the IRS warned that "settlements of will contests will continue to be scrutinized in order to assure that the settlement in question is not an attempt to circumvent . . . [the rule requiring split interests to be in certain forms] by instituting and settling a collusive contest."

Reformations

To qualify for the charitable deduction for a remainder interest, certain provisions must be included in a charitable remainder trust. These requirements apply with respect to the income, estate, and gift tax charitable deductions. There is a procedure, however, by which these trusts—those created both during lifetime and testamentary trusts—can be adjusted to bring them into compliance with the appropriate tax law requirements, for income tax, estate tax, and gift tax consequences.

Federal law permits a charitable deduction for a *qualified reformation* of a trust, when the trust does not meet the requirements of a charitable remainder annuity trust or a charitable remainder unitrust, for purposes of qualifying for the estate tax charitable deduction. The qualified reformation procedure requires that the interest be a *reformable interest* that can be changed (such as by amendment or construction) into a *qualified interest*. Also, for the reformation to be effective:

- Any difference between the actuarial value (determined as of the date of the decedent's death) of the qualified interest and the actuarial value (as so determined) of the reformable interest may not exceed 5 percent of the actuarial value (as so determined) of the reformable interest.
- In the case of a charitable remainder interest, the nonremainder interest (before and after the qualified reformation) must terminate at the same time.
- In the case of any other interest, the reformable interest and the qualified interest must be for the same period.
- The change must be effective as of the date of death of the decedent.

A nonremainder interest (before reformation) for a term of years in excess of 20 years is treated as satisfying the second of these requirements if the interest (after reformation) is for a term of 20 years.

In general, a *reformable interest*, for estate tax law purposes, is any interest for which a charitable deduction would be allowable at the time of the decedent's death but for the requirement that the interest be in one of the specified forms. For example, an interest was ruled not to be a reformable interest because the trustees of the trust had the discretion to transfer trust property to a cemetery association, which would be a noncharitable transfer under federal law.

The term *reformable interest* does not include any interest unless, before the remainder vests in possession, all payments to noncharitable persons are expressed either in specified dollar amounts or a fixed percentage of the property. This rule does not apply, however, to any interest if a judicial proceeding is commenced to change the interest into a qualified interest not later than the 90th day after the last date (including extensions) for filing the return (if an estate tax return is required to be filed), or the last date (including extensions) for filing the income tax return for the first tax year for which a return is required to be filed by the trust (if an estate tax return is not required to be filed).

If, by reason of the death of an individual or by termination or distribution of a trust in accordance with it instrument, a reformable interest goes into a wholly charitable trust or passes to a person for a charitable purpose by the due date for filing the estate tax return (including extensions), an estate tax charitable deduction is allowed for the reformable interest as if it had met the general requirements on the date of the decedent's death.

ASCERTAINABILITY OF CHARITABLE INTERESTS

Another issue that can operate to defeat an estate tax charitable contribution deduction is the rule that the value of a charitable interest must be ascertainable as of the death of the decedent, so that it is severable from the noncharitable interest. This rule is often at issue when there is vague language in the will and/or a substantial amount of discretion is vested in the trustee. The Supreme Court held that the standard must be "fixed in fact and capable of being stated in definite terms of money." A federal court of appeals wrote that the case law on the point "indicate[s] that the test has not been construed to require mathematical certainty such that the dollar amount which the charitable remainderman would receive could be accurately calculated" as of the date of death.

In one instance, a federal court of appeals upheld an IRS determination that claimed federal estate tax charitable contribution deductions were not allowable because the personal representatives of the estate had unfettered discretion to divert the amount provided for the charities to noncharitable beneficiaries. The representatives were empowered by the will to make posthumous gifts to various individuals who had contributed to the decedent's well-being or were otherwise helpful to him. As is typical in these instances, the amount provided for the charitable organizations was the residue of the estate. As noted, the law requires that the amount destined for charity must be presently ascertainable at the time of death; what actually happens to the money and/or property thereafter is irrelevant.

The will involved in this case gave the personal representatives "sole and complete" discretion to make these gifts. The court lamented the absence of any fixed standard to be applied to this discretion. It noted that there was no limit as to the number of persons who might be so compensated; the decedent lived 60 years, and the court observed that many individuals had probably been "helpful" to him during his lifetime. The court did not know how to set limits on the meaning of words such as "well-being" and "helpful." Other unanswered questions plagued the court, such as the size of the various contributions and the period of time over which they were to be made. Wrote the court: "These elements are uncertain and cannot be measured with any precision, and therefore they make the amount going to charity unascertainable at the time of death." This vagueness in the language of the will forced the court to rule that the charitable deduction was not available.

This opinion and others like it do not stand for the proposition that any amount of discretion or lack of certainty will always doom an estate tax charitable contribution deduction. If a standard is fixed and can be stated in definite terms of money, and if there is a reasonable likelihood that money and/or property will in fact be transferred for charitable purposes, the deduction will not be defeated. As the Supreme Court stated years ago on that point, there is "no uncertainty appreciably greater than the general uncertainty that attends human affairs."

What often happens in this area is that the will enables the personal representative to invade the principal of the estate (the amount that is, on the face of the will, going to charity) for the comfort, support, maintenance, and/or happiness of the surviving spouse. On one occasion, the Supreme Court held that the discretion accorded a personal representative to determine elements such as "happiness" defeated the charitable deduction. By contrast, an appellate court in prior (and somewhat similar) cases found ascertainability. In one case, the representative's discretion was limited to the needs and prior lifestyles of the beneficiaries; the court wrote that the "possibility that the charitable bequests would fail or be diminished was so remote as to be nil." In another instance, a court found that the representative's power to pay principal to a beneficiary was limited by an ascertainable standard and "hence there is no argument that the deductibility of the charitable remainder is destroyed by the power of invasion."

In a subsequent case, the decedent's will provided for a charitable remainder in a reformed charitable remainder trust. The will also provided, however, for money for an individual, for improvements on the decedent's house as long as this individual lived there, and for payment of this individual's hospital, medical, dental, and income tax obligations. The government contended that the provisions for improvements to the home and for the individual's personal income taxes failed the ascertainability test. The trial court, however, concluded that any expenses with respect to the residence could be satisfied out of an income interest. The fact that the trust could pay for the income interest beneficiary's unusual and exceptional expenses was neutralized by the facts of his age (87), independent sources of income, and insurance coverage. On appeal, the appellate court agreed, sifting through the precedents to find ascertainability in "comfort" but not "happiness" and an adequate standard in "accident, illness, or other unusual circumstances" but not in "pleasure." It found that "improvements" to the house and the payment of income taxes were closely akin to "comfort" and allowed the charitable contribution deduction.

Thus, when a trustee has considerate discretionary authority as to the making of charitable contributions from the assets of an estate, the estate tax charitable contribution deduction will not be available. When the amount of the bequest is not uncertain and the bequest has a "legal reality" in the will, however, the estate tax charitable contribution deduction will be allowed. By contrast, when a charitable remainder interest in a residuary trust created under a decedent's will was deemed by the IRS not to be presently ascertainable, due to the lack of specificity of charitable beneficiaries, the interest was found to be ineligible for the estate tax charitable deduction.

GENERATION-SKIPPING TRANSFER TAX SYSTEM

Another transfer tax has as its purpose curbing a perceived abuse involving the use of trust vehicles in estate planning. As will be seen, trusts can be used effectively as a means for passing wealth to successive generations at minimum tax cost to the decedent's estate. Indeed, one of the guiding principles of estate planning is the passing down of wealth to "lower" or successive generations at a minimum tax cost.

Because decedents' estates are taxed on the value of their property, and trusts are taxed only on the income they generate, trusts have become convenient vehicles, or depositories, for generational wealth. A decedent's wealth (denominated *first generation*) can be transferred to a trust. The transfer may or may not incur a transfer tax. Typically, the trust retains the property (known as *trust corpus* or *principal*) and distributes income to the next generational level (denominated *second generation*), typically the sons and daughters of the decedent. Tax is paid on the trust income but not the trust property. The trust property is not included in the estate of a child of the decedent on the child's death. Therefore, there is no estate tax at the second generational level. The trust, on the death of a child of the decedent, typically distributes its property to the grandchildren of the decedent (denominated *third generation*) free of transfer tax. Through the use of a trust vehicle, property ownership skips a generation and that generation's level of estate transfer tax.

To curb generation-skipping transfers of wealth through use of trusts and preserve the integrity of uniform generation-to-generation transfer taxes, the generation-skipping transfer tax was adopted.

A transfer tax is imposed on every generation-skipping transfer. The tax rate is a flat amount equal to the maximum unified estate and gift tax rate. The generation-skipping transfer (GST) tax rate is 55 percent. The tax itself, although a transfer tax, is not unified with the estate and gift tax. It is a separate tax on transfers of property. The source for payment of the tax is the property subject to the GST tax.

The federal tax rules determine to which generation a transferor of a generation-skipping transfer belongs. Generally, generational levels are assigned based on lineal descent. Adopted individuals and individuals related by half-blood are treated as lineal descendants. A married individual is assigned to the same generational level as his or her spouse. Nonlineal descendants are assigned to generations based on their age. An individual born within $12\frac{1}{2}$ years of a transferor is assigned to the same generation as the transferor. An individual between $12\frac{1}{2}$ and $37\frac{1}{2}$ years younger than a transferor is assigned to the next lower generational level. New generational levels are created for each additional 25-year difference.

A generation-skipping transfer is defined as any:

- Taxable distribution
- Taxable termination
- Direct skip

Certain Transfer

Certain transfers are excluded from the definition.

- *Taxable distribution* is any distribution from a trust to a skip person, that is, a person two or more generations below the transferor of the interest. The amount of a taxable distribution is the value of the property received by the transferee, reduced by the expenses of the transferee related to the tax.
- *Taxable termination* is any termination of an interest in property held in trust when the interest is for the benefit of a skip person. The taxable amount in the case of a taxable termination is the value of the property received on the termination, reduced by expenses related to the property.
- *Direct skip* is the transfer of an interest in an item of property to a skip person. The amount of the taxable gift is the value received.

The valuation of the transfer is as of the time of the transfer. The estate tax alternate valuation period may apply to direct skips or taxable terminations at death.

An exemption is allowed to every individual with respect to the value of property transferred, with the base amount of the exemption of $1 million. As with the gift tax annual exclusion, spouses are permitted to split the generation-skipping transfer tax exemption. This allows married couples to transfer up to twice the available exemption amount free of GST tax.

Another exemption is permitted for transfers to certain grandchildren. If a parent of a grandchild, who is a lineal descendant of the transferor, is dead, the grandchild is treated as the child of the transferor. In this case, the generation-skipping gap is closed up so that no GST tax applies to the transaction.

Gifts directly to skip persons are exempt from the GST tax to the extent of the gift tax annual exclusion. Gifts to a trust for the benefit of a skip person are exempt from the GST tax to the extent of this annual exclusion only if (1) the income and corpus of the trust can be distributed only to that skip person for whom the trust was created; and (2) if that skip person dies before termination of the trust, the trust's assets are includible in the gross estate of that skip person (typically accomplished by granting that skip person a general power of appointment exercisable by that skip person's will).

Notwithstanding the foregoing, the GST taxes are to be reduced between 2002 and 2009; these taxes are slated to be restored in 2010. The GST tax exemption for a given year (prior to repeal) is equal to the unified credit exemption amount for estate tax purposes. Also, as under prior law, the GST tax rate for a given year will be the highest estate and gift tax rate in effect for that year.

SUMMARY

This chapter provided a summary of the federal estate and gift tax rules, including the law concerning the charitable contribution deductions that are an important element of these rules. The chapter also summarized the basic principles of estate planning. The chapter then explored the generation-skipping transfer tax system and concluded with a review of reformations of trusts with charitable interests, will contests, and the standards for ascertaining charitable interests.

CHAPTER 6

Special Property Rules

The federal tax law concerning charitable gifts of property encompasses much more than gifts of securities or real estate. There are several unique rules in this setting that can be invoked; they are inventoried in this chapter. Specifically, this chapter summarizes the charitable giving rules in relation to:

- Works of art
- Vehicles
- Intellectual property
- Automobile expenses
- Inventory
- Scientific research property
- Computer technology or equipment
- Contributions of license to use patent
- Real property used for conservation purposes
- S corporation stock
- Use of property
- Property subject to debt
- Future interests in tangible personal property

WORKS OF ART

Contributions of works of art may, of course, be made to charitable organizations. Works of art may also be loaned to these organizations.

Gifts

In general, the federal income tax charitable contribution deduction for a gift of a work of art is an amount equal to the fair market value of the property (see Chapter 2). There are, however, three exceptions to this general rule:

1. The charitable deduction for a year may be limited by one of the percentage limitations (see Chapter 4).
2. The work of art that is contributed may be the creation of the donor, in which case the deduction is confined to the donor's basis in the property (see Chapter 7).
3. The work of art may be put to an unrelated use by the charitable recipient, in which case the deduction is confined to the donor's basis in the property (see Chapter 8).

Of these elements, the third situation is the most likely to occur. A work of art, being an item of tangible personal property, is subject to a special rule: When a gift of tangible personal property is made to a charitable organization and the donee's use of it is unrelated to its tax-exempt purposes, the amount of the charitable deduction that would otherwise be determined must be reduced by the amount of gain that would have been long-term capital gain if the property contributed had been sold by the donor at its fair market value, ascertained at the time of the contribution.

The greatest controversy surrounding the charitable deduction of a work of art is likely to be the value of the item. Not infrequently, there is a dispute between the IRS and a donor as to the fair market value of a work of art. Usually these disputes are settled; sometimes they are resolved in court. The appropriate value of an item of property is a question of fact, not law; thus, the testimony of one or more expert witnesses can be significant. A trial court's valuation of an item of property will be set aside on appeal only if the finding of value is clearly erroneous.

Loans

Rather than contribute a work of art to a charitable organization, a person may decide to loan the artwork to a charity. This type of transfer does not give rise to a federal income tax charitable contribution deduction. The transaction is nonetheless a gift. The transaction is disregarded as a transfer for gift tax purposes, however, when (1) the recipient organization is a charitable entity, (2) the use of the artwork by the charitable donee is related to the purpose or function constituting the basis for its tax exemption, and (3) the artwork involved is an archaeological, historic, or creative item of tangible personal property.

VEHICLES

Contributions of motor vehicles, boats, airplanes, and the like to charitable organizations have vexed Congress and the IRS for many years. Although the principal concern has been and continues to be the matter of valuation, this aspect of charitable giving also potentially involves issues directly affecting the charitable donee: private inurement, private benefit, intermediate sanctions, and the unrelated business rules.

Background

Although this subject considerably predates 2000, it is notable that in that year the IRS, analogizing to *A Tale of Two Cities* and the *Star Wars* epic, observed that "there is a dark side in the Exempt Organization Universe." Indeed, the agency on that occasion reflected its view that it is under siege because of evildoing in the realm of charitable giving: The IRS "in recent years has been confronted with a number of aggressive tax avoidance schemes." None of these sometimes abusive giving arrangements, however, has irked the IRS more than the matter of solicitation of contributions to charitable organizations of automobiles and other vehicles. This matter festered over the ensuing years, with Congress legislating on the subject in 2004.

Statutory Regime

The rules entail deductibility and substantiation requirements in connection with contributions to charity of motor vehicles, boats, and airplanes—collectively termed *qualified vehicles*. These requirements supplant the general gift substantiation rules (see Chapter 12) where the claimed value of the gifted property contributed exceeds $500.

Pursuant to these rules, a federal income tax charitable contribution deduction is not allowed unless the donor substantiates the contribution by a contemporaneous written acknowledgment of it by the donee organization and includes the acknowledgment with the donor's income tax return reflecting the deduction. This acknowledgment must contain the name and taxpayer identification number of the donor and the vehicle identification number or similar number. If the gift is of a qualified vehicle that was sold by the donee charitable organization without any "significant intervening use or material improvement," the acknowledgment must also contain a certification that the vehicle was sold in an arm's-length transaction between unrelated parties, a statement as to the gross proceeds derived from the sale, and a statement that the deductible amount may not exceed the amount of the gross proceeds. If there is this type of use or improvement, the acknowledgment must include a certification as to the intended use or material improvement of the vehicle and the intended duration of the use and a certification that the vehicle will not be transferred in exchange for money, other property, or services before completion of the use or improvement. An acknowledgment is *contemporaneous* if the donee organization provides it within 30 days of the sale of the qualified vehicle or, in an instance of an acknowledgment including the foregoing certifications, of the contribution of the vehicle.

The amount of the charitable deduction for a gift of a qualified vehicle depends on the nature of the use of the vehicle by the donee organization. If the charitable organization sells the vehicle without any significant intervening use or material improvement of the vehicle by the organization, the amount of the charitable deduction may not exceed the gross proceeds received from the sale. Where there is a use or improvement, the charitable deduction is based on the fair market value of the vehicle.

The legislative history accompanying this law states that these two exceptions are to be strictly construed. To meet this *significant use* test, the organization must actually use the vehicle to substantially further its regularly conducted activities and the use must be significant. The test is not satisfied if the use is incidental or not intended at the time of the contribution. Whether a use is *significant* also depends on the frequency and duration of use.

A *material improvement* includes major repairs to a vehicle or other improvements to the vehicle that improve its condition in a manner that significantly increases its value. Cleaning the vehicle, minor repairs, and routine maintenance do not constitute material improvements. Presumably this exception is available only when the donee charitable organization expresses its intent at the outset (at least in part by means of the certification) that the donee plans to materially improve the vehicle.

A donee organization that is required to provide an acknowledgment under these rules must also provide that information to the IRS. A penalty is imposed for the furnishing of a false or fraudulent acknowledgment, or an untimely or incomplete acknowledgment, by a charitable organization to a donor of a qualified vehicle.

Regulatory Gloss

The IRS issued interim guidance concerning these rules for deductible charitable contributions of qualified vehicles. This guidance added third exception to these rules, which is for circumstances where the charity gives or sells the vehicle at a significantly below-market price to a needy individual, as long as the transfer furthers the charitable purpose of helping a poor or distressed individual who is in need of a means of transportation. The guidance also explains how the fair market value of a vehicle is determined.

The IRS issued a form (Form 1098-C) to be used by donee charitable organizations to report to the IRS contributions of qualified vehicles and to provide the donor with a contemporaneous written acknowledgment of the contribution. A donor of a qualified vehicle must attach Copy B of this form to the donor's income tax return in order to take a deduction for the contribution of the vehicle where the claimed value is in excess of $500. Generally, the donee must furnish Copies B and C of the form to the donor either no later than 30 days after the date of sale or 30 days after the date of the contribution, depending on the circumstances. Copy A of this form is to be filed with the IRS, Copy C is for the donor's records, and Copy D is retained by the charitable donee.

Other Issues

Appraisal

If the value of the contributed vehicle is in excess of $5,000, the donor is obligated to obtain an independent appraisal of the value of the vehicle (see Chapter 12).

Penalties

Both parties are potentially liable for penalties for aiding and abetting understatements of tax liability, for preparation of false tax returns, and for promoting abusive tax shelters.

Unrelated Business Considerations

When vehicles are contributed to a charitable organization and the organization disposes of them, the charity may be perceived as being in the business of acquiring and selling the vehicles. Nonetheless, this activity is not considered an unrelated business, because of a *donated goods exception*. In some instances, payments to a charitable organization in the context of these programs may be characterized as tax-excludable royalties.

Contributions "to" Charity

To be deductible, a contribution must be to (or for the use of) a qualified charitable organization (see Chapter 8). To be *to* a charity, the gift must be made under circumstances where the donee has full control of the donated money or other property and full discretion as to its use. When a charitable organization utilizes the services of a for-profit company to receive and process donated vehicles, the gift may be deemed to be to the company, rather than the charity, in which case there is no charitable contribution deduction. This situation can be resolved, however, by denominating the company as the agent of the charity for this purpose.

Private Benefit Doctrine

 The IRS has raised the issue of applicability of the private benefit doctrine. The agency posits situations in which an automobile dealer or some other third party is the true beneficiary of a transaction. If the private benefit is more than insubstantial, the charitable organization's tax-exempt status could be jeopardized.

Private Inurement Doctrine

The IRS has also raised the possibility of application, in this setting, of the private inurement doctrine. When such a third party is an insider with respect to the charitable organization, that doctrine could be implicated, thereby endangering the organization's exempt status.

Intermediate Sanctions

The intermediate sanctions rules are applicable when a transaction constitutes an *excess benefit transaction* and the charitable organization's dealings are with a *disqualified person* with respect to it. The IRS may also assess a penalty for willful and flagrant violation of these standards.

INTELLECTUAL PROPERTY

The value of certain intellectual property contributed to charity can be speculative. An item of contributed intellectual property may prove to be worthless or the initial promise of worth may be diminished by subsequent inventions, marketplace competition, or other factors. Even if intellectual property has the potential for significant monetary benefit, this will not be the outcome if the charitable donee does not make the appropriate investment, have the necessary personnel and equipment, and/or have sufficient sustained interest to exploit the intellectual property. Valuation is made yet more difficult in the charitable contribution context because the transferee does not provide full, if any, consideration in exchange for the transferred property pursuant to arm's-length negotiations, and there may not be a comparable sales market for the property to use as a benchmark for valuations.

Congress, in 2004, enacted legislation concerning charitable contributions of intellectual property. This legislation is predicated on the view that excessive charitable contribution deductions enabled by inflated valuations in this context are best addressed by confining the amount of the deduction for gifts of intellectual property to the donor's basis in the property while allowing for additional charitable contribution deductions thereafter if the contributed property generates income for the charitable organization.

Statutory Regime

Contributions of certain types of intellectual property have been added to the list of gifts that give rise to a charitable contribution deduction that is confined to the donor's basis in the property (see Chapter 8), although, as discussed later, in instances of gifts of intellectual property, there may be one or more subsequent charitable deductions. This property consists of patents, copyrights (with exceptions), trademarks, trade names, trade secrets, know-how, software (with exceptions), or similar property, or applications or registrations of such property. Collectively, these properties are termed *qualified intellectual property* (except in instances when contributed to private foundations).

A person who makes this type of gift, denominated a *qualified intellectual property contribution,* is provided a charitable contribution deduction (subject to the annual percentage limitations) equal to the donor's basis in the property in the year of the gift and, in that year and/or subsequent years, a charitable deduction equal to a percentage of net income that flows to the charitable donee as the consequence of the gift of the property. For a contribution to be a qualified intellectual property contribution, the donor must notify the donee at the time of the contribution that the donor intends to treat the contribution as a qualified intellectual property contribution for deduction and reporting purposes. The net income involved is termed *qualified donee income.*

Thus, a portion of qualified donee income is allocated to a tax year of the donor, although this income allocation process is inapplicable to income received by or accrued to the donee after 10 years from the date of the gift; the process is also inapplicable to donee income received by or accrued to the donee after the expiration of the legal life of the property.

The amount of qualified donee income that materializes into a charitable deduction, for one or more years, is ascertained by the *applicable percentage,* which is a sliding-scale percentage determined by this table, which appears in the Internal Revenue Code:

Donor's Tax Year	Applicable Percentage
1st	100
2nd	100
3rd	90
4th	80
5th	70
6th	60
7th	50
8th	40
9th	30
10th	20
11th	10
12th	10

Thus, if following a qualified intellectual property contribution, the charitable donee receives qualified donee income in the year of the gift, and/or in the subsequent tax year of the donor that amount becomes, in full, a charitable contribution deduction for the donor (subject to the general limitations). If such income is received by the charitable donee eight years after the gift, for example, the donor receives a charitable deduction equal to 40 percent of the qualified donee income. As this list indicates, the opportunity for a qualified intellectual property deduction arising out of a qualified intellectual property contribution terminates after the 12th year of the donor ending after the date of the gift.

The reporting requirements rules concerning certain dispositions of contributed property were amended in 2004 to encompass qualified intellectual property contributions.

Notification Requirement

A donor satisfies the notification requirement if he or she delivers or mails to the donee, at the time of the contribution, a statement containing (1) the donor's name, address, and taxpayer identification number; (2) a description of the intellectual property in sufficient detail to identify it; (3) the date of the contribution; and (4) a statement that the donor intends to treat the contribution as a qualified intellectual property contribution.

AUTOMOBILE EXPENSES

A standard mileage rate can be used, rather than itemization of expenses, in calculating the charitable deduction for use of a passenger automobile. That rate is 14 cents per mile.

Rather than deduct automobile expenses, an individual may be reimbursed by the charitable organization involved for the expenses incurred. Generally, one who serves as a volunteer for and who provides services to a charitable organization, and is reimbursed by the organization for the expenses of providing the services, does not receive gross income as a result of the reimbursement. If, however, this type of reimbursement exceeds the amount of the expenses, the excess amount constitutes gross income. There are some relatively narrow exceptions to these rules.

INVENTORY

Special federal tax rules govern charitable contributions of items of inventory of a corporation. The term *inventory* means property that is stock-in-trade of a business enterprise, held for sale to customers. When the property is sold, the resulting income is ordinary income.

In general, the amount of the charitable deduction for contributions of property is measured by using the fair market value of the property (see Chapter 2). When a corporation makes a charitable contribution of property out of its inventory, however, the gift deduction is generally confined to an amount that may not exceed the donor's cost basis in the property. That is, the amount that might otherwise be deductible must be reduced by the amount of ordinary income that would have resulted had the items been sold.

Nevertheless, a special rule provides an augmented deduction under certain circumstances, pursuant to which the charitable deduction for contributions of inventory may be an amount equal to as much as twice the cost basis in the property. These gifts of inventory are known as *qualified contributions.*

Basic Rules

The charitable contribution deduction for a gift of inventory generally must be reduced by an amount equal to one-half of the amount of gain that would not have been long-term capital gain if the property had been sold by the donor at fair market value at the date of the contribution. If, after this reduction, the amount of the deduction would be more than twice the basis in the contributed property, the amount of the deduction must be further reduced to an amount equal to twice the cost basis in the property.

This augmented deduction is available under eight circumstances:

1. The gift is of property that is properly be included in the donor's inventory.
2. The donor is a corporation (other than a small business corporation).
3. The donee is a charitable organization (other than a private foundation).
4. The donee's use of the property is related to the donee's tax-exempt purposes.

5. The property is to be used by the donee solely for the care of the ill, the needy, or infants.
6. The property is not transferred by the donee in exchange for money, other property, or services.
7. The donor receives from the donee a written statement representing that its use and disposition of the property will be in accordance with these rules.
8. The property is in compliance with all applicable requirements of the Federal Food, Drug, and Cosmetic Act.

Restrictions on Use

For a contribution to qualify under these rules, the contributed property must be subject to certain restrictions on use. If the transferred property is used or transferred by the donee organization (or by any subsequent transferee that furnished to the donee the requisite written statement) in a manner inconsistent with the requirements of these rules, the donor's deduction is only the amount allowable with regard to gifts of inventory in general. As noted, this general deduction is confined to the donor's cost basis.

If the donor is, however, able to establish that, at the time of the contribution, the donor reasonably anticipated that the property would be used in a manner consistent with these requirements, then the donor's deduction will nonetheless be computed using two special rules.

Exempt Purpose Use

The use of the property must be related to the purpose or function constituting the ground for tax exemption as a charitable entity of the organization to which the contribution is made. The gift property may not be used in connection with any activity that gives rise to unrelated business property.

Ultimate Beneficiaries

The gift properties must be used for the care of the ill, needy, or infants. The property itself must ultimately either be transferred to (or for the use of) the ill, needy, or infants for their care or be retained for their care. No other individual may use the contributed property except as incidental to primary use in the care of the ill, needy, or infants. The donee organization may satisfy these requirements by transferring the property to a relative, custodian, parent, or guardian of the ill or needy individual or infant, or to any other individual if it makes a reasonable effort to ascertain that the property will ultimately be used primarily for the care of the ill or needy individual or infant, and not for the primary benefit of any other person.

The donee organization may transfer the gift properties to other qualified tax-exempt public charitable organizations, within or outside the United States. For these rules to be satisfied, however, the transferring organization must obtain a written statement from the transferee organization. If the property is ultimately transferred to, or used for the benefit of, ill or needy persons or infants who are outside the United States, the organization that transfers the property outside the United States must be a corporation. For these purposes, if the donee organization charges for its transfer of contributed property (other than an allowable fee), the requirements of these rules are not met.

Restrictions on Transfer of Contributed Property

In general, a contribution will not satisfy these rules if the donee organization or any transferee of it requires or receives any money, property, or services for the transfer or use of the property contributed. A contribution may qualify under these rules if the donee organization charges a fee to another organization in connection with its transfer of the donated property, if (1) the fee is nominal in relation to the value of the transferred property, and (2) the fee is reimbursement of the donee organization for its administrative, warehousing, or similar costs.

Requirements of Written Statement

Statement to Donor

The donee organization must furnish each donor with a written statement that (1) describes the contributed property, stating the date of its receipt; (2) represents that the property will be used in compliance with this body of law; (3) represents that the donee organization is a charitable organization and is not a private foundation; and (4) represents that adequate books and records will be maintained and made available to the IRS on request.

Statements to Transferring Organization

If an organization that received a contribution under these rules transfers the contributed property to another organization, the transferee organization must furnish to the transferring organization a written statement containing the information referenced in the first, second, and fourth requirements for a statement to a donor. This statement must also represent that the transferee organization is a charitable organization that is not a private foundation (or, if a foreign organization, that it would meet that test). This written statement must be furnished within a "reasonable period" after the transfer.

Compliance with Food, Drug, and Cosmetic Act

If the contributed property is subject to the Federal Food, Drug, and Cosmetic Act, the property must comply with that law at the date of contribution and for the immediately preceding 180 days. In the case of specific items of contributed property not in existence for the entire 180-day period immediately preceding the date of contribution, this requirement is met if the contributed property complied with that law during the period of its existence and at the date of contribution and if, for the 180-day period prior to contribution, other property (if any) held by the donor at any time during that period (which property was fungible with the contributed property) was in compliance with that law during the period held by the donor.

Amount of Reduction

The amount of the charitable contribution under these rules must be reduced before application of the percentage limitation on the charitable deduction (see Chapter 4). These rules mandate two reductions. The amount of the first reduction is equal to one-half of the amount of gain that would not have been long-term capital gain if the property had been sold by the donor at fair market value on the date of its contribution. If the amount of the charitable contribution remaining after this reduction exceeds twice the basis of the contributed property, then the amount of the charitable contribution is reduced a second time to an amount equal to twice the amount of the basis of the property.

SCIENTIFIC RESEARCH PROPERTY

Special federal tax rules govern the deductibility of corporate char-itable contributions of scientific research property. To qualify un-der these rules, the property that is the subject of the gift must be from the donor's inventory.

In addition, for this charitable deduction to be available, all of these seven requirements must be satisfied:

1. The contribution must be to an eligible institution of higher education or an eligible scientific research organization.
2. The property must be constructed by the donor corpo-ration.
3. The contribution must be made not later than two years af-ter the date on which construction of the property is sub-stantially completed.
4. The original use of the property must be by the charitable recipient.
5. The property must be scientific equipment or apparatus substantially all of the use of which by the charitable recip-ient is for research or experimentation, or for research training, in the United States in physical or biological sciences.
6. The property must not be transferred by the charitable recipient in exchange for money, other property, or serv-ices.
7. The corporation receives from the charitable recipient a written statement representing that its use and disposition of the property will be in accordance with the fifth and sixth of these requirements

This deduction is computed in the same manner as is the case with respect to the special rule concerning gifts of inventory, dis-cussed earlier.

COMPUTER TECHNOLOGY OR EQUIPMENT

Special federal tax rules govern the deductibility of charitable con-tributions of computer technology or equipment. The property that is eligible for this education must be computer software, com-puter or peripheral equipment, and fiber-optic cable related to computer use. The contribution must be made by a corporation and satisfy these eight criteria:

1. The recipient must be an educational institution, a tax-exempt entity that is organized primarily for purposes of supporting elementary and secondary education, or a public library.
2. The contribution must be made no later than three years after the date the donor acquired the property (or, in the case of property constructed by the donor, the date on which construction of the property was substantially completed).
3. The original use of the property must be by the donor or the donee.
4. Substantially all of the use of the property by the donee must be for use within the United States for educational purposes that are related to the purpose or function of the donee organization.
5. The property may not be transferred by the donee in exchange for money, other property, or services, except for shipping, installation, and transfer costs.
6. The property must fit productively into the donee's education plan.
7. The donee's use and disposition of the property must be in accordance with the fourth and fifth of these requirements.
8. The property involved must meet any standards that the IRS may promulgate to assure that the property meets minimum functionality and suitability standards for educational purposes.

This deduction is computed in the same manner as is the case with respect to the special rule concerning gifts of inventory, discussed earlier.

LICENSE TO USE PATENT

The IRS has addressed various aspects of contributions to qualified charitable organizations of licenses to use patents. This guidance came in the form of a ruling, which posited three situations.

In the first situation, a person contributes to a tax-exempt university a license to use a patent but retains the right to license the patent to others.

In the second situation, a person contributes a patent to an exempt university subject to the condition that a faculty member of the university who is an expert in the technology covered by the patent continue to be a member of the faculty of the institution during the remaining life of the patent. If this condition is not satisfied, the patent is to revert to the donor. The patent will expire 15 years after the date of the gift. On the date of the contribution, the likelihood that this individual will cease to be a member of the faculty before the patent expires was not so remote as to be negligible (see Chapter 8).

In the third situation, a person contributes to an exempt university all of the person's interest in a patent. The transfer agreement provides that the university may not sell or license the patent for three years. This restriction does not result in any benefit to the donor; under no circumstances can the patent revert to the donor.

A charitable contribution deduction is denied for certain contributions of partial interests in property. A charitable deduction is denied for a contribution of less than the taxpayer's entire interest in property unless the value of the interest contributed would be allowable as a deduction if the donor were to transfer the interest in trust. This rule does not disallow a deduction for a contribution of an interest that, even though partial, is the taxpayer's entire interest in the property. If, however, the property in which the partial interest exists was divided in order to create the interest, the deduction is not allowed (see Chapters 7 and 9).

A charitable deduction is available for a contribution, not in trust, of a partial interest that is less than the donor's entire interest in property if the partial interest is an undivided portion of the donor's entire interest.

A contribution of the right to use property that the donor owns (see next section), such as a contribution of a rent-free lease, is a contribution of less than the donor's entire interest in the property. As an illustration, if a person contributes an interest in motion picture films but retains the right to make reproductions of the films and exploit the reproductions commercially, the contribution is less than the donor's entire interest in the property.

The IRS ruled that the contribution in the first of these situations was a transfer of a partial interest, for which no charitable contribution deduction is allowable. The license granted to the university was deemed similar to the rent-free lease and the partial interest in motion picture films, in that it constituted neither the person's entire interest in the patent nor a fraction or percentage of each and every substantial interest or right that the person owns in the patent.

If, as of the date of a gift, a transfer of property for charitable purposes is dependent on the performance of an act or the happening of a precedent event to become effective, there is no charitable deduction, unless the possibility that the charitable transfer will not become effective is so remote as to be negligible. If, as of the date of a gift, a transfer of property for charitable purposes may be defeated by the performance of an act or the happening of an event, no deduction is allowable unless the possibility that the act or event will occur is so remote as to be negligible (see Chapter 8). Thus, a charitable deduction was not allowed in the second situation.

When a donor places a restriction on the marketability or use of property, the amount of the charitable contribution deduction is the fair market value of the property at the time of the contribution, determined in light of the restriction. Generally, then, in the third situation, there is a deductible contribution. The restriction, however, reduced what would otherwise have been the fair market value of the patent and therefore reduced the amount of the charitable contribution.

REAL PROPERTY USED FOR CONSERVATION PURPOSES

Special federal tax rules pertain to contributions to charity of real property for conservation purposes. These rules are an exception to the general rule that there is no charitable contribution deduction for contributions of partial interests in property (see Chapter 7).

These rules are in the context of the income tax charitable contribution deduction for qualified conservation contributions. There are, however, somewhat comparable rules in the estate tax and gift tax charitable deduction settings (see Chapter 5). An estate may claim a charitable contribution deduction for the value of the portion of a conservation easement includible in the estate; individuals claim an income tax charitable deduction for the balance of the easement.

A *qualified conservation contribution* has three fundamental characteristics: (1) it is a contribution of a qualified real property interest, (2) to a qualified organization, (3) exclusively for conservation purposes.

The amount allowed as a charitable contribution deduction for a qualified conservation easement is the difference between the fair market value of the burdened property before the gift and the value of it following the gift.

Qualified Real Property Interests

A *qualified real property interest* is one of these three interests in real property: (1) the donor's entire interest in the property other than a qualified mineral interest, (2) a remainder interest (see Chapter 9), or (3) a restriction (granted in perpetuity) on the use that may be made of the real property. A *qualified mineral interest* is the donor's interest in subsurface oil, gas, or other minerals, and the right to access to these minerals.

A real property interest is not treated as an entire interest in the property (other than a qualified mineral interest) if the property in which the donor's interest exists was divided prior to the contribution to enable the donor to retain control of more than a qualified mineral interest or to reduce the real property interest donated. Minor interests that will not interfere with the conservation purposes of the gift, such as rights-of-way, may, however, be transferred prior to the conservation contribution without adversely affecting the treatment of a property interest as a qualified real property interest. An entire interest in real property may consist of an undivided interest in the property.

Qualified Organizations

A *qualified organization* is a unit of government, a publicly supported charitable organization, or a supporting organization that is controlled by one or more of the foregoing two types of entities. In addition, an organization must have a commitment to protect the conservation purposes of the donation and have the resources to enforce the restrictions. A qualified organization is not required to set aside funds to enforce the restrictions that are the subject of the contribution.

A deduction is allowed for a contribution under these rules only if, in the instrument of conveyance, the donor prohibits the donee from subsequently transferring the easement (or, in the case of a remainder interest or the reservation of a qualified mineral interest, the property), whether for consideration or not, unless the donee, as a condition of the subsequent transfer, requires that the conservation purposes which the contribution was originally intended to advance be carried out. Moreover, subsequent transfers must be restricted to organizations qualifying, at the time of the subsequent transfer, as eligible donees. Nonetheless, when a later unexpected change in the conditions surrounding the property that is the subject of a donation makes impossible or impractical the continued use of the property for conservation purposes, these requirements will be met if the property is sold or exchanged and any proceeds are used by the donee organization in a manner consistent with the conservation purposes of the original contribution.

Conservation Purpose

The term *conservation purpose* means:

- Preservation of land areas for outdoor recreation by, or for the education of, the general public
- Protection of a relatively natural habitat of fish, wildlife, or plants, or similar ecosystem
- Preservation of open space (including farmland and forest land), when the preservation is for the scenic enjoyment of the general public, is pursuant to a clearly delineated federal, state, or local governmental policy, and/or will yield a significant public benefit
- Preservation of a historically important land area or a certified historic structure

Exclusivity Requirement

To satisfy these rules, a contribution must be *exclusively* for conservation purposes. A conservation deduction will not be denied, however, when an incidental benefit inures to the donor merely as a result of conservation restrictions limiting the uses to which the donor's property may be put. In general, a conservation deduction will not be allowed if the contribution would accomplish one of the enumerated conservation purposes but would also permit destruction of other significant conservation interests. Nonetheless, a use that is destructive of conservation interests will be permitted if the use is necessary for protection of the conservation interests that are subject of the contribution.

A contribution cannot be treated as being exclusively for conservation purposes unless the conservation purpose is protected in perpetuity. Thus, any interest in the property retained by the donor (and the donor's successors in interest) must be subject to legally enforceable restrictions that will prevent uses of the retained interest that are inconsistent with the conservation purposes of the donation. A deduction is not permitted for a contribution of an interest in property that is subject to a mortgage, unless the mortgagee subordinates its rights in the property to the right of the charitable organization to enforce the conservation purposes of the gift in perpetuity. A conservation deduction will not be disallowed, however, merely because the interest that passes to, or is vested in, the donee charitable organization may be defeated by the performance of some act or the happening of some event, if on the date of the gift it appears that the possibility that the act or event will occur is so remote as to be negligible.

Valuation

The amount of the charitable contribution deduction, in the case of a contribution of a donor's entire interest in conservation property (other than a qualified mineral interest), is the fair market value of the surface rights in the property contributed. The value for the deduction is computed without regard to the mineral rights. In the case of a contribution of a remainder interest in real property, depreciation and depletion of the property must be taken into account in determining the value of the interest. The value of a charitable contribution of a perpetual conservation restriction is the fair market value of the restriction at the time of the contribution. In the case of a contribution of a qualified real property interest for conservation purposes, the basis of the property retained by the donor must be adjusted by the elimination of that part of the total basis of the property that is properly allocable to the qualified real property interest granted.

Substantiation

If a donor makes a qualified conservation contribution and claims a charitable contribution deduction for it, the donor must maintain written records of the fair market value of the underlying property before and after the contribution, and the conservation purpose furthered by the donation. This information may have to be part of the donor's income tax return.

S CORPORATION STOCK

S corporations are small business corporations that, for federal income tax purposes, are treated as partnerships. Charities are eligible to receive gifts of stock of these closely held businesses. The major tax problem in this regard for charitable organizations is that this type of interest is regarded as ownership in an unrelated business. Items of income, loss, or deduction of an S corporation flow through to charitable organization shareholders as unrelated business income. A charity is taxed on its share of an S corporation's income, as determined for accounting purposes, rather than simply on the corporation's actual cash distributions. Gain or loss on the disposition of stock in an S corporation results in unrelated business income.

Gifts from Donor's Perspective

A donor must initially determine whether he or she is willing to contribute S corporation stock to a charitable organization. This donor will consider many of the same factors that he or she would for a gift of an ownership interest in any type of closely held business. Two of these are (1) whether the donor would be comfortable with a charity having the legal rights of a minority shareholder and (2) whether the stock is subject to a transfer restriction that would prevent the charity from selling or granting the stock to another party without the shareholder's approval.

The income tax deduction usually will be less than the appraised value of the stock. The tax law mandates that the income tax deduction for a charitable gift of S corporation stock be reduced under rules that are analogous to charitable gifts of partnership interests. It may be possible to avoid a reduced deduction by having the donor terminate the S corporation status shortly before making the gift of stock. The step transaction doctrine may, however, foil this approach (see Chapter 2).

Otherwise, the charitable contribution deduction available to the donor is contingent on compliance with the gift substantiation rules and, most likely, the appraisal requirements (see Chapter 12). If the charitable donee sells or otherwise disposes of the stock within two years of its receipt, reports must be provided to the IRS and the donor.

Gifts from Donee's Perspective

A charitable organization that is contemplating receiving or that holds stock of an S corporation faces both tax and nontax issues.

Nontax Issues

Charitable organizations readily accept contributions of publicly traded marketable securities. A charity should, however, treat offers of S corporation stock in a manner similar to prospective gifts of real estate. Just as each parcel of real estate is unique, an S corporation is a separate business, the success or failure of which depends primarily on the management skills of the corporation's directors and shareholders. Although ownership of S corporation stock does not incur the maintenance responsibilities associated with real estate, a charity can incur additional bookkeeping burdens as the result of owning and selling this type of stock.

The crucial issue is whether the stock looks like an attractive investment in relation to the potential burdens that ownership of the stock could impose. Questions to be asked (in advance of the gift) include how soon the stock can be sold and converted into productive marketable investments, and, if the stock is to be held for a period of time, if it can produce net cash flow (after payment of the unrelated business income tax) for use for charitable purposes. The tax consequences will generally be secondary to the basic economics of the transaction.

As a general rule, charities prefer to sell interests in closely held businesses that have been contributed to them, as these assets usually do not conform to charities' overall investment philosophy. Stock in an S corporation is not an exception to this basic policy; the charitable donee is almost certain to want to sell it. (Imposition of the unrelated business income tax will likely make the charity even more eager to sell the asset.)

Donors may, however, expect the charity to hold the S stock for a significant period of time. Moreover, there is a restricted market for selling this type of stock; it is frequently confined to the corporation itself, existing shareholders, or purchasers who have been preapproved by the existing shareholders. Inasmuch as a charitable organization is almost certain to be a minority shareholder, it must rely on the controlling shareholders for fair treatment. For example, the charity should satisfy itself that the control group will not engage in practices that may prove damaging (or embarrassing) to the charity.

Consequently, a charity is well advised not to accept a gift of S corporation stock unless it is reasonably satisfied that there will not be any resulting material financial difficulties. A charity should also investigate the possibility of problems under state law concerning ownership of S corporation stock. If the stock is to be sold several years after the contribution, the charity should be assured (by means including procurement of a timely appraisal) that it is receiving a fair price for the stock.

Another nontax issue is the credit to be given a donor of S corporation stock in the context of a fundraising campaign. The choice is between the full fair market value of the stock or that value reduced by the amount of the unrelated business income tax burden. Likewise, if the stock is donated in exchange for a charitable gift annuity (see Chapter 9), the choice is essentially already made: As only the after-tax amount will be left to pay the annuity, the annuity should be based on the amount of the after-tax proceeds.

Tax Issues

The greatest potential tax burden that owning and selling S corporation stock presents to a charity is payment of the tax on unrelated business income.

If the income from the S corporation is minimal, tax problems in that context are avoided. The first $1,000 of unrelated business income is not taxable (and the unrelated business income tax return, Form 990-T, need not be filed). Quarterly estimates of the tax need not be filed (on Form 99-W) if the total tax liability for the year is less than $500. The charity can assess this situation by asking questions of the prospective donor and by examining the Schedule K-1 information returns that the S corporation issued to the donor in recent years. Otherwise, the tax return must be filed and taxes paid; quarterly estimates of the tax will have to be paid to avoid penalties.

If the gift of S corporation stock is accepted, the charity should be provided the donor's adjusted basis in the stock, because that will be used in determining the amount of taxable gain the charity will have on the sale of the stock. A low basis could cause normally tax-exempt cash distributions to be taxable and could prevent the charity from deducting the business operating losses. Various administrative requirements, such as gift substantiation and an independent appraisal, have been mentioned already.

Generally, the income of an S corporation is allocated to each shareholder in proportion to the number of shares owned by that shareholder. If a shareholder acquires or disposes of S corporation stock during a year, he or she is taxed on a portion of the year's income based on the number of days that the shareholder owned the stock during that year.

Unrelated business taxable income in this context consists of the charity's share of the accounting income shown on the shareholder's Schedule K-1, which the corporation attaches to its annual tax return (Form 1120S). The accounting income is rarely the same as the cash distributions that the charity receives (if any) from the S corporation. It is common for an S corporation to retain part of its profits to reinvest in growing the business. With rare exceptions, the cash distributions that the charity receives from the S corporation will be nontaxable, because the tax is levied on the accounting-based income instead.

To the extent that the unrelated business income tax cannot be avoided, a charity's primary tax concern should be assurance that it has sufficient money available to pay the tax as it comes due, usually in quarterly estimated tax payments. Although most S corporations distribute sufficient cash to their shareholders to enable them to pay the income tax attributable to that income, a charity should address this issue before accepting a gift of S corporation stock. A charity should avoid accepting stock of an S corporation that is like a burned-out partnership tax shelter, with substantial accounting income and little in the way of actual cash distributions to pay the unrelated business income tax.

When the stock is sold, the charity should be certain that it is selling the stock for a fair price. Sales made close to the date of the gift usually can be done at a price that is at or near the original appraised value of the stock. If the sale is several years later, the original appraisal will be outdated and the charity will require some other proof (most likely, a contemporaneous appraisal) that the price is appropriate. A charitable organization can sell the stock at a below-value price if it makes a valid business judgment that it should rid itself of the asset because of tax liabilities (particularly if these liabilities are greater than originally anticipated).

Unlike most other assets held by tax-exempt organizations, gain from the sale of S corporation stock is subject to the unrelated business income tax that the charity must pay. The amount of the gain from the sale of S corporation stock, however, is usually much less than that from comparable C (regular) corporation stock, because the basis of S corporation stock is usually increased by the amount of corporate profits that were retained by the S corporation.

Other Tax Issues

As noted, actual distributions of cash and property by an S corporation (as contrasted with accounting-based income) are generally nontaxable. There are, however, three situations in which a distribution from an S corporation can be taxable:

1. When the distribution is greater than the basis in the stock, the excess is taxable as capital gain.
2. When the S corporation previously was a C corporation, a distribution of accumulated profits attributable to the C corporation years could be a taxable dividend to taxpaying shareholders, but it is probably not taxable as unrelated business income to a tax-exempt shareholder in the year paid. A tax-exempt shareholder that purchased S corporation stock may, however, ultimately have to pay tax on the a distribution in the year the stock is sold, because the distribution reduces the basis in the stock.
3. This situation can be the most serious: when the S corporation distributes appreciated property (such as real estate) to its shareholders. This type of distribution can trigger taxable income, irrespective of whether it is distributed as an ongoing distribution or a liquidation. This could pose a burden for all shareholders, including charities, because they will have to spend money to pay the tax when all they might have received is illiquid property.

When a charitable organization engages in a business that generates unrelated business income, it can claim a charitable deduction for an amount contributed to an unrelated charity. The question thus arises as to whether an S corporation's charitable gifts are deductible by the charitable organization/shareholder in the same manner. A related question is whether there is any reduction in the benefit of the charitable gift if the S corporation makes a gift to the charity that owns some of its stock. There certainly is a problem if the S corporation is a subsidiary of the charity, but the tax outcome is unclear when the charity owns only a small percentage of the stock.

USE OF PROPERTY

It is common for donors to make gifts of property *to* charities. It is far less likely that a donor will make a gift of property *for the use of* a charitable organization (see Chapter 8). These two approaches may be contrasted with a gift, to a charity, of the *right to use* an item of property for a period of time. An example of this is a contribution, by an owner of an office building, of the rent-free use of office space to a charitable organization for a period of time. Another example is a gift by an owner of vacation property of the right to use the property for a period of time (such as two weeks). There is, however, no federal income tax charitable deduction for this type of gift.

The reason for the lack of a deduction for a gift of this nature is the fact that the contribution is of a partial interest in the property; this is not one of the forms of partial interests the gift of which gives rise to a charitable deduction (see Chapters 7 and 9). Also, because the donor of the right to use an item of property rarely takes the value of the use of the property into income as imputed rent, to allow a charitable deduction for the use of the property by a charitable organization would be to allow a double deduction under the circumstances.

The IRS provided an example of the application of this rule. The example concerns a common situation: an auction sponsored by a charitable organization, where one of the items that is donated to the charity is the right to use a vacation home for one week, with the donor of the home being its owner. The value of the fair rental amount forgone by the property owner is not the basis for a federal income tax charitable contribution deduction. (Moreover, use of the property by the successful bidder at the auction is considered "personal use" by the owner, for purposes of determining any business expense deduction allowable with respect to the property.)

PROPERTY SUBJECT TO DEBT

As discussed throughout, charitable gifts may be made using property. When, however, the property is subject to a debt, unique tax consequences are likely to arise.

One of these consequences is that the transaction is likely to be a bargain sale. This is because the transfer of property that was subject to a debt relieved the donor of that obligation, which is a form of consideration, so the donor received something in return for the gift (namely, relief from the debt). This topic has been the subject of litigation.

The federal tax law is clear that gain from the sale or other disposition of property is the excess of the amount realized over the adjusted basis. The general rule is that the adjusted basis for determining the gain or loss from the sale or other disposition of property is the basis for federal tax law purposes, as "adjusted." The phrase *other disposition of property* includes a gift of property. Thus, a disposition of property includes a gift of the property or a transfer of the property in satisfaction of the liabilities to which it is subject. The bargain sale rules, however, entail a somewhat different definition of the term *basis*, which is that, if a deduction is allowed for a federal income tax charitable contribution deduction by reason of a sale, then the adjusted basis for determining the gain from the sale is that portion of the adjusted basis which bears the same ratio to the adjusted basis as the amount realized bears to the fair market value of the property. Thus, the general rule uses the phrase *sale or other disposition*, while the bargain sale rule only uses the term *sale*. This fact led to a contention that a sale occurs in this setting only when the transferor receives a direct benefit from the transaction, such as cash on mortgaging the property or a depreciation deduction with respect to the property prior to transferring it to a charity. This argument leads to the collateral contention that the general rule for determining basis applies rather than the bargain sale rule.

A Supreme Court opinion made it clear, however, that taxation on relief from debt is not dependent on any theory of economic benefit; rather, it applies to situations such as those not involving the taking of any depreciation deductions. The Court stated: "This, however, does not erase the fact that the mortgagor received the loan proceeds tax free and included them in his basis on the understanding that he had an obligation to repay the full amount. . . . When the obligation is cancelled, the mortgagor is relieved of his responsibility to repay the sum he originally received and thus realizes value to that extent within the meaning of . . . [the tax law defining *amount received*]. From the mortgagor's point of view, when his obligation is assumed by a third party who purchases the encumbered property, it is as if the mortgagor first had been paid with cash borrowed by the third party from the mortgagee on a nonrecourse basis, and then had used the cash to satisfy his obligation to the mortgagee."

The Court put the matter this way (as a contrast): "When a taxpayer receives a loan, he incurs an obligation to repay that loan at some future date. Because of this obligation, the loan proceeds do not qualify as income to the taxpayer. When he fulfills the obligation, the repayment of the loan likewise has no effect on this tax liability."

Another court subsequently completed this argument: "But when someone else relieves him of his obligation to pay the loan, it is as though the taxpayer had received cash and the transfer of the encumbered property to the charity is the equivalent of a sale without regard to any tax benefit theory."

In the case, individuals contributed mortgaged property to a college, which took the property subject to the debt. The court wrote that "it was as if the taxpayers had been paid with cash borrowed by . . . [the college] from the mortgagee on a nonrecourse basis, and then had used the cash to satisfy their obligation to the mortgagee."

The IRS consistently interprets the term *sale* in the bargain sale context to include gifts of mortgaged property to a charity. Thus, "[i]f property is transferred subject to an indebtedness, the amount of indebtedness must be treated as an amount realized for purposes of determining whether there is a sale or exchange. . . , even though the transferee does not agree to assume or pay the indebtedness." This approach was upheld by a court as being reasonable.

This doctrine of law causes the transaction to be partially a purchase and partially a gift. The tax basis of the property must, as noted, be allocated to both the purchase and gift portions of the transaction in determining the capital gain to be reported.

For these purposes, it is immaterial whether the donee organization pays the debt or agrees to assume it. The relief from the obligation is regarded as an item of consideration in either event.

This principle of law also applies in the planned giving context (see Chapter 9). Thus, the contribution to a charitable organization, by means of a pooled income fund, of an item of property that is subject to a debt causes the donor to be treated as if he or she had received income in an amount equal to the amount of the debt. The taxable gain is determined using the bargain sale rules, which require allocation of the basis in the property to the purchase and gift elements.

It appears that these rules apply in the context of charitable giving by means of charitable remainder trusts. In the setting of these trusts, the consequences of transferring property encumbered with debt can be more severe than is the case with pooled income funds. Unrelated business income received by tax-exempt organizations includes unrelated debt-financed income; a gift of mortgaged property to a charitable remainder trust can cause the trust to receive unrelated debt-financed income. When a charitable remainder trust receives unrelated business taxable income in a year, it loses its tax exemption for the year. If an individual transfers mortgaged property to a charitable remainder trust, and the individual is personally liable on the mortgage, the trust may become disqualified on the ground that discharge of the obligation causes the donor to become the owner of the trust.

FUTURE INTERESTS IN TANGIBLE PERSONAL PROPERTY

A charitable contribution consisting of a transfer of a future interest in tangible personal property is treated as made only when all intervening interests in, and rights to the actual possession or enjoyment of, the property have expired, or are held by persons other than the donor or those related to the donor.

The term *future interest* includes:

- Reversions, remainders, and other interests or estates, whether vested or contingent, and whether or not supported by a particular interest or estate, which are limited to commence in use, possession, or enjoyment at some future date or time
- Situations in which a donor purports to give tangible personal property to a charitable organization but has an understanding, arrangement, agreement, or the like, whether written or oral, with the charitable organization which has the effect of reserving to, or retaining in, the donor a right to the use, possession, or enjoyment of the property

These rules do not apply with respect to a transfer or an undivided present interest in property. For example, a contribution of an undivided one-quarter interest in a painting with respect to which the charitable donee is entitled to possession during three months of each year is treated as made on receipt by the donee of a formally executed and acknowledged deed of gift. The period of initial possession by the donee may not, however, be deferred for more than one year.

Thus, these rules do not apply with respect to a transfer of a future interest in intangible personal property or of a transfer of a future interest in real property. A fixture that is intended to be severed from real property is, however, treated as tangible personal property. For example, a contribution of a future interest in a chandelier attached to a building is considered to consist of a future interest in tangible personal property if the transferor intends that it be detached from the building at or prior to the time when the charitable organization's right to possession or enjoyment of the chandelier is to commence.

In the case of a charitable contribution of a future interest, the other rules of the federal tax law of charitable giving are inapplicable to the contribution until the time the contribution is treated as made under these rules.

SUMMARY

This chapter summarized the federal tax law relating to unique situations concerning charitable gifts of property. The types of property that can be the subject of charitable contributions reviewed are works of art (including those created by the donor), vehicles (including boats and airplanes), intellectual property, inventory, scientific research property, computer technology or equipment, licenses to use patents, real property used for conservation purposes, small business (S) corporation stock, property subject to debt, and future interests in tangible personal property. The chapter also addressed the deductibility of automobile expenses when the use is for charitable ends and explored the matter of gifts of the use of property.

CHAPTER 7

Unique Charitable Gift Situations

The purpose of this chapter is to summarize the federal tax law pertaining to unique (if not unusual) charitable gift situations. That is, as noted there is more to the tax law than contributions to charity of money, securities, and real estate. Specifically, this chapter will describe the law concerning charitable gifts in the context of:

- Contributions from retirement accounts
- Contributions of materials or items created by the donor
- Charity auctions
- Gifts of services
- Unreimbursed expenses
- Travel where there may be an element of pleasure
- Bargain sales
- Contributions by trusts
- Partial interests
- Use of charitable family limited partnerships
- Applicability of the foreign tax credit

CONTRIBUTIONS FROM RETIREMENT ACCOUNTS

An eligible individual may make deductible contributions to a traditional retirement arrangement (IRA). Other individuals with taxable income may make nondeductible contributions to a traditional IRA. Earnings and pretax contributions in a traditional IRA are includible in the recipient's gross income when withdrawn. Withdrawals made before age $59\frac{1}{2}$ are subject to a 10 percent excise tax (absent an exception).

Individuals with adjusted gross incomes below certain levels may make nondeductible contributions to a Roth IRA. Amounts withdrawn from a Roth IRA as a qualified distribution are not includible in gross income. A *qualified distribution* is a distribution made after five years and after the holder has attained age $59\frac{1}{2}$, died, or become disabled; the distribution also is made for first-time home buyer expenses up to $10,000. Distributions from a Roth IRA that are not qualified distributions are includible in income to the extent the distributions are attributable to earnings; they are also subject to the 10 percent early withdrawal tax (unless an exception is available).

Individuals who itemize their deductions may claim a deduction for contributions made to qualified charitable organizations (see Chapter 1). Total deductible contributions may not exceed 50 percent of the donor's adjusted gross income; lower deductibility limits apply in the case of contributions of appreciated property and contributions to certain private foundations (see Chapter 4). Excess amounts may be carried forward and deducted in subsequent years. Also, the total of most categories of itemized deductions, including charitable contribution deductions, is reduced by 3 percent of adjusted gross income in excess of a certain threshold ($150,000 for joint filers in 2006).

An individual who wishes to donate otherwise taxable IRA assets to charity must first include the taxable amounts in income and then claim a deduction for the charitable contributions. Not all individuals can deduct the full amount of their charitable contributions; this aspect of the law discourages some individuals from contributing their IRA assets to charity. A popular proposal would allow donors to exclude from gross income direct transfers from IRAs to eligible charitable organizations.

DONORS' CREATIONS

An individual may contribute, to a charitable organization, an item of property that the donor created, such as a painting or a manuscript. The charitable deduction for this type of gift is not based on the general rule, which uses the fair market value of the property (see Chapter 2); instead, the deduction is confined to the donor's cost basis in the property.

This tax law result is mandated by the rule that requires a reduction in the charitable contribution deduction, created by a gift of property, by an amount equal to the amount of gain that would not have been long-term capital gain had the property been sold by the donor at its fair market value at the time of the contribution (see Chapter 8). The federal tax law excludes from the definition of the term *capital asset* a "copyright, a literary, musical, or artistic composition, a letter or memorandum, or similar property," held by (1) an individual whose "personal efforts" created the property; (2) in the case of a letter, memorandum, or similar property, an individual for whom the property was prepared or produced; or (3) an individual in whose hands the basis of the property is determined, for purposes of ascertaining gain from a sale or exchange, in whole or in part by reference to the basis of the property in the hands of an individual described in either of the foregoing two categories. Thus, this charitable deduction is confined to the amount equal to the cost incurred by the donor in the course of creating the item of property.

As an illustration of this rule, a retired athlete decided to contribute various memorabilia accumulated over his career to a charitable organization, which in turn planned to construct a museum housing these items. Among the gifted properties were autographed photographs presented to him over the years as gifts from celebrities. The IRS held that the photographs were created in part by his efforts, and thus the charitable contribution deduction for the gift of them was confined to his basis in the items. The IRS also similarly ruled in connection with diaries of his performances. By contrast, collectibles (such as artworks and crystal), sports equipment, plaques, trophies, and awards given to him were considered by the IRS to be capital assets, so that the charitable deduction for these properties was not limited by this basis-only rule.

CHARITY AUCTIONS

There is considerable confusion and misunderstanding as to the federal tax law applicable to the conduct of charity auctions, particularly regarding how the charitable gift substantiation and quid pro quo contribution rules (see Chapter 12) apply. This uncertainty was colorfully manifested in a personal finance magazine, where it was written that a "special circle of tax hell has been carved out for you if you're involved in one of today's hottest fund-raising activities: charity auctions."

This body of law concerning the charitable deduction has four elements:

1. The charitable contribution deduction available to those who contribute something to be auctioned
2. The charitable contribution deduction that may be available to those who acquire an item at a charity auction
3. The substantiation rules
4. The quid pro quo contribution rules

(Three other bodies of tax law concern the tax treatment, with respect to the charitable organization, of the funds expended by the patrons at the auction; the rules for reporting the event to the IRS; and the state sales tax rules.) There can be different and additional complexities when the fundraising event is a lottery, raffle, or other game of chance.

Charitable Contribution Deductions

Donors of Items to Be Auctioned

In general, the contribution of an item of property to a charitable organization, for the purpose of being auctioned, gives rise to a charitable contribution deduction. The usual rule is that the deduction is equal to the fair market value of the contributed property.

Note: This analysis is based on the assumption that the charity conducting the auction is a public charity and not a private foundation (see Chapter 1).

If the item donated is tangible personal property that has appreciated in value, the charitable deduction is confined to the donor's basis in the property (see Chapter 8). This is because the gift was made for an unrelated purpose-immediate resale by the donee.

If the donated property has a value in excess of $5,000, a charitable deduction is allowed only where there is an independent bona fide appraisal (see Chapter 12). An appraisal summary must be included with the donor's tax return. The charitable organization must report its sale of the property to the IRS if the auction took place within two years of the gift.

There is no charitable deduction for a gift of the right to use property (see next section). Thus, for example, if an individual contributes the opportunity to use his or her vacation property for two weeks, there is no charitable deduction equal to the fair rental value of the property. Moreover, the period of time during which the property is used by the winning bidder must be considered by the donating individual(s) as personal time for purposes of the rules regarding the deductibility of business expenses in connection with the property.

There is no charitable deduction for a gift to a charitable organization of services (see next section). Thus, for example, if a lawyer donates his or her will-drafting services, there is no charitable deduction equal to the hourly rate the lawyer would normally charge for his or her time in preparing wills. Notwithstanding this denial of the deduction as stated in the tax regulations, there would be no deduction in any event, because there is no deduction of any consequence for gifts of property created by the donor.

Further, special rules apply when a business makes a charitable contribution of items from its inventory (see Chapter 6). The substantiation rules apply with respect to gifts of items with a value of $250 or more to be auctioned by a charitable organization (see Chapter 12).

Charitable Contribution Deductions

Acquisition of Items at Auction

The law, as sometimes applied in this area, is that for a payment of money or the transfer of property to a charitable organization to be deductible as a gift, the payor had to have donative intent. Were that an absolute requirement, almost no payments made at a charity auction would be deductible as charitable gifts. The law usually emphasizes a more mechanical computation: In general, deductible payments to a charity are those that exceed the fair market value of anything that the "donor" may receive in return, other than items of insignificant value.

Whether one who acquires an item of property or services at a charity auction is entitled to a charitable contribution deduction is, consequently, problematic. Thus, the above-noted article correctly observed that, as to the enactment of the substantiation and quid pro quo rules, "[I]t was widely assumed that Congress was after folks who buy stuff at auctions and then deduct most or even all of the price as a charitable contribution."

There are two schools of thought on this point, both of which are facially valid. One is that the auction is the marketplace, so that whatever is paid for an item at an auction is its fair market value at that time. Pursuant to this view, the transaction is always a purchase in its entirety; there is no gift element and thus no charitable deduction.

The other school of thought is that an item auctioned at a charity has a fair market value irrespective of the amount paid for it at the auction. This approach allows a charitable deduction for an amount paid at a charity auction that is in excess of the value of the property.

In actual practice, most items disposed of at a charity auction are acquired for a value that does not involve any gift element (because the amount paid is roughly equal to the value of the item, or perhaps less); thus there is no charitable deduction. If an individual wishes to claim a charitable deduction, the burden of proof is on the putative donor to prove that what was paid was in excess of the fair value of the property. This burden of proof can probably be met when it is relatively easy to prove the fair market value of the item, such as an appliance or automobile. But when the value of an item is difficult to discern, it is likely to be a struggle for an auction patron to convince the IRS that a portion of the amount paid was a deductible gift.

The determination of the fair market value of an item is the work of appraisers. Essentially, they look at comparables. For example, if a house sold for $200,000, all other factors being equal, that is the value at the time of sale of the neighboring houses. Thus, the critical factor is the determination of the market, which involves geographical, economical, and timing elements.

Some disparage the idea that the value of an item sold at a charity auction is set at the time of purchase. There cannot be any dispute that an auction constitutes a market, but critics assert it should not be presumed that the price paid for an item at a charity auction is its fair market value. This is particularly the case when, as noted, the value is ascertainable commercially; if the amount paid at an auction for an item of property is in excess of that value, it is easier to make the case that the difference in amounts was a contribution. For example, if a charitable organization auctioned an automobile with a sticker price of $20,000 and received $25,000 for the vehicle, it is reasonable to assume that the individual who acquired the vehicle is entitled to a charitable deduction of $5,000.

The tax regulations contain an example concerning an individual who attends an auction held by a charitable organization. Prior to the auction, the organization publishes a catalog that meets the requirements for a written disclosure statement under the quid pro quo rules (see Chapter 12), including the charity's good faith estimate of the value of the items that will be available for bidding. A copy of the catalog is provided to all in attendance at the auction. This individual reads in the catalog that the charitable organization's estimate of the value of a vase is $100. The individual has no reason to doubt the accuracy of this estimate. The individual successfully bids and pays $500 for the vase. Because this individual knew, prior to making the payment, that the estimate in the catalog was less than the amount of the payment, the individual satisfies the required element of intent. Thus, this individual may treat the charity's estimate of the value of the vase as its fair market value in determining the amount of the charitable deduction (which, in general, would be $400).

Substantiation Rules

The position of the IRS on charity auctions can be found in the agency's rulings harking as far back as 1967. There is little question, however, that charitable organizations and their donors have not, over the intervening years, understood the IRS's stance, which has been clear, consistent, and sensible. Consequently, Congress believed it had to enact legislation in this area and, in 1993, it did.

This subject needs to be placed in context. It can rarely honestly be said that an individual who attends an auction sponsored by a charitable organization is there for the purpose of making a gift. Obviously, someone who wants to contribute to the charitable organization can do so without attending its auction. Individuals participate in these auctions to help support the charitable organization *and* to *purchase* items.

The statutory substantiation rule is this: To be able to deduct a gift, a donor who makes a separate charitable contribution of $250 or more in a year must obtain the requisite written substantiation from the donee charitable organization (see Chapter 12). This substantiation must be an acknowledgment of the gift and must contain this information: (1) the amount of money and a description (but not value) of any property other than money that was distributed; (2) whether the donee organization provided any goods or services in consideration, in whole or in part, for any money or property contributed; and (3) a description and good faith estimate of the value of any goods or services so provided.

Clearly, these substantiation rules are applicable with respect to gifts of items to be auctioned (assuming a charitable contribution deduction is available or desired). Also, as far as acquisition of an item at a charity auction is concerned, if there is no gift element, it is clear that the rules do *not* apply.

When the patron at a charity auction is, however, of the view that he or she has made a charitable contribution in the course of acquiring an item, and the ostensible gift element is $250 or more and a charitable deduction is desired, these rules come into play. The donor should notify the charitable organization that he or she believes a gift was made at the auction, with the intent of receiving the necessary acknowledgment. If the charity agrees that a gift was made, it will issue a written substantiation showing the amount that was "contributed" (here, the full amount of the winning bid) and a description and good faith estimate of the value of the item acquired. The difference, then, would be the amount deductible as a charitable gift.

This process will not function smoothly if the charitable organization believes (or is uncertain in the matter) that no part of the payment was in fact a charitable gift. Certainly a charity in this position could refuse to issue the acknowledgment or refuse to commit itself to a good faith estimate of the value of the item auctioned; as a practical matter, relations with donors and patrons are such that a charity usually cannot be so cavalier.

These rules place considerable pressure on charitable organizations. To return to the preceding example, is the charitable organization willing to issue a substantiation acknowledgment that the auctioned automobile has a value of $20,000, so that the winning bidder can claim a charitable deduction of $5,000? A charitable organization that knowingly provides a false written substantiation to a donor may be subject to a penalty for aiding and abetting an understatement of tax liability.

Quid Pro Quo Contribution Rules

When a person makes a payment to a charitable organization in excess of $75 and receives something of material value in return, the charitable entity is required to make a good faith estimate of the value of the item and notify the donor that only the difference between the fair market value of the item and the amount paid for it (if any) is deductible as a charitable contribution (see Chapter 12). The charitable organization is not, however, expected to function as an appraiser.

Here the application of the tax rules in the charity auction context become less clear. Superficially, the quid pro quo rules would seem to apply in the charity auction setting when the amount transferred is in excess of $75 and there is a gift element.

A *quid pro quo contribution* is a payment "made partly as a contribution and partly in consideration for goods or services provided to the payor by the donee organization." Thus, it can be argued that the purchase of an item at an auction, at a price known to be in excess of the fair market value of the item, is both a contribution and a payment made in consideration of something (a purchase). This law, however, contemplates a transfer that is predominantly a contribution, with the purchase or consideration element being minor.

Nonetheless, if the donor and the donee are in harmony on this point, and if the amount paid at an auction is in excess of $75, the charity can make the necessary disclosure, notifying the donor that the deductible amount is confined to the payment less the value of the item.

SERVICES

An individual may contribute his or her services to a charitable organization. This is, of course, the action of a volunteer. A federal income tax charitable deduction is not, however, available for the contribution of services.

Because the donor of services rarely takes the value of the services into account as income (imputed income), to allow a charitable deduction for the contribution of the services to a charitable organization would be to permit a double deduction under the circumstances. Also, it is the IRS's view that the difficulties associated with the valuation of donated services are in themselves a policy reason for not allowing this type of deduction (along with the associated revenue loss).

In one case, a lawyer performed legal services for charitable organizations over a three-year period, for which he was not compensated. For each of these years, he deducted amounts reflecting the value of his time expended in rendering the services. The court involved found the tax regulation barring this type of deduction to be valid and held that the lawyer was not entitled to a charitable deduction for the gift of his time devoted to charity. The court rejected the argument that the lawyer was donating property, namely, the product of his services in the form of pleadings, resolutions, opinion letters, reports, deeds, and the like.

In other instances, the IRS ruled that there is no tax deduction for the gift by a radio station to a charitable organization of broadcast time as part of the station's programming and that the contribution to a charitable organization by a newspaper of space in the newspaper is not deductible. This rule of law should be contrasted with the rule that a contribution of a contract right to receive purchased services is deductible, because it is not a contribution of the donor's services.

Under the facts of the case that gave rise to this rule, a radio station received lodging and transportation rights from hotels and airlines in exchange for the provision of advertising time. The radio station included the value of the lodging and transportation in its gross income, and the hotels and airlines included in their gross incomes the value of the advertising time. The radio station donated the lodging and transportation rights to a governmental agency.

The IRS concluded that the radio station was entitled to a charitable deduction for the fair market value of the donated rights. In so doing, the IRS made an analogy to an earlier ruling, in which it upheld the deductibility of a gift to a charitable organization of a right to receive dance lessons that the donor purchased from a dance school. Again, the gift was of property, namely, a purchased contract right to receive dance lessons.

UNREIMBURSED EXPENSES

Unreimbursed expenditures incurred by an individual, in the course of rendering services that augment or further the program activities of one or more charitable organizations, may be deductible as charitable contributions. This type of deduction, which may be thwarted if an element of personal pleasure is involved, is in contrast to the rules that preclude a charitable contribution deduction for a gift of the services themselves or for payments made directly to individuals by those who are assisting these individuals in their charitable endeavors.

The range of expenditures that can be deductible in this regard is potentially sweeping, embracing expenses for the cost of a uniform without general utility, which is required to be worn in performing donated services; transportation expenses necessarily incurred in performing donated services; and meals and lodging necessarily incurred while away from home in the course of performing donated services. The rationale for this deduction is that these expenses are not incurred for the benefit of the individual performing the services but rather for the benefit of the charitable organization or organizations involved.

These unreimbursed expenses, incurred by volunteers, have been ruled to be deductible as charitable contributions:

- Expenses incurred by civil defense volunteers in the performance of their duties (such as traveling expenses and expenses of attending meetings)
- Expenses incurred by a member of the Civil Air Patrol that are directly attributable to the performance of services (such as the expenses of acquiring and maintaining uniforms, and of maintenance and repair of a telescope)
- Expenses incurred by elected or appointed government officials that are directly connected with and solely attributable to the performance of their official duties
- Expenses incurred while rendering services to the American Red Cross as a nurses' aide (such as local transportation costs and expenses of acquiring and maintaining uniforms)
- Expenses incurred while assisting underprivileged juveniles selected by a charitable organization (such as admission costs and expenses of meals)
- Expenses incurred by an individual while participating in a church-established program
- Expenses incurred by volunteer pilots in providing training services for an organization that promotes, fosters, and engages in aviation education activities

There may be as many as six elements of this analysis: (1) whether the activities involved are exempt functions of the charitable organization; (2) the inherent nature of the services provided; (3) the substance of the services; (4) the duration of the services; (5) whether the outlays are excessive; and (6) the extent of any pleasure derived by the service provider.

Exempt Functions

Thus, these expenses, to be deductible, must be directly connected to the performance of services in enhancement of a charitable organization's exempt functions. In most of the court opinions and IRS rulings on this subject, this aspect of the matter has not been at issue. Nonetheless, even in this area, some aspects of volunteer service may entail nondeductible expenses. For example, even though expenses incurred in connection with the rendering of services to a church may be deductible, the expenses of individuals attending church conventions, assemblies, or other meetings in accordance with their rights, privileges, or obligations as members of a church are not deductible. Likewise, although unreimbursed expenses incurred by a volunteer for a charitable organization for the operation, maintenance, and repair of an automobile or airplane may be deductible, items such as the proportionate share of general maintenance and repairs, liability insurance, or depreciation in connection with use of an automobile for charitable purposes are not deductible.

Inherent Nature of Services

In general, anyone can serve as a volunteer for a charitable organization and be entitled to a charitable contribution deduction for unreimbursed expenses incurred. In other words, the individual who is a volunteer incurring expenses does not have to be a professional or other expert in a field to serve a charity that is functioning in that field. Thus, an individual may be a trustee, director, and/or officer of a charitable organization and incur deductible unreimbursed expenses in that capacity. Likewise, an individual serving as a lay member of a church may incur deductible unreimbursed expenses.

At the same time, the fact that an individual is a professional or other expert in a field does not, in and of itself, preclude deductibility of unreimbursed expenses. This factor may, however, increase the likelihood that pleasure, undue or otherwise, is being derived from the experience.

Substance of Services

It has been held that one element of the "relevant inquiry" in this area is the "*extent*" of the charitable services provided by the volunteer. The term *substance* probably is preferable to the term *extent*.

This subjective factor looks to the inherent value to the charitable organization of the services provided. This aspect of the matter is more fully developed in the context of the rules concerning permissible and impermissible pleasure.

Nonetheless, as an illustration, it has been held that expenses incurred by a lay member of a church in attending a church convention as a delegate may be deductible as a charitable gift. Similarly, expenses incurred by a member of the American Legion who is appointed as a delegate to and attends an American Legion convention may be deductible. In limiting the reach of this aspect of deductibility, the IRS makes much of the word *delegate*, stating that the term is used in its "general meaning of one appointed and sent by another, with authority to transact business as his [or her] representative." In other words, the IRS is, in this setting, equating a *delegate* with an *agent*. This position enabled the IRS to rule that expenses were not deductible when incurred by an individual in connection with a "study mission," when the charity directly served did not conduct the mission, the travel arrangements were made by the individual, and the "itinerary also covered other points of interest that are ordinarily a part of tourist sight-seeing schedules."

Duration of Services

It has also been held that one element of the relevant inquiry in this area is the *duration* of the charitable service provided by the volunteer. The little law there is on this point, and the law that may be extrapolated from related contexts, suggests that to give rise to deductible expenses, the charitable services must be carried on for the duration of the day (eight hours). Thus, an individual was allowed to deduct expenses incurred in attending the meetings of and otherwise providing services for a charitable organization when he, in the words of a court, "routinely spent a full day" doing so.

This factor also relates to the matter of pleasure entailed by the activities. The more time provided for recreational and personal undertakings, the less time there is for the provision of substantive services and the more opportunity for impermissible pleasure and no charitable contribution deduction.

Excessive Expenditures

Unreimbursed expenditures for items such as meals and lodging, incurred in connection with charitable activities, must be *reasonable* to be deductible. These outlays, and also those for transportation, must be *necessarily* incurred. Inasmuch as a requirement of *reasonableness* is inherent in the concept of *necessary*, these expenses for travel, meals, and lodging must be both reasonable and necessary.

In one case, an individual was active with three charitable organizations and undertook considerable travel in connection with his volunteer work for them. The IRS disallowed some of his deductions for unreimbursed expenses, in part on the ground that they were lavish or extravagant. The IRS asserted that he stayed in "deluxe" hotels; a court, however, allowed the deductions because, although the outlays were not "frugal," they were for the hotels that hosted the particular meetings (or similarly priced ones nearby), and thus were "convenient" and saved him additional travel expense. The rental of a hotel suite was found to be reasonable because the individual stayed one week and used the suite as a meeting place for officials of one of the charitable organizations. Also, this individual "held relatively prestigious positions in large charitable organizations, such that staying in quality lodgings may have been acceptable practice." The court was of the view, however, that this individual was overly generous in his practice of dispensing gratuities and disallowed most of those outlays.

Element of Pleasure

As noted, the rationale for the deductibility of these expenses is that they are incurred for the benefit of the charitable organization involved, not for the benefit of the participating individual. Thus, the more the individual derives pleasure from his or her undertakings for a charitable organization, the less likely it is that the related unreimbursed expenses will be deductible. In one case, the court concluded that an individual who traveled to attend folk dance festivals could not deduct the expenses as a charitable contribution, even though he acquired knowledge that he used in rendering services to a charitable organization, because he derived "substantial personal pleasure" from participation in the festivals.

This principle is more fully developed in the body of law summarized in the next section.

LIMIT ON DEDUCTION DUE TO PLEASURE

There is no charitable contribution deduction for expenses incurred for traveling, meals, and lodging while away from home, whether paid directly or by reimbursement, unless, as provided in a statute, there is "no significant element of personal pleasure, recreation, or vacation" involved. This rule also applies when the expenses are paid by an "indirect means such as by contribution to the charitable organization that pays for the taxpayer's travel [and other] expenses."

This body of law focuses on three of the six elements summarized earlier: the substance of the services, the duration of the services, and the extent of any pleasure derived by the individual providing the services.

Substance of Services

As noted, one element of the relevant inquiry in this area is the *extent*—or *substance*—of the charitable services provided by the volunteer. The legislative history of this law states that the individual must be "on duty in a genuine and substantial sense throughout the trip" to be entitled to the deduction for unreimbursed expenses; the deduction is not available when the individual "only has nominal duties relating to the performance of services for the charity." This history also indicates that Congress was concerned about situations in which the "value of the services performed appeared to be minimal compared to the amount deducted."

For example, the IRS states that an individual "who sails from one Caribbean Island to another and spends eight hours a day counting whales and other forms of marine life as part of a project sponsored by a charitable organization generally will not be permitted a charitable deduction." Aside from the unexplained insertion of the word *generally,* the implication is that whale-watching and like undertakings are not sufficiently substantive to constitute the type of charitable services that give rise to deductible unreimbursed expenses. Similarly, in the other setting, the IRS took the same position with respect to "study missions."

The IRS also stated that an individual who "works on an archaeological excavation sponsored by a charitable organization for several hours each morning, with the rest of the day free for recreation and sightseeing, will not be allowed a deduction even if the taxpayer works very hard during those few hours." Although this statement is intended to illustrate the element of *duration*, it appears to indicate that the expense deduction would be available if the volunteer worked "very hard" on the archaeological dig eight hours a day. Consequently, the IRS view seems to be that whale-watching is too passive whereas full-time hard work at an archaeological evacuation site amounts to sufficient charitable service to support a charitable deduction for the related unreimbursed expenses.

The IRS further wrote that a "member of a local chapter of a charitable organization who travels to New York City and spends an entire day attending the organization's regional meeting will not be subject to this provision [denial of the charitable deduction] even if he or she attends the theatre in the evening." This example illustrates that attending meetings for the benefit of a charitable organization constitutes substantive services that support the expense deduction.

In one case, an individual was denied a charitable deduction for unreimbursed travel expenses when he traveled as an "official representative" of a charitable organization or when he was merely an "observer."

Duration of Services

As noted, another element of the relevant inquiry in this area is the *duration* of the charitable services provided by the volunteer. The legislative history of this law states that Congress was concerned about situations in which the "amount of time spent during the day on activities benefiting the charitable organization was relatively small compared to the amount of time during the day available for recreation and sightseeing activities." As discussed, at least eight hours of charitable services per day appear to be necessary to meet the standard and support this aspect of the expense deduction. This is so irrespective of whether the services are provided out-of-doors or in meeting rooms.

In one case, an individual stayed at resort hotels to attend meetings of charitable organizations. Although golf and tennis tournaments were held, he "routinely spent a full day attending meetings or otherwise providing services while attending conferences," which "preclud[ed] participation in the recreational activities." The deduction for his unreimbursed expenses was upheld.

As previously indicated, there cannot be an allocation of services in support of an expense deduction for a portion of unreimbursed expenses. The legislative history of this law states that there is no deduction in a situation involving an individual "who for significant portions of the trip is not required to render services." For example, at least according to the IRS's view of the law, an individual cannot provide substantive services for the benefit of a charitable organization for four hours a day and properly claim a charitable deduction for one-half of the unreimbursed expenses incurred for travel, meals, and lodging.

Element of Pleasure

As noted, no charitable contribution deduction is available for expenses incurred for traveling, meals, and lodging while away from home, whether paid directly or by reimbursement, "unless there is no significant element of personal pleasure, recreation or vacation" involved. This requires identification and quantification of a pleasure element. Inexplicably, in interpreting this rule, a court wrote that the "relevant inquiry is the extent and duration of the charitable services provided by the taxpayer, and not some quantum measure of pleasure derived by the taxpayer." Given the language of the statute, an assessment of a "quantum measure of pleasure" derived by a service provider in this setting seems unavoidable.

The only conceivable explanation for this dismissal of the pleasure element must be found in an analysis of the context in which it was written. In the case, the court allowed the claimed deduction for expenses for travel to a resort location, where golf and tennis activities were featured, because the individual service provider served on the charitable organization's executive committee and was forced to participate in meetings all day, and thus could not partake of social activities except in the evening. This approach correlates with the IRS's view that the expense deduction is available when the service provider participates in substantive meetings all day for the benefit of a charitable organization, notwithstanding pleasurable undertakings (such as the theater) after hours (such as in the evening). The import of this approach seems to be that the element of pleasure, recreation, or vacation does not become *significant* when the day also includes at least eight hours of substantive activities engaged in for the advancement of charitable purposes. (This exercise nonetheless cannot ignore a "quantum measure of pleasure," but rather should lead to a conclusion that the pleasure component is *insignificant.*)

In another case, an individual incurred expenses in connection with participation in a safari, in which he collected animals and donated them to a museum. The court allowed the deduction, emphasizing the factor of the individual's intent, that is, whether he undertook the trip primarily for furtherance of charitable purposes or for his "personal pleasure, welfare or economic benefit or entertainment." Yet a series of cases holds that the expenses of participating in "People-to-People" tours are not deductible, because the individual travelers are the primary beneficiaries of the payments.

Another aspect of this analysis is whether the individual *enjoys* providing the services to the charitable organization. Presumably, because these individuals are serving as volunteers, this type of enjoyment is always present, although there may be degrees of it. The legislative history of this law states that, in determining whether travel away from home involves a significant element of personal pleasure, recreation, or vacation, the "fact that a taxpayer enjoys providing services to the charitable organization will not lead to denial of the deduction." The example is given of a troop leader for a tax-exempt youth group who takes children belonging to the group on a camping trip; the leader's travel expenses in this connection are deductible if he or she is "on duty in a genuine and substantial sense throughout the trip, even if he or she enjoys the trip or enjoys supervising children."

BARGAIN SALES

The charitable deduction for an item of capital gain property is often based on the fair market value of the property; the donor is not required to recognize gain on the capital gain element in the property (see Chapter 2). One of the exceptions to that rule involves the bargain sale.

Definition of *Bargain Sale*

A *bargain sale* is a transfer of property to a charitable organization, when the transaction is in part a sale or exchange of the property and in part a charitable contribution of the property. Basically, a bargain sale is a sale of an item of property to a charitable organization at a price that is less than the fair market value of the property; the amount equal to the fair market value of the property, less the amount that is the sales price, is regarded as a contribution to the charitable organization.

A court upheld a bargain sale transaction in which persons sold stock to a city for less than the fair market value of the securities. The city wanted the property represented by the stock for use as part of a sewage treatment program. The stock had a value of $7.9 million and was sold for $4 million. In another case, two individuals sold a custom flybridge steel fishing trawler to a charitable organization for $25,000, to be used to teach delinquent youths individual responsibilities by going on sea cruises; the vessel was custom-made for the sellers, with a fair market value of $160,000.

Disputes can arise as to whether a transaction is a bargain sale or a regular sale of property at fair market value. In one of these instances, a court held that the conveyance to a county of an easement restricting the development of land gave rise to a bargain sale and thus a charitable contribution deduction, despite the IRS's contention that the amount paid by the county for the transfer was its fair market value. The county acquired the easement pursuant to an agricultural land preservation program; the donors were paid $309,000. The court found the value of the easement to be $518,000, resulting in a charitable deduction in the amount of $209,000. The IRS contended that the easement was worth only the $309,000 the government paid for it, that sum being in line with amounts the county generally paid for development rights under the program.

Allocation of Basis

The charitable deduction arising from the making of a bargain sale may be an amount equal to the value of the gift portion of the property transferred. The charitable deduction may be less, however, inasmuch as a deduction reduction rule potentially applies to the contribution element in a bargain sale. (The deduction rule requires that, under certain circumstances, the amount is equal to the fair market value of the property be reduced by the ordinary income or capital gain element in the property [see Chapter 8].)

There must be allocated to the contribution portion of the property that element of the adjusted basis of the entire property that bears the same ratio to the total adjusted basis as the fair market value of the contributed portion of the property bears to the fair market value of the entire property. Further, for these purposes, there must be allocated to the contributed portion of the property the amount of gain that is not recognized on the bargain sale, but that would have been recognized if the contributed portion of the property had been sold by the donor at its fair market value at the time of its contribution to the charitable organization.

The amount of long-term capital gain or ordinary income that would have been recognized if the contributed portion of the property had been sold by the donor at its fair market value at the time of its contribution is the amount that bears (1) the same ratio to the ordinary income (or long-term capital gain) that would have been recognized if the entire property had been sold by the donor at its fair market value at the time of its contribution (2) as the fair market value of the contributed portion of the property at that time bears to the fair market value of the entire property at that time. The fair market value of the contributed portion of the property is the amount determined by subtracting from the fair market value of the entire property the amount realized on the sale.

The contributed element arising from a bargain sale is the subject to the percentage limitations (see Chapter 4). The gain generated as the consequence of a bargain sale transaction must be recognized in the year of the sale.

A bargain sale will also arise when the property transferred to a charitable organization is subject to a debt, even though the donor does not receive any payment for the transfer of the property.

Interplay with Deduction Reduction Rule

A court ruled that the federal tax regulations accompanying the appreciation reduction rule were invalid to the extent that they required reduction of a donor's charitable deduction, arising by reason of a bargain sale, by the amount of the unrealized appreciation of the sale portion of the property. The donors sold appreciated long-term capital gain property to a charitable organization in a bargain sale. The regulations accompanying these rules provided that, in the case of a bargain sale to which the deduction reduction rule applies, no deduction is allowable unless the gift exceeds the appreciation reduction amount for all of the property. Because this interpretation of the rules would have eliminated any charitable contribution deduction, the donors contended that the deduction reduction rule only causes a reduction in their charitable deduction of the inherent gain in the donated portion of the property. In agreeing with the donors, the court parsed the language of the deduction reduction rule, which speaks of the "property contributed," and concluded that Congress referenced, in connection with bargain sales, only the property donated and not the property sold as well. Therefore, the court pronounced the regulations unreasonable and thus invalid. The regulations were subsequently revised to reflect this opinion.

Interplay with Carryover Rules

In a case, a donor made a bargain sale of capital gain property to a charitable organization. Earlier in the same year, the same donor made another gift of different capital gain property to another charitable recipient, resulting in a charitable deduction (prior to application of the percentage limitations). This deduction exceeded the amount allowable for the donor for gifts of capital gain property for the year, thus forcing all of the deduction attributable to the bargain sale to be carried forward.

The tax regulations state that a charitable deduction arising from a bargain sale of property is an "allowable" deduction, even if part or all of the contribution must be carried forward, irrespective of whether the portion carried over is ever used as a deduction. In this case, the donors challenged the regulation, claiming that the deduction resulting from the first gift must be made in its entirety before any part of the contribution for the second gift can be deducted. If that were true, it would have worked out that the entire allowable deduction relating to capital gain property in the year of the gift and in the subsequent year would have been charged against the first contribution, leaving nothing to be deductible that was attributable to the second contribution. But the court held that there is no basis in law for the "first-in first out" rule as the donors suggested.

The court construed the term *allowable* in the context of the five-year carryover rule. That is, the deductibility of a gift may not be known until the expiration of six years—long after the expiration of the period of limitations for assessment of a deficiency in respect to the year of contribution. The court wrote: "We think it unlikely that Congress intended the substantive rights of taxpayers and the government to be imperiled by a rule providing that no deduction was 'allowable' for [these] purposes . . . unless it eventually turned out, long after the taxable year, that the contribution actually reduced the taxpayer's taxable income in any of the 5 succeeding tax years." The court continued: "We think that if the statute is read in the context of all relevant provisions, the word 'allowable' must be interpreted as referring to a contribution available for deduction even though the contribution does not ultimately result in a deduction by reason of future events entirely unrelated to the nature of the charitable contribution. This interpretation of the law," concluded the court, "strongly supports" the regulation.

CONTRIBUTIONS BY TRUSTS

Contributions to charitable organizations may be made by trusts. The federal tax law differentiates between simple trusts and complex trusts. A trust may qualify as a simple trust in one year and be a complex trust in another year.

General Rules

The terms of a simple trust provide that all of the trust income is to be distributed currently and do not provide that any amounts are to be paid, permanently set aside, or used for charitable purposes. A simple trust is not considered to be a trust that may pay, permanently set aside, or use any amount for charitable purposes for any tax year in which the trust is not allowed a charitable deduction.

A complex trust is allowed a deduction, in computing its taxable income, for an amount of gross income, without limitation, that pursuant to the terms of the governing instrument is, during the tax year, paid for a charitable purpose.

A trust is allowed a deduction for distributions to beneficiaries up to the amount of *distributable net income* of the trust for the tax year. A complex trust may deduct, up to its distributable net income ceiling for the year, the sum of any income for the tax year required to be distributed currently and any other amounts, whether income or principal, properly paid or credited or required to be distributed for that tax year.

A trust beneficiary must include in income the amount distributed to the beneficiary as well as any amount credited or required to be distributed by the trust to the beneficiary. Any amount paid or permanently set aside or otherwise qualifying for the charitable deduction is not encompassed by these rules.

Amounts paid, permanently set aside, or to be used for charitable purposes are deductible by trusts only to the extent provided by the applicable charitable deduction rules. Thus, a trust is not entitled to a charitable contribution deduction (or a distribution deduction) for a contribution to a charitable organization when the gift is of some or all of the trust principal. For example, the IRS ruled that a trust cannot claim a charitable contribution deduction for gifts of trust principal that satisfy the requirements of a qualified conservation contribution (see Chapter 6).

For a trust to claim a charitable deduction for an amount of gross income that it contributes for charitable purposes, the governing instrument of the trust must accord the trustee(s) the authority to make charitable contributions. In the case of an investment by a trust in a partnership, the partnership may make a charitable contribution from the partnership's gross income. Although that income is never available to the trust, for federal tax purposes, the trust must take into account its distributive share of the partnership's income, gain, loss, deductions (including for charitable contributions), and credits (see Chapter 3). Under these circumstances, a trust's deduction for its distributive share of a charitable contribution made by a partnership will not be disallowed merely because the trust's governing instrument does not authorize the trustee to make charitable contributions.

Gifts of Interests in Properties

A charitable deduction is not allowed for the fair market value of a contribution of any interest in property that is less than the donor's entire interest in the property and that is transferred in trust, unless the transfer meets certain requirements. If a donor's entire interest in the property is transferred in trust and contributed to a charitable organization, however, a charitable deduction is allowed. For example, if an item of property is transferred in trust, with the requirement that the income of the trust be paid for a term of 20 years to a church and thereafter the remainder is to be paid to an educational institution, a deduction is allowed for the value of the property.

These rules do not apply with respect to a contribution of a partial interest in property if the interest is the donor's entire interest in the property (an income interest or remainder interest). If the property in which a partial interest exists was divided in order to create the interest and thus avoid these rules, however, a charitable deduction is not allowable.

A charitable contribution deduction is precluded when the ineligible partial interests are created on or about the same time. This ban is not necessarily permanent, however; when there is a substantial time gap between the creation of a trust and the contribution in question, a charitable deduction may be available. One instance in which this occurred involved the contribution of a fraction of an income interest in a charitable remainder trust to a charitable organization that was the remainder interest beneficiary (leading to a partial termination of the trust). The IRS was persuaded that the six-year gap spanning creation of the trust and the fractional interest gift demonstrated that the donors did not inappropriately divide their interest in the trust.

A charitable contribution deduction is not allowed for the fair market value of a gift, to a charitable organization, of a remainder interest in property that is less than the donor's entire interest in the property and that the donor transfers in trust, unless the trust is a charitable remainder annuity trust, a charitable remainder unitrust, or a pooled income fund (see Chapter 9).

A charitable contribution deduction is not allowed for the fair market value of a gift, to a charitable organization, of an income interest in property that is less than the donor's entire interest in the property and that the donor transfers in trust, unless the income interest is a guaranteed annuity interest or a unitrust interest, and the grantor is treated as the owner of the interest.

Guaranteed Annuity Interests

An income interest is a *guaranteed annuity interest* only if it is an irrevocable right, pursuant to the governing instrument of the trust, to receive a guaranteed annuity. A guaranteed annuity is an arrangement under which a determinable amount is paid periodically (but not less than annually), for a specified term and/or for the life or lives of an individual or individuals, each of whom must be living at the date of transfer and can be ascertained at that date. For example, the annuity may be paid for the life of an individual plus a term of years. An amount is *determinable* if the exact amount that must be paid under the conditions specified in the governing instrument of the trust can be ascertained as of the date of transfer. For example, the amount to be paid may be a stated sum for a term, or for the life of an individual, at the expiration of which it may be changed by a specified amount but may not be redetermined by reference to a fluctuating index, such as a cost of living index. The amount to be paid may be expressed in terms of a fraction or percentage of the cost of living index on the date of transfer.

An income interest is a guaranteed annuity interest only if it is a guaranteed annuity interest in every respect. For example, if the income interest is the right to receive from a trust each year a payment equal to the lesser of a sum certain or a fixed percentage of the net fair market value of the trust assets, determined annually, the interest is not a guaranteed annuity interest.

When a charitable interest is in the form of a guaranteed annuity interest, the governing instrument of the trust may provide that income of the trust, which is in excess of the amount required to pay the guaranteed annuity interest, may be paid to or for the use of a charitable organization. Nevertheless, the amount of the charitable deduction is limited to the fair market value of the guaranteed annuity interest.

If the present value on the date of transfer of all the income interests for a charitable purpose exceeds 60 percent of the aggregate fair market value of all amounts in the trust (after the payment of liabilities), the income interest will not be considered a guaranteed annuity interest unless the governing instrument of the trust prohibits both the acquisition and the retention of assets that would give rise to a tax on jeopardizing investments by a private foundation if the trustee had acquired assets of that nature.

An income interest consisting of an annuity transferred in trust is not a guaranteed annuity interest if any amount other than an amount in payment of a guaranteed annuity interest may be paid by the trust for a private purpose before the expiration of all the income interests for a charitable purpose, unless the amount for a private purpose is paid from a group of assets that, pursuant to the governing instrument of the trust, are devoted exclusively to private purposes and to which the split-interest trust rules are inapplicable by reason of an exception to them. This exception applies only if the obligation to pay the annuity for a charitable purpose begins as of the date of creation of the trust, and the obligation to pay the guaranteed annuity for a private purpose does not precede the obligation to pay the annuity for a charitable purpose, and only if the governing instrument of the trust does not provide for any preference or priority in respect of any payment of the guaranteed annuity for a private purpose as opposed to any payment for a charitable purpose. In this context, an amount is not paid for a private purpose if it is paid for what the tax regulations term an "adequate and full consideration" in money or money's worth.

Unitrust Interests

An income interest is a *unitrust interest* only if it is an irrevocable right pursuant to the governing instrument of the charitable remainder unitrust to receive payment, not less often than annually, of a fixed percentage of the net fair market value of the trust assets, determined annually. In computing the net fair market value of the trust assets, all assets and liabilities must be taken into account without regard to whether particular items are taken into account in determining the income of the trust. The net fair market value of the trust assts may be determined on any date during the year or by taking the average of valuations made on more than one date during the year, provided that the same valuation date or dates and valuation methods are used each year. When the governing instrument of the trust does not specify the valuation date or dates, the trustee is to select the date or dates and indicate the selection on the first return that the trust is required to file with the IRS (Form 1041). Payments in connection with a unitrust interest may be paid for a specified term or for the life or lives of an individual or individuals, each of whom must be living at the date of transfer and can be ascertained at that date. For example, a unitrust interest may be paid for the life of an individual plus a term of years.

An income interest is a unitrust interest only if it is a unitrust interest in every respect. For example, if the income interest is defined as the right to receive from a trust each year a payment equal to the lesser of a sum certain or a fixed percentage of the net fair market value of the trust assets, determined annually, the interest is not a unitrust interest.

When a charitable interest is in the form of a unitrust interest, the governing instrument of the trust may provide that income of the trust in excess of the amount required to pay the unitrust interest is to be paid to or for the use of a charitable organization. Nevertheless, the amount of the deduction under these rules is limited to the fair market value of the unitrust interest.

An income interest in the form of a unitrust interest is not a unitrust interest if any amount other than an amount in payment of a unitrust interest may be paid by the trust for a private purpose before the expiration of all the income interests for a charitable purpose, unless the amount for a private purpose is paid from a group of assets that, pursuant to the governing instrument of the trust, are devoted exclusively to private purposes and to which the split-interest trust rules are inapplicable by reason of an exception. This exception applies only if the obligation to pay the unitrust interest for a charitable purpose begins as of the date of creation of the trust, and the obligation to pay the unitrust interest for a private purpose does not precede the obligation to pay the unitrust interest for a charitable purpose, and only if the governing instrument of the trust does not provide for any preference or priority in respect of any payment of the unitrust interest for a private purpose as opposed to any payment for a charitable purpose. In this context, an amount is not paid for a private purpose if it is paid for an adequate and full consideration in money or money's worth.

Valuation

The charitable contribution deduction for a gift of a guaranteed annuity interest or unitrust interest is limited to the fair market value of the interest on the date of the contribution. The fair market value of a unitrust interest is determined by subtracting the present value of all interests in the transferred property, other than the unitrust interest, from the fair market value of the transferred property. If, by reason of all the conditions and circumstances surrounding a transfer of an income interest in property in trust, it appears that the charitable organization may not receive the beneficial enjoyment of the interest, a charitable deduction is allowed only for the minimum amount it is evident the charity will receive.

Recapture

If the donor of an income interest in property, at any time before termination of the interest, ceases to be treated as the owner of the interest (such as by reason of death), the donor must be considered as having received, on the date of cessation of ownership, an amount of income equal to (1) the amount of any charitable deduction that was allowed to the donor for the contribution of the interest, reduced by (2) the discounted value of all amounts that were required to be, and actually were, paid with respect to the interest under the terms of the trust to the charitable organization before the time at which the donor ceased to be treated as the owner of the interest.

The discounted value of these amounts is computed by treating each amount as a contribution of a remainder interest after a term of years and valuing each amount as of the date of contribution of the income interest by the donor, consistent with the manner in which the fair market value of the income interest was determined. This rule is not to be construed to disallow a deduction to the trust for amounts paid by the trust to the charitable organization after the time at which the donor ceased to be treated as the owner of the trust.

Denial of Deduction for Certain Contributions

If a charitable contribution deduction is allowed for the fair market value of an income interest transferred in trust, not the grantor of the income interest, nor the trust, nor any other person may be allowed a charitable or any other type of deduction for the amount of any charitable contribution made by the trust with respect to, or in fulfillment of, the income interest. This rule is not to be construed, however, to disallow a deduction to the trust for amounts paid by the trust after the grantor ceased to be treated as the owner of the income interest that are not taken into account in determining the amount of recapture, or disallow a deduction to the grantor for a charitable contribution made to the trust in excess of the contribution required to be made by the trust under the terms of the trust instrument with respect to, or in fulfillment of, the income interest.

PARTIAL INTERESTS

As a general rule, there is no federal income tax deduction for a contribution of a partial interest in property to a charitable organization. This rule is, however, largely engulfed by exceptions. The principal exception is for qualified transfers made in trust form (see previous section and Chapter 9). Additional exceptions cover certain gifts for conservation purposes, contributions of a remainder interest in a personal residence or farm, and contributions of an undivided portion of the donor's entire interest in property (see Chapters 6 and 9).

A charitable deduction is, however, allowed for a contribution of a partial interest in property, without regard to this rule, when the interest is less than the entire interest in the property, if the interest is the donor's entire interest in the property. Nonetheless, if the property in which the partial interest exists was divided to create this type of partial interest and thus avoid the general rule, the charitable deduction will not be allowed.

The purpose of this general rule is to preclude a claimed charitable contribution deduction in an amount greater than the value of the interest contributed. Illustrations of partial interests include:

- The contribution of voting stock to a charitable organization, with the donor retaining the right to vote that stock. The IRS, however, considered a similar set of facts and reasoned that, because the voting rights were transferred to an unrelated individual for a valid business purpose, the contribution of stock subject to a voting agreement was eligible for the charitable contribution deduction, because the donor's interest in the stock was not divided to avoid the partial interest rule.
- An irrevocable assignment to a charity of the cash surrender value of life insurance, with the donor retaining the right to designate the beneficiary and to assign the balance of the policy subject to the charity's right to the cash surrender value.

For example, a contribution of the right to use property that the donor owns, such as a contribution of a rent-free lease, is treated as a contribution of less than the person's entire interest in the property. Likewise, if a person contributes an interest in motion picture films, but retains the right to make reproductions of the films and exploit the reproductions commercially, the contribution is regarded as one that is less than the person's entire interest in the property. In both instances, the contribution is not deductible.

Another example involved the contribution to a tax-exempt university of a license to use a patent, with the donor retaining the right to license the patent to others. The IRS analogized this arrangement to the rent-free lease and the partial interest in motion picture films just mentioned, in that the license did not constitute the donor's entire interest in the patent. This gift was ruled to be one of a nondeductible partial interest, with the IRS observing that the result would have been the same had the donor retained any other substantial right in the patent, such as a gift whereby the patent (or license to use the patent) was contributed solely for use in a particular geographic area while the donor retained the right to use the patent (or license) in other geographic areas.

Still another illustration concerned railroads that conveyed, to a charitable organization, their interests in certain railroad rights-of-way for interim trail use pursuant to the Rails to Trails Act. This law causes this use of these rights-of-way (easements) to not be treated as a permanent abandonment of the right-of-way for railroad purposes, thus preserving the railroad right-of-way in case of future need. The railroads sought charitable contribution deductions for these conveyances. The IRS's lawyers concluded, however, that the railroads contributed only a partial interest in the property, retaining the right to use the easement in the case of reactivation of rail service. It is possible, nonetheless, that the value of the retained interest was insubstantial, on the ground that the possibility of reactivation was so remote as to be negligible (see next section).

If, as of the date of a gift, a transfer of property for charitable purposes may be defeated by the performance of an act or the happening of an event, a charitable deduction is not allowable unless the possibility that the act or event will occur is so remote as to be negligible. In application of this rule, the IRS held that a deduction was not allowable for a contribution of a patent to a tax-exempt university on the condition that an individual, who was a faculty member of the institution and an expert in the technology covered by the patent, continue to be a member of the faculty of the university during the remaining life of the patent. If the individual ceased to be a member of the university's faculty before the patent expired, the patent was to revert to the donor. The patent was to expire 15 years after the date of the contribution. On the date of the gift, the likelihood that this individual would cease to be a member of the faculty of the university before the patent expired was not so remote as to be negligible.

In one case, a gift was made of the long-term capital gains portions of commodities futures contracts to a charitable organization. The donors retained a right to the income from the contracts representing short-term capital gain. The IRS asserted, in litigation, that this was a nondeductible gift of a partial interest. The court, however, did not view these portions of gains as substantial interests or rights owned by the donors that could not be divided in donating a portion of a futures contract. The charitable deduction was allowed, inasmuch as the donors did not retain any interest in the portion of the futures contracts that they donated to the charitable organization. The contribution was held to be of an undivided portion of the donors' entire interest in the futures contracts, namely, the segment of the contracts representing long-term capital gain.

The IRS stated that, in enacting this rule, Congress "was concerned with situations in which taxpayers might obtain a double benefit by taking a deduction for the present value of a contributed interest while also excluding from income subsequent receipts from the donated interest." Also, the agency wrote that Congress "was concerned with situations in which, because the charity does not obtain all or an undivided portion of significant rights in the property, the amount of a charitable contribution deduction might not correspond to the value of the benefit ultimately received by the charity." The legislative solution, said the IRS, "was to guard against the possibility that such problems might arise by denying a deduction in situations involving partial interests, unless the contribution is cast in certain prescribed forms." The scope of this rule "thus extends beyond situations in which there is actual or probable manipulation of the non-charitable interest to the detriment of the charitable interest, or situations in which the donor has merely assigned the right to future income."

CHARITABLE FAMILY LIMITED PARTNERSHIPS

The IRS has expressed its concern about the growing use of a charitable giving technique involving what is known as *charitable family limited partnerships*. The agency wrote in 2000 that the charitable family limited partnership is a "planned giving scheme" that "may be this year's favorite charity scam." The IRS's view of this use of a charitable family limited partnership has not abated since that time.

With this approach, a donor having substantially appreciated assets, which often are not readily marketable (such as real estate or a proprietary interest in a closely held business), establishes a family limited partnership. The donor transfers the appreciated assets to the partnership in exchange for a general and limited partnership interest. The general partnership interest constitutes 1 or 2 percent of the total partnership interests. The partnership agreement usually provides for a term of 40 to 50 years.

The donor contributes a large percentage (often as much as 98 percent) of the partnership interest to a charity, in the form of a limited partnership interest. The donor usually retains the general partnership interest. The donor may also retain a modest limited partnership interest or transfer such an interest to his or her children. An independent appraisal of the value of the partnership interests is done to establish fair market value for purposes of the federal income tax charitable contribution deduction. The charity receives whatever assets are held by the partnership at the end of the partnership term, assuming that the partnership interest is not sold prior to the expiration of the term.

A donor in this situation claims an income tax charitable deduction based on the value of the gift of the partnership interest to the charity. The value likely has been discounted to take into account (1) the lack of the charity's control and management of partnership operations, and (2) lack of marketability of the limited partnership interest in the context of a closely held business.

The IRS, in evaluating these transactions, wrote that the "key point is control." Here control remains with the donor as the general partner. The charity, a limited partner, lacks any voice in the day-to-day management or operations of the partnership. (This is ironic, by the way, in that, when public charities first began functioning as general partners in limited partnerships, the IRS tried to insist that the charities *not* have any day-to-day involvement in the operation of the partnerships.)

If the partnership sells the appreciated property it holds, most of the gain escapes taxation because of the charity's tax-exempt status. Only the modest limited or general partnership interests held by the donor and the donor's family are subject to capital gain taxation. The donor generally receives a management fee as compensation for operating and managing the partnership.

The charity holds an interest that may produce current income (although the IRS has noted that many of these limited partnerships produce little or no income). The charity also holds an interest in an asset (an appreciating asset, one hopes) that will be sold or exchanged no later than the expiration of the partnership term, usually 40 to 50 years.

Often the partnership agreement gives the partnership the right to sell the property to the donor or the donor's family at a price specified in the agreement. The IRS has observed that, while this type of an option "may serve to benefit" the charity, the option is "often viewed by critics of this technique as working more for the benefit of" the donor or the donor's family. This technique, the IRS noted in an understatement, "raises a number of tax issues." One is that the "operation of the partnership may cross over into the area of clear tax abuse." Other problematic areas include the extent of the charitable deduction (if any).

In one instance, a court upheld the basic validity of this type of partnership, sustaining the claim for federal gift tax charitable contribution deductions (although not in the amounts sought by the donors). The court concluded that all that had been assigned were the economic rights with respect to the partnership, and thus that the assignment did not cause the assignees to be admitted as substitute limited partners. One of the dissenters in this case (indeed, the trial judge) faulted the majority's analysis of the transaction, writing (somewhat reflecting the IRS's view of these transactions) that, "[u]ndaunted by the facts, well-established legal precedent, and [the agency's] failure to present sufficient evidence to establish [its] determinations, the majority allow their olfaction to displace sound legal reasoning and adherence to the rule of law." Another dissenter was of the view that the public policy doctrine, or step transaction doctrine, would preclude the gift tax charitable deduction (see Chapters 1 and 2).

FOREIGN TAX CREDIT

Current tax regulations permit U.S. donors to allocate and apportion all of their deductible charitable contributions to U.S.-source income for purposes of calculating the foreign tax credit. These regulations changed the method of allocating and apportioning these deductions from ratable apportionment on the basis of gross income to apportionment on the basis of income from sources within the United States.

These regulations provide that the deduction for charitable contributions is definitely related and allocable to all of the donor's gross income and is apportioned between the statutory grouping (or among the statutory groupings) of gross income and residual grouping on the basis of the relative amounts of gross income from sources in the United States in each grouping. For example, where a deduction for charitable contributions is allocated and apportioned for purposes of the foreign tax credit limitation, the charitable deduction is allocated to all of the donor's gross income and apportioned solely to the residual grouping consisting of U.S.-source gross income.

This revision of the law was intended to ensure that multinational corporations are not discouraged from making charitable contributions, which are deductible for federal income tax purposes, simply because the allocation and apportionment rules would reduce the donor's foreign source income and, as a result, the donor's foreign tax credit limitation.

The regulations also provide that, where a charitable contribution is made by a member of an affiliated group, the deduction for the charitable contribution is related to and allocated to the income of all of the members of the affiliated group and not to any subset of the group.

SUMMARY

This chapter provided analyses of unique charitable gift situations. The topics explored were contributions of property from retirement accounts, contributions of property created by the donor, the rules applicable in the context of charity auctions, gifts of services, the treatment of unreimbursed expenses, situations where there was an element of pleasure, bargain sales, contributions by trusts, gifts of partial interests, the use of charitable family limited partnerships, and applicability of the foreign tax credit rules.

CHAPTER 8

Other Aspects
of Deductible Giving

The purpose of this chapter is to summarize other aspects of the federal tax law pertaining to deductible charitable giving. Specifically, this chapter will:

- Summarize the law concerning charities' use of agents
- Describe the law pertaining to gifts for the use of a charity
- Discuss the matter of conditional gifts
- Summarize the law concerning the earmarking of gifts for individuals
- Summarize the deduction reduction rules
- Summarize the twice basis deduction rules
- Address the impact of the alternative minimum tax
- Discuss the interrelationship with the business expense deduction
- Discuss the interrelationship with certain lobbying rules
- Summarize the law concerning gifts to noncharitable organizations
- Briefly note the law concerning reallocation of deductions
- Discuss rules concerning the funding of terrorism
- Note the statute of limitations law
- Summarize the concept of trust income
- Enumerate the various tax law penalties in the charitable giving setting

CONTRIBUTIONS BY MEANS OF AGENT

Deductible charitable contributions can be made *to* or *for the use of* the recipient organization (see Chapter 4 and the following section). In connection with the former approach, a charitable organization may receive charitable contributions by means of an agent. The IRS wrote that it is "well established" that a charity can use an agent for this purpose. In fact, however, there is little law on the point, although the matter has come to the fore in the context of charitable contributions of used vehicles (see Chapter 6).

Agency is a fiduciary relationship resulting from the manifestation of consent by one person (the *principal*) to another (the *agent*) that the agent shall act on behalf of the principal and be subject to the principal's control, and consent by the agent to function in that capacity. The IRS observed that an agent's general fiduciary duties to the principal include the "duty to account for profits arising out of the employment, the duty to not act as (or on account of) an adverse party without the principal's consent, the duty to not compete with the principal on his own account or for another in matters relating to the subject matter of the agency, and the duty to deal fairly with the principal in all transactions between them."

As an example, if an individual unconditionally delivers or mails a properly endorsed stock certificate to a charitable donee or the donee's agent, the gift is completed on the date of delivery; if the certificate is received in the ordinary course of the mail, the gift is completed on the date of mailing. In another illustration, a utility company was authorized by a charitable organization to act as its agent in receiving contributions from customers of the company. In appropriate circumstances, a charitable organization may use an agent to perform functions other than receipt of contributions. Although the contract terms setting forth the parties' rights and obligations are of major importance to the IRS, all of the facts and circumstances must be considered in determining the existence of a principal-agent relationship.

In connection with a property donation program reviewed by the IRS, a charitable organization desired to appoint a company as its agent for the purpose of assisting the charity in the solicitation, acceptance, processing, and sale of personal property (principally, vehicles) donated by the public. The IRS looked primarily to the terms of a proposed contract between the parties, which, the IRS observed, "clearly purports" to establish an agency relationship pursuant to state law. The agreement showed that the company would be acting on the charity's behalf and subject to its control in the general performance of the activities. The amount of discretion that the company was to exercise was said to not be in conflict with an agency relationship. The charity was, and was to remain, the equitable owner of the property until an authorized sale occurred. The vehicle titling process was found to be in accord with agency treatment; on the sale of an item of donated property, the proceeds were to become the property of the charity, net of the fee payable to the company. Until a sale occurred, the risk of accidental loss, damage, or destruction of the donated property was to be borne by the charity, subject to the company's obligation to pay the cost of insurance coverage. The company was to provide monthly accounting reports to, in a form and in detail satisfactory to, the charity. The company was to provide weekly advertising reports to the charity. The charity reserved the right to audit and inspect the company's property donation program financial statements at any time during normal business hours. The IRS held that if the actual course of dealing between the parties was in accord with their written agreement, there would be a valid agency relationship, so that contributions could be made to the charity by means of the company.

GIFTS FOR THE USE OF CHARITY

In addition to gifts *to* a charitable organization, the federal tax law concerning charitable giving frequently makes reference to gifts *for the use of* a charitable organization. The statutory definition of a *charitable contribution* for federal income tax law purposes states that it is a "contribution to or for the use of" qualified charitable organizations.

There is little law on the point. One court had occasion to peruse the legislative history of the law that added this phrase to the Internal Revenue Code (in 1921) and concluded that the words mean "roughly the equivalent of" the words "in trust for." In the previous year, the then Bureau of Internal Revenue had ruled that charitable deductions could not be taken for contributions to trusts, community chests, and other types of charitable foundations, on the ground that these organizations were not organized and operated for charitable purposes but merely served as a conduit for contributions to charitable organizations. These organizations were common law trusts; legal title to the contributions remained vested in a trustee that invested the funds prior to disbursement to various charitable organizations.

The legislative history of this phrase indicates that Congress intended by this law change to make contributions in trust for the benefit of charitable organizations eligible for deduction as charitable gifts. Over the intervening years, courts and the IRS have adhered to this interpretation of the words *for the use of*.

The matter was taken to the Supreme Court, in connection with an issue as to whether funds transferred by parents to their children while the children served as full-time, unpaid missionaries for a church were deductible as charitable contributions. Inasmuch as the gifts were not to the church, the argument advanced by the parents turned on whether the gifts were for the use of the church. The Supreme Court, in reaffirming that the words mean "in trust for," concluded that the payments were not deductible as charitable contributions.

The Court observed that while this interpretation of the phrase "does not require that the qualified [charitable] organization take actual possession of the contribution, it nevertheless reflects that the beneficiary must have significant legal rights with respect to the disposition of donated funds." The Court rejected the claim that a charitable deduction should be allowed merely because the charitable organization has a "reasonable opportunity to supervise the use of contributed funds." The Court observed that the IRS would "face virtually insurmountable administrative difficulties in verifying that any particular expenditure benefited a qualified donee," were a looser interpretation of the phrase utilized. This larger interpretation would, wrote the Court, "create an opportunity for tax evasion that others might be eager to exploit," although the Court was quick to note that "there is no suggestion whatsoever in this case that the transferred funds were used for an improper purpose."

Under these facts, the Supreme Court found that the funds were not transferred "in trust for" the church. The money was transferred to the children's personal bank accounts as to which they were the sole authorized signatories. No trust or "similar legal arrangement" was created. The children lacked any legal obligation to use the money in accordance with guidelines of the church, nor did the church have any legal entitlement to the money or a cause of action against missionaries who used their parents' money for purposes not approved by the church.

A charitable contribution deduction is not allowed for a gift of services (see Chapter 7). Unreimbursed expenses made incident to the rendition of services to charitable organizations can, however, be deductible. At the outset, the IRS's position was that expenses incurred for charitable purposes were gifts for the use of, and not to, charitable organizations. This position was reviewed in litigation and the government lost the cases. The IRS thereafter abandoned this position and ruled that unreimbursed expenses incurred by an individual in rendering gratuitous services to a charitable organization are gifts to the charity.

A contribution of an income interest in property, whether the contributed interest is transferred in trust or not, for which a charitable deduction is allowed must be construed as made for the use of, rather than to, a charitable organization. A contribution of a remainder interest in property, whether the contributed interest is transferred in trust or not, for which a charitable deduction is allowed must generally be considered as made to the charitable organization. If, however, a remainder interest is transferred in trust and, pursuant to the terms of the trust instrument, the interest contributed is, on termination of the predecessor estate, to be held in trust for the benefit of the organization, the contribution must be considered as made for the use of the organization.

CONDITIONAL GIFTS

A donor may make a contribution to a charitable organization but place one or more conditions on the gift. Depending on the type of condition, there may not be a charitable deduction for the transfer, at least not until the condition is satisfied. Conversely, a condition may not have any bearing on the deductibility of the charitable gift.

There are three types of conditions in this regard:

1. A condition (sometimes termed a *contingency*) that is material, so that the transfer is not considered complete until the condition is satisfied
2. A condition involving a possible occurrence, when the likelihood of the event occurring is so remote as to be negligible, in which case the condition is disregarded for purposes of deductibility
3. A condition that is material but that is in furtherance of a charitable purpose, so that the condition, which is more in the nature of a *restriction*, does not adversely affect the deduction

Material Conditions—Nondeductibility

As to the first two of the just-cited categories, the standard is this: If, as of the date of a gift, a transfer for charitable purposes depends on the performance of some act or the happening of a precedent event in order that it might become effective, no deduction is allowable unless the possibility that the charitable transfer will not become effective is so remote as to be negligible. If the possibility is not negligible, if it occurs, and if the charitable transfer becomes effective, the charitable deduction (if any) arises at the time the condition is satisfied or eliminated.

As an illustration, a charitable organization wishes to construct a building to be used for its program purposes. It has developed a building fund that is sufficient to cover 90 percent of the construction costs of the building; the organization will seek the remaining funds from the public. The organization represents to donors that, if the contributions are not sufficient to meet the balance of the costs of construction, the contributions will be returned to the donors. If the contributions received exceed the necessary amount, the organization will retain the excess funds for general program purposes. Thus, as of the date of the gifts, the transfers for charitable purposes depend on the performance of an act or the happening of a precedent event to become effective. Furthermore, whether the contributions will be returned depends solely on whether the donors contribute an amount equal to the difference between the cost of constructing the building and the amount already in the building fund. Under these circumstances, the possibility that the charitable transfer will not become effective is not so remote as to be negligible. Consequently, the gifts are not deductible as of the time of the transfer, but will become deductible at the time the condition is satisfied or eliminated (i.e., when the public gifts are transferred to the building fund, because the needed amount was raised, or are retained by the organization to be expended for general program purposes).

As another example, a person contributed a patent to a tax-exempt university, subject to the condition that a named faculty member of the institution (who was an expert on the technology covered by the patent) continue to be a member of the faculty of the university during the remaining life of the patent. Under the terms of this gift, if the individual ceased to be a faculty member of the university before the patent expired, the patent would revert to the donor. The patent was to expire 15 years after the date of the contribution. On the date of the contribution, the likelihood that the specified individual would cease to be a member of the faculty of this university before the patent expired was not so remote as to be negligible. The IRS ruled that a charitable contribution deduction was not allowable for this gift.

In some instances, a condition may affect only a portion of the gift. For example, the department of parks and tourism of a state obtained sponsors who agreed to pay any deficit that the department might incur in conducting an international steeplechase race to promote tourism. The department represented to the sponsors that any funds not used to meet the deficit would be returned to the sponsors on a pro rata basis. Thus, only the pro rata portion of any sponsorship advance that the department used for racing expenses was a payment to the state for exclusively public purposes. Therefore, only the portion of each advance actually used to meet the deficit was held deductible by the sponsor as a charitable contribution. No portion of the advance was considered to be a payment of a contribution until the time the net amount actually going to the state was definitely determined by a final accounting.

A condition or battery of conditions may be so extensive that the matter goes to the question of the donor's intent. In one instance, a gift of land was burdened with so many conditions, including sale of the land, that a court found that the "donor," at best, had an intent to make a gift of future sales proceeds rather than an intent to make a present gift of the land.

Negligible Conditions

As noted, a condition that is *so remote as to be negligible* is ignored for gift deductibility purposes. This phrase was defined by a court as a "chance which persons generally would disregard as so highly improbable that it might be ignored with reasonable safety in undertaking a serious business transaction." It was also defined by another court as a "chance which every dictate of reason would justify an intelligent person in disregarding as so highly improbable and remote as to be lacking in reason and substance."

In one case, a court found conditions that were not so remote as to be negligible. One condition was found to have a "good chance" of occurring. Another condition was characterized as "certainly foreseeable" and "quite likely." Still another condition was labeled as having a "high probability," "probable," and "quite possible." Thus, a charitable gift was not deductible at the time originally made. In another case, a charitable deduction was not allowable because there was a "realistic possibility" that the condition involved would occur. The IRS examined the terms and conditions of a trust established to advance charitable ends and concluded that the possibility that trust assets would be used for noncharitable purposes was not so remote as to be considered negligible. Thus, it disallowed the claimed charitable contribution deductions.

Further, if an interest has passed to, or is vested in, a charitable organization on the date of a gift, and if the interest would be defeated by the performance of some act or the happening of some event, the possibility of occurrence of which appeared on that date to be so remote as to be negligible, the charitable contribution deduction would be available.

If it is determined that a condition is a negligible one, the amount of the gift for deduction purposes still may have to be discounted by the present value of the condition.

Material Conditions—Deductibility

There is one type of material condition that will not defeat a charitable deduction and, indeed, must be satisfied if the deduction is to be allowed. This is a condition that the gift be used for one or more program purposes; as noted, this is frequently known as a *restricted* gift. Some examples of restricted gifts include a gift to a:

- Charitable organization restricted to use for scholarships
- University restricted to a fund underlying a chair in a particular department
- Museum restricted to the museum's endowment fund
- Hospital restricted to the hospital's building fund

These types of conditions or restrictions will not cause a charitable contribution deduction to be disallowed.

EARMARKING OF GIFTS FOR INDIVIDUALS

A charitable contribution deduction is not allowed if the charitable organization involved is used merely as a conduit, so that a payment to the charity is *earmarked* or similarly designated for the benefit of one or more specified individuals, even if these recipients are members of the charitable class the charity is intended to benefit. This aspect of the law comprises other, related elements, such as the concept of a gift, gifts for the use of a charity, and conditional gifts.

For example, an individual claimed charitable contribution deductions for payments made to a tax-exempt college. He had previously indicated to a prospective student at the college that he would like to aid the student financially; he wrote that he would try to arrange for a scholarship for this student. In a letter to the director of admissions of the college, accompanying the gifts, this individual wrote: "I am aware that a donation to a [s]cholarship [f]und is only deductible if it is unspecified, however, if in your opinion and that of the authorities, it could be applied to the advantage of [the particular student], I think it would be constructive." A court found that these gifts were earmarked for the student; the ostensible donor was not aided by the fact that the college never awarded the student a scholarship but simply applied the payments to his account at the college.

Likewise, an individual made payments for the maintenance and education of a child who was a ward of a tax-exempt children's home. Rejecting the claim of a charitable deduction for the payments, a court, while conceding that the payments relieved the home of the financial obligation of furnishing the child with its services, wrote that the deduction could not be sustained because the payments were for a designated individual and "for no other individuals or for no other purpose" of the home. The court wrote that "[c]harity begins where certainty in beneficiaries ends, for it is the uncertainty of the objects and not the mode of relieving them which forms the essential elements of charity."

The IRS has ruled in this context. In one instance, an individual contributed money to a tax-exempt university, with the requirement that the funds be used to further the research project of a particular professor. Inasmuch as the university lacked discretion over the use of the funds, the IRS concluded that it was only a conduit, so that the true donee was the professor. The IRS ruled that the gift was not deductible. Similarly, an individual made a contribution to a missionary fund that was intended to reimburse missionaries for approved expenses not covered by amounts received from the missionaries' parents, friends, relatives, or personal savings; the donor's son was one of the missionaries. The IRS ruled that contributions to the missionary fund that were earmarked for a particular individual would be treated as gifts to that individual and were not deductible.

The pivotal test in this setting is whether the charitable organization receiving the contribution has full control of the donated funds and discretion as to their use, so as to ensure that the funds will be used to carry out the charity's functions and purposes. Contributions are deductible unless they are distinctly earmarked by the donor so that they may be used only for the benefit of a designated individual or are received by the charity pursuant to a commitment or understanding that they will be so used.

For example, a corporation established a scholarship program, selecting the universities from which it drew a substantial number of its employees. The universities selected the recipients of the scholarship, although there was no employment commitment between the corporation and the scholarship recipients. The IRS observed that, for purposes of determining that a contribution is made to or for the use of a charitable organization rather than to a particular individual who ultimately benefits from the contribution, the organization must have full control of the use of the donated funds, and the contributor's intent in making the payment must be to benefit the organization, not the individual recipient.

In another instance, students at a religious educational institution had their tuition paid by "sponsors," which in many cases were the students' parents. The sponsors signed a commitment form that set the contribution amount and the payment schedule, and indicated the names of the sponsor and the student; space was provided on the payment envelopes for the student's name. The form provided that use of the contributions was "solely at the discretion of" the organization. The IRS denied charitable contribution deductions because deductibility requires both full control of the gift funds by the charitable organization and an intent by the donor to benefit the charity and not a particular recipient. The agency concluded that the commitment form and envelopes indicated that the payments were designated for the benefit of particular students. The control the school had over the use of the funds was considered to be no different from the control any school has over tuition payments.

Another court opinion nicely illustrates the subtleties that can arise in making distinctions in this area. The charity involved was a tax-exempt charitable and religious mission. Donors sent many checks to the mission, on many of which were entered the names of particular missionaries; the receipts from the mission reflected "support" for missionaries identified by name. Sometimes the checks were accompanied by letters that identified missionaries by name, indicating that the contribution was for their support. The mission sent the donors a pamphlet stating that contributions were allocated equally for the missionaries, in terms of personal allowances and service support. The donors' contributions were placed in a common pool used for missionary support and were disbursed in accordance with the policy of the mission as described in the pamphlet.

A court concluded that this mission had exclusive control, pursuant to its policy, over the administration and distribution of the funds contributed. The donors' designation of the missionaries to be supported by their contributions was portrayed by the court as "no more than a manifestation of [the donors'] desire to have their donations credited to the support allowance of those individuals." The court found that the donors "knew and intended that their funds would go into a common pool to be distributed only as the [m]ission itself determined."

The court thus rejected the IRS's assertion that these contributions were not deductible because they were made for the support of certain designated individuals. That position was dismissed: "It seems to us that [the IRS] has chosen the wrong case to be puristic in [its] effort to collect the sovereign's revenue." Indeed, the court concluded that the IRS was "hoist with [its] own petard," in that a revenue ruling issued by the agency had reached a conclusion similar to the court's.

The IRS considered a situation concerning a tax-exempt charitable and educational organization that provided support for the composition and performance of musical works. A married couple expressed interest in supporting a particular composer's work; six months later, the couple made a contribution to the charity. At the time of the gift, the charity did not make any commitment to use the funds to commission a work by the composer. Five months later, however, the charity, the composer, and an orchestra entered into an agreement by which the charity paid the composer a fee to commission a work and to reimburse his expenses for appearing at the premiere of the work; the amount of the donors' gift was "sufficient" to enable the charity to pay these costs. The IRS ruled that the gift was not impermissibly earmarked for the benefit of the composer and thus was deductible.

DEDUCTION REDUCTION RULES

A donor (individual or corporation) who makes a gift of *ordinary income property* to a charitable organization (public or private) must confine the charitable deduction to an amount equal to the donor's cost basis in the property. The deduction is not based on the fair market value of the property; it must be reduced by the amount that would have been gain (ordinary income) if the property had been sold. As an example, if a donor gave to a charity an item of ordinary income property having a value of $1,000, for which he or she paid $600, the resulting charitable deduction would be $600.

Any donor who makes a gift of *capital gain property* to a public charity generally can compute the charitable deduction using the property's fair market value at the time of the gift, regardless of the basis amount and with no taxation of the appreciation (the capital gain inherent in the property). Suppose, however, a donor makes a gift of capital gain tangible personal property (such as a work of art) to a public charity, and the use of the gift property by the donee is unrelated to its tax-exempt purposes (see Chapter 7). The donor must reduce the deduction by an amount equal to all of the long-term capital gain that would have been recognized had the donor sold the property at its fair market value as of the date of the contribution.

Generally, a donor who makes a gift of capital gain property to a private foundation must reduce the amount of the otherwise allowable deduction by all of the appreciation element (built-in capital gain) in the gift property. An individual, however, is allowed full fair market value for a contribution to a private foundation of certain publicly traded stock (known as *qualified appreciated stock*).

TWICE-BASIS DEDUCTIONS

As a general rule, when a corporation makes a charitable gift of property from its inventory, the resulting charitable deduction cannot exceed an amount equal to the donor's cost basis in the donated property. In most instances this basis amount is rather small, being equal to the cost of producing the property. Under certain circumstances, however, corporate donors can receive a greater charitable deduction for gifts out of their inventory. Where the tests are satisfied, the deduction can be equal to cost basis plus one-half of the appreciated value of the property. The charitable deduction may not, in any event, exceed an amount equal to twice the property's cost basis.

Five requirements have to be met for this twice-basis charitable deduction to be available:

1. The donated property must be used by the charitable donee for a related use.
2. The donated property must be used solely for the care of the ill, the needy, or infants.
3. The property may not be transferred by the donee in exchange for money, other property, or services.
4. The donor must receive a written statement from the donee representing that the use and disposition of the donated property will be in conformance with these rules.
5. Where the donated property is subject to regulation under the Federal Food, Drug, and Cosmetic Act, the property must fully satisfy the act's requirements on the date of transfer and for the previous 180 days.

For these rules to apply, the donee must be a public charity; that is, it cannot be a private foundation or a private operating foundation (see Chapter 3). An S corporation—the tax status of many businesses—cannot utilize these rules.

Similarly computed charitable deductions are available for contributions of scientific property used for research and contributions of computer technology and equipment for educational purposes.

ALTERNATIVE MINIMUM TAX CONSIDERATIONS

The federal tax law includes an alternative minimum tax. This tax is termed an *alternative* tax because it may be paid instead of the regular income tax. It is called a *minimum* tax because it is designed to force persons of wealth to pay some federal tax, notwithstanding the sophistication of their tax planning. (This tax is, today, rather controversial, because it is now being applied to taxpayers of more moderate means.)

Some persons are able to avoid taxation, in whole or in part, through the use of deductions, credits, exemptions, and the like. These items are generally known as *items of tax preference* or *tax preference items*. A general summary of the alternative minimum tax is that it is a tax, computed with some adjustments, on many of a person's tax preference items.

The charitable community and the alternative minimum tax have a precarious coexistence. This is because, as a general rule, the donor of an item of appreciated property contributed to a public charity escapes taxation on the capital gain inherent in the property (see Chapter 2). This feature of the federal income tax law is a major incentive for charitable giving. There are those, however, who assert that—if only as a matter of pure tax policy—this capital gain should be subject to some taxation. One option in this regard is to subject this gain to the alternative minimum tax. Congress experimented with this approach. Thus, for a period of about six years, the appreciation element inherent in a charitable contribution of appreciated property was considered an item of tax preference for purposes of the alternative minimum tax.

In 1986 a rule was adopted that, for purposes of computing alternative minimum taxable income, the deduction for charitable contributions of capital gain property (real, tangible personal, or intangible personal) is disallowed to the extent that the fair market value of the property exceeds its adjusted basis. This rule was a compromise in the face of an effort to subject this type of appreciation element to the regular capital gains tax. The charitable community that is highly dependent on contributions of appreciated property (such as institutions of higher education and museums) thereafter experienced a substantial decline in giving of property and began to work to change, if not eliminate, the rule.

This effort was successful. First Congress created a partial and temporary exception in 1990. Then Congress attempted to permanently repeal the application of the alternative minimum tax to charitable giving in 1992, although this undertaking failed. Nonetheless, the legislative history of this potential law change offered this explanation: "The [Senate Finance] [C]ommittee believes that the temporary AMT [alternative minimum tax] exception for contributions of appreciated tangible personal property has induced additional charitable giving. Thus, by permanently extending this rule and expanding it to apply to all appreciated property gifts, taxpayers will be allowed the same charitable contribution deduction for both regular tax and alternative minimum tax purposes. This will provide an additional incentive for taxpayers to make contributions of appreciated property."

Success in this regard arrived in 1993, which brought permanent repeal of this alternative minimum tax rule in relation to gifts of all categories of property. Thus, an inducement for charitable giving, in the form of the appreciated property contribution rules, is today embedded in the Internal Revenue Code. From time to time, nonetheless, proposals surface to treat the charitable deduction for gifts of appreciated property as an item of tax preference.

BUSINESS EXPENSE DEDUCTION

A charitable contribution deduction is not allowed for a gift of property for which the donor has claimed a business expense deduction. For example, a retired athlete cannot claim a charitable contribution deduction for donating gifts of clothing and supplies used during his or her career to a museum, if he or she previously claimed a business expense deduction with respect to the items. This limitation also applies to the deduction for depreciation.

An individual or a corporation is not permitted a deduction for a contribution as a business expense if any part of it is deductible as a charitable contribution. For example, if an individual made a contribution of $5,000 and only $4,000 was deductible as a charitable contribution (whether because of the percentage limitations [see Chapter 4], the requirements as to timing of the payment [see Chapter 3], or both), there cannot be a business expense deduction for the remaining $1,000. For this rule to apply, the payment must in fact be a charitable contribution. Thus, in the language of the tax regulations, contributions to organizations other than charitable ones "which bear a direct relationship to the taxpayer's business and are made with a reasonable expectation of a financial return commensurate with the amount of the donation may constitute allowable deductions as business expenses."

LOBBYING ACTIVITIES

The business expense deduction is denied for amounts incurred in an attempt to influence federal or state (but not local) legislation through communication with members or employees of legislative bodies or other government officials who may participate in the formulation of legislation. A flow-through rule disallows a business expense deduction for a portion of the membership dues paid to a trade, business, or professional association or other noncharitable organization that engages in lobbying (unless the organization elects to pay a so-called *proxy tax* on its lobbying expenditures).

An anti-avoidance rule has been designed to prevent persons from using charitable organizations as a conduit for the conduct of lobbying activities, the costs of which would not be deductible if conducted directly by the donor. That is, a deduction is not allowed—either as a charitable contribution deduction or as a business expense deduction—for amounts contributed to a charitable organization that conducts lobbying activities, if (1) the charity's lobbying activities concern matters of direct financial interest to the donor's business, and (2) a principal purpose of the contribution is to avoid the general disallowance rule that would apply if the contributor directly had conducted the lobbying activities.

The application of this anti-avoidance rule to a contributor does not adversely affect the tax-exempt status of the charitable organization as long as the activity qualifies as nonpartisan analysis, study, or research or was not substantial. The determination regarding a principal purpose of the contribution is based on the facts and circumstances surrounding the gift, including the existence of any formal or informal instructions relating to the charitable organization's use of the contribution for lobbying efforts (including nonpartisan analysis), the temporal nexus between the making of the contribution and the conduct of the lobbying activities, and any historical pattern of contributions by the donor to the charity.

CORPORATE SPONSORSHIPS

A for-profit corporation can provide substantial financial support to a tax-exempt (almost always charitable) entity, as sponsorship of a program, event, or other function of the entity—or of the organization in its entirety. The business corporation receives considerable favorable publicity in exchange for its largesse. The law struggles to differentiate between treatment of the payment as a gift, with the publicity merely an acknowledgment of the contribution, and treatment of it as a payment for advertising services, in which case it would likely be unrelated business income. Unique statutory rules address the tax law aspects of *corporate sponsorships*.

In general, the receipt of a qualified sponsorship payment by a tax-exempt organization is not the receipt of income that is considered unrelated business income. These rules hinge, in considerable part, on two concepts: the qualified sponsorship payment and the substantial return benefit.

A *qualified sponsorship payment* is any payment of money, transfer of property, or performance of services, by a person engaged in a trade or business to an exempt organization, with respect to which there is no arrangement or expectation that the person will receive any substantial return benefit. For this purpose, it is irrelevant whether the sponsored activity is related or unrelated to the recipient organization's exempt purposes. It is also irrelevant whether the sponsored activity or other function is temporary or permanent.

A *substantial return benefit* is any benefit, other than goods, services, or other benefits of substantial value that are disregarded, or certain uses and acknowledgments. A substantial return benefit includes advertising; the provision of facilities, services, or other privileges to the payor or persons designated by the payor (collectively, the payor) (with exceptions, discussed in the next section); and granting the payor an exclusive or nonexclusive right to use an intangible asset (such as a trademark, patent, logo, or designation) of the exempt organization.

A substantial return benefit does not include the use or acknowledgment of the name or logo (or product lines) of the payor's trade or business in connection with the activities of the exempt organization. Use or acknowledgment does not include advertising but may include logos and slogans that do not contain qualitative or comparative descriptions of the payor's products, services, or facilities; a list of the payor's locations, telephone numbers, or Internet address; value-neutral descriptions, including displays or visual depictions, of the payor's product line or services; and the payor's brand or trade names and product or service listings.

Logos or slogans that are an established part of a payor's identity are not considered to contain qualitative or comparative descriptions. Mere display or distribution, whether without charge or for remuneration, of a payor's product by a payor or the exempt organization to the general public at the sponsored activity is not considered an inducement to purchase, sell, or use the payor's product and thus will not affect the determination of whether a payment is a qualified sponsorship payment.

An arrangement that acknowledges the payor as the exclusive sponsor of an exempt organization's activity, or the exclusive sponsor representing a particular trade, business, or industry, generally does not, alone, result in a substantial return benefit. For example, if in exchange for a payment, an organization announces that its event is sponsored exclusively by the payor (and does not provide any advertising or other substantial return benefit to the payor), the payor has not received a substantial return benefit.

By contrast, an arrangement that limits the sale, distribution, availability, or use of competing products, services, or facilities in connection with an exempt organization's activity generally results in a substantial return benefit. For example, if in exchange for a payment, an exempt organization agrees to allow only the payor's products to be sold in connection with an activity, the payor has received a substantial return benefit. Thus, the tax law distinguishes between an exclusive sponsor and an exclusive provider.

For these purposes, the term *advertising* means a message or other programming material that is broadcast or otherwise transmitted, published, displayed, or distributed, and that promotes or markets any trade or business, or any service, facility, or product. Advertising includes messages containing qualitative or comparative language, price information or other indications of savings or value, an endorsement, or an inducement to purchase, sell, or use any company, service, facility, or product. A single message that contains both advertising and an acknowledgment is nonetheless considered advertising.

Goods, services, or other benefits are disregarded under two sets of circumstances. One situation is where the benefits provided to the payor have an aggregate fair market value that is not more than 2 percent of the amount of the payment or $75 (adjusted for inflation), whichever is less.

The other situation where benefits are disregarded is where the only benefits provided to the payor are token items (such as bookmarks, calendars, key chains, mugs, posters, or T-shirts) bearing the exempt organization's name or logo that have an aggregate cost within the limit established for low-cost articles. Token items provided to employees of a payor, or to partners of a partnership that is the payor, are disregarded if the combined total cost of the token items provided to each employee or partner does not exceed the low-cost article limit.

If the fair market value of the benefits (or, in the case of token items, the cost) exceeds the amount just specified or the limit, then (unless they constitute a use or acknowledgment) the entire fair market value of the benefits, not merely the excess amount, is a substantial return benefit.

If there is an arrangement or expectation that the payor will receive a substantial return benefit with respect to a payment, then only the portion of the payment (if any) that exceeds the fair market value of the substantial return benefit is a qualified sponsorship payment. The fair market value is determined on the date on which the sponsorship arrangement was created. If, however, the exempt organization does not establish that the payment exceeds the fair market value of any substantial return benefit, then no portion of the payment constitutes a qualified sponsorship payment.

The unrelated business income tax treatment of any payment (or portion of one) that is not a qualified sponsorship payment is determined by application of the general unrelated business rules. For example, payments related to the exempt organization's provision of facilities, services, or other privileges to the payor, advertising, exclusive provider arrangements, a license to use intangible assets of the exempt organization, or other substantial return benefits are evaluated separately in determining whether the exempt organization realizes unrelated business income.

To the extent necessary to prevent avoidance of this allocation rule, where the exempt organization fails to make a reasonable and good faith valuation of any substantial return benefit, the IRS is empowered to determine the portion of a payment allocable to the substantial return benefit. The agency can treat two or more related payments as a single payment.

Qualified sponsorship payments in the form of money or property (but not services) are treated as contributions received by the exempt organization for purposes of determining public support. This is the case irrespective of whether the donative organization or the service provider organization rules are applicable (see Chapter 1).

The fact that a payment is a qualified sponsorship payment that is treated as a contribution to the payee organization is not determinative of whether the payment is a business expense or a charitable contribution from the standpoint of the payor.

The existence of a written corporate sponsorship agreement does not, in itself, cause a payment to fail to be a qualified sponsorship payment. The terms of the agreement—not the fact of its existence or degree of detail—are relevant to the determination of whether a payment is a qualified sponsorship payment. Likewise, the terms of the agreement and not the title or responsibilities of the individuals negotiating the agreement determine whether a payment (or a portion of one) made pursuant to the agreement is a qualified sponsorship payment.

The term *qualified sponsorship payment* does not include any payment where the amount is contingent, by contract or otherwise, on the level of attendance at one or more events, broadcast ratings, or other factors indicating the degree of public exposure to the sponsored activity. The fact that a payment is contingent on sponsored events or activities actually being conducted does not, alone, cause the payment to fail to be a qualified sponsorship payment.

These rules do not apply with respect to payments made in connection with qualified convention and trade show activities. These rules also do not apply to income derived from the sale of advertising or acknowledgments in exempt organization periodicals. For this purpose, the term *periodical* means regularly scheduled and printed material published by, or on behalf of, the exempt organization. A periodical is not related to, or primarily distributed in connection with, a specific event conducted by the exempt organization.

GIFTS TO NONCHARITABLE ORGANIZATIONS

It is possible for a contribution to be treated as a deductible charitable contribution when the gift is made to a noncharitable (including for-profit) organization. This occurs when the recipient of the gift is a pass-through entity and a charitable organization is the ultimate donee. In some instances the initial payee organization is regarded as the agent of the organization that is the ultimate recipient of the organization, and the payor is considered, for federal tax law purposes, to have made the payment directly to the ultimate transferee, notwithstanding the flow of the payment through one or more intermediate (or conduit) entities (see previous section).

For example, contributions to a tax-exempt social club were held to be deductible as charitable contributions, because the club functioned as an authorized agent for one or more charitable organizations, enabling the members of the club, when purchasing tickets for a social event, (1) to direct that the amount of their total payment in excess of the price of the tickets be transferred to charitable organizations and (2) to deduct, as charitable gifts, that portion of the payment to the club that was paid to the charitable organizations. This is a common practice among trade, business, and professional associations that encourage members to make gifts to related charitable organizations at the same time they pay their annual membership dues. The payments to both entities are made as a single transaction because the gift element of the payment is flowed through the association to the charitable recipient.

Charitable gift deductibility treatment was accorded to additional amounts paid by customers of a utility company, when paying their bills to the company, where the additional amounts were earmarked for a charitable organization that assisted individuals with emergency-related energy needs. Again, the utility company was considered the agent of the charitable organization; the company did not exercise any control over the funds and segregated them from its own funds. In a similar situation, contributions paid to a title-holding company for purposes of maintaining and operating a historic property were ruled by the IRS to be deductible as charitable gifts, when the gifts were segregated from the company's funds and were otherwise clearly devoted to charitable ends. In this instance, however, the ruling was subsequently withdrawn (for unknown reasons), although the effect of the withdrawal was not made retroactive.

While not in the charitable giving context, a comparable set of rules offers some guidelines for this type of pass-through giving. The law is that amounts paid to a tax-exempt organization (such as a membership association) for transfer to a political action committee do not, when promptly and directly transferred, constitute political campaign expenditures by the transferor organization. A transfer is considered *promptly and directly* made if (1) the procedures followed by the organization satisfy the requirements of applicable federal and state campaign laws; (2) the organization maintains adequate records to demonstrate that the amounts transferred do in fact consist of political contributions or dues, rather than investment income; and (3) the political contributions or dues transferred were not used to earn investment income for the transferor organization.

One of the issues reflected in the political action committee rules is the element of *promptness* of the transfer of the funds. Although this generally is a facts-and-circumstances test, in one instance the IRS imported the concept into the charitable field. The case involved facts similar to those in the utility company matter. Although the IRS wrote that the payments were "initially commingled" with the utility's funds, it added that they were "earmarked and transferred" to the charity's account on a "frequent and regular basis." In both of these instances, the transfers were made weekly.

Based on the foregoing law (such as it is), it may be concluded that a payment made to a noncharitable entity can be deductible as a charitable gift under five sets of circumstances:

1. The amount that is the charitable gift is clearly so designated by the donor.
2. The intermediate organization is clearly functioning as the agent of the charity.
3. The gift component of the payment is promptly transferred to the charity.
4. The intermediate entity does not earn any investment income on the amounts destined for charity.
5. The intermediate organization directly transfers the appropriate funds to the charitable organization.

These factors, in summary, make it clear that the intermediate entity is functioning as a conduit on behalf of the charitable organization.

REALLOCATION OF DEDUCTIONS

The IRS has broad statutory authority to undo a person's "creative" tax planning by readjusting the facts to more correctly state the person's tax position. This authority empowers the IRS to closely scrutinize transactions between mutually controlled parties. This process is known as *reallocation* of items of income, deductions, and credits; it is done when necessary to prevent the evasion of taxes or to ensure the clear reflection of each person's income. The IRS can use this authority to reallocate, in the charitable giving context, to adjust (reduce) a claimed charitable contribution deduction.

In one instance, two partners, who were an individual and a corporation wholly owned by him, caused their partnership to distribute to them a parcel of land in the form of two tracts of approximately equal value but not equal size. The individual, who held a 49 percent interest in the partnership, received a 76 percent interest in one tract and a 24 percent interest in the other. The land was donated to a city; the individual claimed a charitable contribution deduction based on a 76 percent interest in the real estate. (He also reported 24 percent of the gain from the sale of the other tract.) The IRS reallocated the amount of the charitable con-

tribution deduction (and the capital gain) between the two partners on the basis of their respective percentage interests in the partnership. The IRS was successful in court in forcing this donor to
confine his deduction to an amount equal to the 49 percent interest in the land.

FUNDING OF TERRORISM

National security concerns, certainly those arising in the aftermath
of the terrorist attacks on September 11, 2001, can add federal governmental regulatory constraints and prohibitions on charitable organizations that attract contributions for use in countries other
than the United States. While the law in this area is emerging, a key
element of it is an executive order signed by the president a few
days after the attacks. Actions by the Office of Foreign Assets
Control (OFAC), which is within the Department of the Treasury,
entail a variety of sanctions, including denial of the deductibility of
contributions to an organization. The broad authority of OFAC is
being upheld by the courts.

These developments also have led the Treasury Department
to issue "voluntary" guidelines for charitable organizations to follow so as to avoid ties to terrorist organizations. These sweeping
guidelines have attracted considerable attention and criticism, in
part because they embody precepts that are not required by the
federal tax law or state corporate law.

Moreover, the tax-exempt status of an organization that has
been designated, pursuant to federal law, as supporting or engaging in terrorist activity or supporting terrorism is suspended.
Contributions made to an organization during the period of sus-
pension of exemption are not deductible for federal tax purposes.

STATUTE OF LIMITATIONS

The general rule is that the statute of limitations establishes a three-
year period within which the IRS can assess or collect any deficiencies or additions to tax as determined by it. In the case of a
fraudulent return, however, the period of limitations is extended
indefinitely. On many occasions, the IRS has been allowed to assess
and collect tax deficiencies and additions to tax after expiration of

the general three-year period, because of fraud committed by abuse of the charitable contribution deduction.

CONCEPT OF TRUST INCOME

Basic Principles

The definition of what constitutes *income* of a trust reverberates throughout the tax law of charitable giving as well as the federal tax law generally. This definition affects ordinary trusts, estates, charitable remainder trusts, pooled income funds, trusts that qualify for the gift and estate tax marital deduction, and trusts that are subject to the generation-skipping transfer rules. This aspect of the law is of concern to grantors, beneficiaries, and fiduciaries.

The statutory law generally provides that, for these purposes, the term *income* means the amount of income of the estate or trust for the year determined under the terms of the governing instrument and applicable local law. This concept of income is used as the measure of the amount that must be distributed from a trust in order for the trust to qualify for certain federal tax treatments. Trusts that are classified as simple trusts, net income charitable remainder unitrusts, pooled income funds, and qualified subchapter S trusts are required to make distributions measured, at least in part, by the amount of trust accounting income. A similar concept applies to trusts that qualify for the gift and estate tax marital deductions.

A trust instrument may provide for any amount to be distributed to beneficiaries currently. Trust provisions that measure the amount of the distribution by reference to income but define the term *income* differently from the state statutory definition of the term generally are recognized for state law purposes. Various provisions of the Internal Revenue Code that require the current distribution of income to qualify the trust for certain federal tax treatment, however, are based on the assumption that the income beneficiary will receive what is traditionally considered to be income. In some situations, such as with qualified subchapter S trusts and marital deduction trusts for spouses who are U.S. citizens, the income beneficiary is also permitted to receive distributions of principal as long as all of the income is currently distributed. In other instances, such as with net income charitable remainder unitrusts and pooled income funds, only the income may be distributed.

In all of these situations, the determination as to what is income is critical. Thus, a core concept in this concept is this: The definition of *income* under the terms of the governing instrument and applicable local law must not depart fundamentally from traditional concepts of income and principal, if the desired federal tax treatment is to be secured.

In recent years, state law has been changing dramatically on this point. These statutes are in the process of altering traditional concepts of income and principal in response to investment strategies that seek total positive return on trust assets. These statutes are designed to ensure that when a trust invests in assets that may generate little income in the traditional sense (such as dividends, interest, and rent), the income and remainder beneficiaries are allocated reasonable amounts of the total return of the trust (including traditional income and capital appreciation of trust assets), so that both classes of beneficiaries are treated impartially.

Some state statutes permit the trustee to pay an income beneficiary a unitrust amount—a fixed percentage of the fair market value of the trust assets. Other statutes accord the trustee the discretion to make adjustments between income and principal so as to treat the beneficiaries fairly and objectively.

The Department of the Treasury and the IRS are of the view that an allocation to principal of traditional income items should be respected for federal tax law purposes only if applicable state law has specifically authorized the allocation, in circumstances such as when necessary to ensure impartiality regarding a trust investing for total return. A state statute authorizing certain unitrust payments in satisfaction of an income interest or certain powers to adjust satisfy that requirement, as does a decision by a state's highest court announcing a general principle or rule of law that would apply to all trusts administered under the laws of that state.

Definition of *Income*

For federal tax law purposes, the term *income,* other than when modified, means the amount of income of an estate or trust for the year determined under the terms of the governing instrument and applicable local law. Trust provisions that depart fundamentally from traditional principles of income and principal generally will not be recognized. Thus, items such as dividends, interest, and rent generally are allocated to income, and proceeds from the sale or exchange of trust assets generally are allocated to principal.

Nonetheless, an allocation of amounts between income and principal pursuant to local law will be respected if that law provides for a reasonable apportionment between the income and remainder beneficiaries of the total return of the trust for the year, including ordinary and tax-exempt income, capital gains, and appreciation. For example, a state statute providing that income is a unitrust amount (see Chapters 7 and 9) of no less than 3 percent and no more than 5 percent of the fair market value of the trust assets, determined annually or averaged on a multiple-year basis, is a reasonable apportionment of the total return of the trust.

Generally, these adjustments are permitted by state statutes when (1) the trustee invests and manages the trust assets under the state's prudent investor standard; (2) the trust document describes the amount that may or must be distributed to a beneficiary by reference to the trust's income; and (3) the trustee, after applying the state law rules regarding the allocation of receipts and disbursements, is unable to administer the trust impartially. Allocations pursuant to methods prescribed by these state statutes for apportioning the total return of a trust between income and principal will be respected regardless of whether the trust provides that the income must be distributed to one or more beneficiaries or may be accumulated in whole or in part, and regardless of which alternate permitted method is actually used, as long as the trust complies with all requirements of the state statute for switching methods.

A switch between methods of determining trust income authorized by state statute will not constitute a recognition of tax liability and will not result in a taxable gift from the trust's grantor or any of the trust's beneficiaries. A switch to a method not specifically authorized by state statute, but valid under state law, may constitute a recognition event to the trust or its beneficiaries and may result in taxable gifts from the trust's grantor and beneficiaries, based on the relevant facts and circumstances.

An allocation to income of all or a part of the gains from the sale or exchange of trust assets generally will be respected if the allocation is made either pursuant to the terms of the governing instrument and local law, or pursuant to a reasonable and impartial exercise of a discretionary power granted to the fiduciary by local law or by the governing instrument, if not prohibited by local law.

Capital Gains and Losses

Gains from the sale or exchange of capital assets generally are excluded from distributable net income to the extent that the gains are allocated to corpus. Capital gains allocated to corpus are, however, include in distributable net income if they are paid, credited, or required to be distributed to a beneficiary during the year, or paid, permanently set aside, or to be used for a charitable purpose.

Capital gains can be included in distributable net income if the terms of the governing instrument and local law permit it. That can also be the outcome pursuant to a reasonable and impartial exercise of discretion by the fiduciary, in accordance with a power granted to the fiduciary by applicable local law or by the governing instrument if not prohibited by local law.

PENALTIES

The federal tax law contains a variety of penalties that can be applied for a violation of various aspects of the law of charitable giving. These penalties are part of a broader range of *accuracy-related penalties.*

The accuracy-related penalty is determined as an amount to be added to the income tax equal to 20 percent of the portion of the underpayment of tax. This body of law relates to the portion of any underpayment that is attributable to one or more specified acts, including negligence, disregard of rules or regulations, any substantial understatement of income tax, any substantial income tax valuation misstatement, and/or any substantial estate or gift tax valuation understatement.

The term *negligence* includes any failure to make a reasonable attempt to comply with the applicable law. The term *disregard* includes "any careless, reckless, or intentional disregard."

A *substantial understatement* occurs when the amount of the understatement of tax for the year exceeds the greater of 10 percent of the tax that is required or $5,000. When the violation is by a regular corporation, the penalty is the greater of 10 percent of the required tax or $10,000. The term *understatement* means the excess of (1) the amount of tax required to be shown on the tax return for a year over (2) the amount of tax imposed, which is shown on the tax return, less certain rebates. These rules apply with respect to *tax shelters*; that term is defined to include any "plan or arrangement" (including a partnership) if the principal purpose of it is the "avoidance or evasion" of federal income tax.

An *income tax substantial valuation misstatement* generally occurs if the value of any property (or the adjusted basis of any property) claimed on a tax return is 200 percent or more of the amount determined to be the correct amount of the valuation (or adjusted basis). For this penalty to be imposed, the substantial misstatement must exceed $5,000 ($10,000 for most corporations).

This penalty may be increased in the event of a *gross valuation misstatement*, which is an amount equal to 40 percent of the portion of the underpayment. An income tax gross valuation misstatement generally occurs if the value of any property (or the adjusted basis of any property) claimed on a tax return is 400 percent or more of the amount determined to be the correct amount of the valuation (or adjusted basis).

There is *substantial estate or gift tax valuation understatement* if the value of any property claimed on a tax return is 50 percent or less of the amount determined to be the correct amount of the valuation. This penalty applies when the underpayment exceeds $5,000. A gross valuation misstatement in this context takes place if the value of any property claimed on a tax return is 25 percent or less of the amount determined to be the correct amount of the valuation.

There is a fraud penalty, which is an addition to tax of an amount equal to 75 percent of the portion of the underpayment that is attributable to fraud. If the IRS establishes that any portion of an underpayment is attributable to fraud, the entire underpayment is treated as attributable to fraud, except with respect to any portion of the underpayment that the person can prove, by a preponderance of the evidence, is not attributable to fraud.

These penalties often hinge on the existence of an *underpayment*. This term is defined as the amount by which the tax imposed exceeds the excess of the sum of:

- The amount shown as the tax by the person on his, her, or its tax return, plus
- Amounts not so shown, which were previously assessed (or collected without assessment), over
- The amount of rebates made.

A penalty cannot be imposed with respect to any portion of an underpayment, however, if it is shown that there was a reasonable cause for the portion and the person acted in good faith.

In this regard, there is a special rule for *charitable deduction property*, which is an item of property contributed by a person in a contribution for which an income tax charitable contribution deduction was claimed. This rule is: In the case of an underpayment of tax attributable to a substantial overstatement or a gross valuation overstatement with respect to charitable deduction property, the reasonable cause exception is not applicable unless (1) the claimed value of the property was based on a qualified appraisal made by a qualified appraiser (see Chapter 12) and (2) the contributor made a good faith investigation of the value of the contributed property.

Still other federal tax penalties may be applied in the context of charitable giving. Among them is the penalty for the promotion of a tax shelter. Specifically, a person is liable for a penalty if he or she:

- Organizes or assists in the organization of:
  - A partnership or other entity
  - Any investment plan or arrangement
  - Any other plan or arrangement

- Participates, directly or indirectly, in the sale of any interest in this type of an entity, plan, or arrangement, and
- Makes, furnishes, or causes another person to make or furnish (in connection with such an entity or sale):
  - A statement with respect to the allowability of any tax deduction or tax credit, the excludability of any income, or the securing of any other tax benefit by reason of holding an interest in the entity or participating in the plan or arrangement, which the person knows or has reason to know is false or fraudulent as to any material matter
  - A gross valuation overstatement as to any material matter

In this setting, a *gross valuation overstatement* is any statement as to the value of any property or services if (1) the value so stated exceeds 200 percent of the amount determined to be the correct valuation and (2) the value of the property or services is directly related to the amount of any tax deduction or tax credit allowable under the federal income tax law to any participant. The penalty is, with respect to each tax shelter promotion activity, the greater of $1,000 or 100 percent of the gross income derived (or to be derived) by the person from the activity. A tax shelter promotion activity, with respect to each entity or arrangement, is treated as a separate activity for this purpose, as is each participation in each sale. The IRS is empowered to waive all or any part of this penalty with respect to a gross valuation overstatement, on a showing that there was a reasonable basis for the valuation and that the valuation was made in good faith. This penalty may be imposed in addition to any other tax penalty.

There is a penalty for aiding and abetting an understatement of tax liability. This penalty may be imposed on any person who:

- Aids or assists in, procures, or advises with respect to the preparation or presentation of any portion of a return, affidavit, claim, or other document.
- Knows (or has reason to believe) that the portion of a document will be used in connection with any material matter arising under the federal tax laws.
- Knows that the portion of a document (if so used) would result in an understatement of the liability for tax of another person. This penalty may be separately levied with respect to each document.

For this purpose, the term *procures* includes (1) ordering (or otherwise causing) a subordinate to do an act and (2) knowing of, and not attempting to prevent, participation by a subordinate in an act. In general, the amount of this penalty is $1,000; if a document relates to the tax liability of a corporation, however, the amount of the penalty is $10,000. This penalty may be applied whether the understatement is with the knowledge or consent of the persons authorized or required to present the return, affidavit, claim, or other document or not.

Still other pertinent penalties are those imposed for a failure to: file a tax return, file a correct information return, furnish a correct payee statement, or comply with other information-reporting requirements.

It may appear unlikely or even far-fetched that a donor or someone serving on behalf of a charitable organization—or a charitable organization itself—could reasonably be subjected to one or more of these penalties. Such penalties have been applied by the courts, however. There have been several court opinions concerning the application of these penalties in the charitable giving setting. These include:

- Application of an underpayment penalty when a lawyer intentionally disregarded the tax regulations in claiming a charitable contribution deduction for gifts of legal services (see Chapter 7)

- Application of penalties when the claimed values were based on "financial fantasies"
- Application of a penalty when the gift property was valued at $45,600 and the court found the value to be $4,211
- Application of penalties when the value of the gift property was deliberately inflated and the transactions were tax-motivated
- Application of the negligence penalty when the parties participated in a circular flow-of-funds arrangement, including charitable gifts, designed for tax avoidance
- Application of the penalty for substantial underpayment of federal income tax when a charitable gift of gravesites was made as part of a tax avoidance promotion program
- Application of the valuation overstatement penalty in a case involving a charitable contribution of wild game trophy mounts

A penalty may be imposed in a person who (1) aids or assists in, procures, or advises with respect to the preparation or presentation of any portion of a return, affidavit, claim, or other document; (2) knows (or has reason to believe) that the portion will be used in connection with any material matter arising under the federal tax laws; and (3) knows that the portion (if so used) would result in an understatement of the tax liability of another person. The penalty applies with respect to each document. The amount of the penalty for persons other than corporations is $1,000; for corporations, the amount of the penalty is $5,000. This penalty is applicable, for example, in an instance of violation of the charitable contribution substantiation rules (see Chapter 12).

There is a penalty for violation of the rules concerning disclosures to donors in the case of quid pro quo contributions. Penalties of $10 per contribution, capped at $5,000 per particular fundraising event or mailing, may be imposed on charitable organizations that fail to make the required disclosure, unless the failure was due to reasonable cause. The penalty applies if an organization either fails to make any disclosure in connection with a quid pro quo contribution or makes a disclosure that is incomplete or inaccurate (such as an estimate not determined in good faith of the value of goods or services furnished to the donor).

SUMMARY

This chapter provided information concerning aspects of deductible charitable giving not covered in other chapters. Subjects summarized were the laws pertaining to charities' use of agents, gifts for the use of a charity, conditional gifts, earmarking of gifts for individuals, the deduction reduction rules, the twice-basis deduction rules, the alternative minimum tax, the interrelationship with the business expense deduction, certain lobbying rules, gifts to noncharitable organizations, reallocation of deductions, funding of terrorism, statutes of limitations, the concept of trust income, and the plethora of penalties that can apply in the charitable giving setting.

CHAPTER 9

Planned Giving

The purpose of this chapter is to summarize the tax law pertaining to planned giving, which is the most sophisticated form of charitable giving, in that it usually involves trusts and/or agreements. For the most part, planned gifts are partial interest gifts (see Chapter 7). In a broader sense, planned giving encompasses contributions made by means of decedent's estates (see Chapter 5) and by use of life insurance (see Chapter 10). Specifically, this chapter will:

- Provide an introduction to the concept of planned giving
- Summarize the law concerning charitable remainder trusts
- Address emerging rules concerning premature termination of remainder trusts
- Summarize the law concerning pooled income funds
- Summarize the law concerning charitable gift annuities
- Summarize the law concerning other gifts of remainder interests
- Summarize the law concerning charitable lead trusts
- Explain the application of the federal securities law
- Explain the application of the antitrust law

INTRODUCTION

There are two basic types of planned gifts for charitable purposes. One type is a legacy: Under a will, a gift passes from an estate (as a bequest or a devise) to a charitable organization. The other type is a charitable gift made during a donor's lifetime, using a trust or other form of agreement.

These gifts once were termed *deferred gifts* because the actual receipt of the contribution amount by the charity is deferred until the happening of some event (usually the death of the donor or subsequent death of the donor's spouse). This term, however, has fallen out of favor, because some donors (to the chagrin of the gift-seeking charities) gained the impression that it was their tax benefits that were being deferred.

A planned gift usually is a contribution of a donor's interest in money or an item of property rather than an outright gift of the money or property in its entirety. (The term *usually* is used because gifts involving life insurance do not neatly fit this definition and because an outright gift of property, in some instances, is treated as a planned gift.) Technically, this type of gift is a conveyance of a partial interest in property; planned giving, as noted, is (usually) partial interest giving.

An item of property conceptually has within it two interests: an income interest and a remainder interest.

The *income interest* within an item of property is a function of the income generated by the property. A person may be entitled to all of the income from a property or to some portion of the income—for example, income equal to 5 percent of the fair market value of the property, even though the property is producing income at the rate of 7 percent. This person is said to have the (or an) income interest in the property. Two or more persons (such as spouses or siblings) may have income interests in the same property; these interests may be held concurrently or consecutively.

The *remainder interest* within an item of property is equal to the projected value of the property, or the property produced by reinvestments, at some future date. That is, the remainder interest in property is an amount equal to the present value of the property (or its offspring) when it is to be received at a subsequent point in time.

These interests are measured by the value of the property, the age of the donor(s), the period of time that the income interest(s) will exist, and the frequency and type of the income payout. The computation of these interests is made by means of actuarial tables, usually those promulgated by the Department of the Treasury.

An income interest or a remainder interest in property may be contributed to charity, but a deduction is almost never available for a charitable gift of an income interest in property. (Such a gift is more of an estate planning technique [see Chapter 5].) By contrast, the charitable contribution of a remainder interest in an item of property will—assuming all of the technical requirements are satisfied—give rise to a (frequently sizable) charitable deduction.

When a gift of a remainder interest in property is made to a charity, the charity will not acquire that interest until the income interest(s) in the property have expired. The donor receives the charitable contribution deduction for the tax year in which the recipient charity's remainder interest in the property is established. On the occasion of a gift of an income interest in property to a charity, the charity acquires that interest immediately and retains it until such time as the remainder interest commences.

Basically, under the federal tax law, a planned gift must be made by means of a trust if a charitable contribution deduction is to be available. The trust that facilitates a planned gift is known as a *split-interest trust* because it is the mechanism used to create and maintain the income and remainder interests. In other words, this type of trust is the medium for—in use of a legal fiction—splitting the property into its two component categories of interests. Split-interest trusts are charitable remainder trusts, pooled income funds, and charitable lead trusts. There are some exceptions to the general requirements regarding the use of a split-interest trust in the planned giving context. The principal exception is the charitable gift annuity, which entails a contract rather than a trust. Individuals may give a remainder interest in their personal residence or farm to charity and receive a charitable deduction without utilizing a trust. (Each of these planned giving techniques is summarized in the following section.)

A donor, although desirous of financially supporting a charity, may be unwilling or unable to fully part with property, either because of a present or perceived need for the income that the property generates and/or because of the capital gains taxes that would be experienced if the property were sold. The planned gift is likely to be the solution in this type of situation: The donor may satisfy his or her charitable desires and yet continue to receive income from the property (or property that results from reinvestment). The donor also receives a charitable deduction for the gift of the remainder interest, which will reduce or eliminate the tax on the income from the gift property. There is no tax imposed on the capital gain inherent in the property. If the gift property is not throwing off sufficient income, the trustee of the split-interest trust may dispose of the property (usually without taxation) and reinvest the proceeds in more productive property. The donor may then receive more income from the property in the trust than was received prior to the making of the gift.

CHARITABLE REMAINDER TRUSTS

The most widespread form of planned giving involves a split-interest trust known as the *charitable remainder trust.* This term is nearly self-explanatory: The entity is a trust by which a remainder interest destined for charity has been created. Each charitable remainder trust is designed specifically for the particular circumstances of the donor(s), with the remainder interest in the gift property designated for one or more charities. (Occasionally, because of miscommunication with the donor[s], lack of skill in use of a word processor, or incompetence, a remainder trust will be drafted that is the wrong type. The IRS generously characterizes these trusts as the product of a *scrivener's error* and will recognize the qualification of the corrected trust, which must be undertaken by court-supervised reformation.)

Income Interests

A qualified charitable remainder trust must provide for a specified distribution of income, at least annually, to or for the use of one or more beneficiaries (at least one of which is not a charity). This flow of income must be for life or for a term of no more than 20 years, with an irrevocable remainder interest to be held for the benefit of the charity or paid over to it. The income beneficiaries are those deriving income from the trust (those holding an income interest); the charity has the remainder interest.

   How the income interests in a charitable remainder trust are ascertained depends on whether the trust is a charitable remainder annuity trust or a charitable remainder unitrust. (Recently promulgated tax regulations have changed the concept of trust income, doing away with the traditional precepts of income and principal, with as yet-unknown consequences for some charitable remainder unitrusts.)

Types of Remainder Trusts

With a charitable remainder annuity trust, income payments are in the form of a fixed amount, an annuity. For example, an individual may contribute a sum of money and/or property to a charitable remainder annuity trust, with the trust structured to pay that individual an annual amount of $5,000.

Income payments from a charitable remainder unitrust are in the form of an amount equal to a percentage of the fair market value of the assets in the trust, determined annually. For example, an individual may contribute a sum of money and/or property to a charitable remainder unitrust, with the trust structured to pay that individual an annual amount based on 5 percent of the value of the trust assets on a particular date.

Of the four types of charitable remainder unitrusts, the one just described is known as the *standard charitable remainder unitrust* or the *fixed percentage charitable remainder unitrust*. Two types of unitrusts are known as *income exception charitable remainder unitrusts*. One of these types enables income to be paid to the income interest beneficiary once there is any income generated in the trust; this is the *net income charitable remainder unitrust*. The other type of income-exception unitrust is akin to the previous one but can make catch-up payments for prior years' deficiencies once income begins to flow; this is the *net income make-up charitable remainder unitrust*. The fourth type of unitrust is allowed to convert (flip) once from one of the income exception methods to the fixed percentage method for purposes of calculating the unitrust amount; this is the *flip charitable remainder unitrust*.

Income Payout Rules

The income payout of both of these types of trusts is subject to a 5 percent minimum. That is, the annuity must be an amount equal to at least 5 percent of the value of the property initially placed in the trust. Likewise, the unitrust amount must be an amount equal to at least 5 percent of the value of the trust property, determined annually. These percentages may not be greater than 50 percent. Also, the value of the remainder interest in the property must be at least 10 percent of the value of the property contributed to the trust.

Distributions from charitable remainder trusts are treated as having these four tax characteristics in the hands of the recipients (whether the trust is tax-exempt or not):

1. The amounts are treated as ordinary income, to the extent of the sum of the trust's ordinary income for the tax year of the trust and its undistributed ordinary income for prior

years. An ordinary loss for the current year must be used to reduce undistributed ordinary income for prior years and any excess must be carried forward indefinitely to reduce ordinary income for future years.

2. The amounts are treated as capital gain, to the extent of the charitable remainder trust's undistributed capital gain.

If, in any tax year of a charitable remainder trust, the trust has both undistributed short-term capital gain and undistributed long-term capital gain, the short-term capital gain must be deemed distributed prior to any long-term capital gain.

If a charitable remainder trust has capital losses in excess of capital gains for any tax year, any excess of the net short-term capital loss over the net long-term capital gain for the year must be a short-term capital loss in the succeeding tax year, and any excess of the net long-term capital loss over the net short-term capital gain for the year must be a long-term capital loss in the succeeding tax year.

If a charitable remainder trust has capital gains in excess of capital losses for any tax year, any excess of the net short-term capital gain over the net long-term capital loss for the year must be, to the extent not deemed distributed, a short-term capital gain in the succeeding tax year, and any excess of the net long-term capital gain over the net short-term capital loss for the year must be, to the extent not deemed distributed, a long-term capital gain in the succeeding tax year.

3. The amounts are treated as other income to the extent of the sum of the trust's other income for the tax year and its undistributed other income for prior years. A loss in this category for the current year must be used to reduce undistributed income in this category for prior years, and any excess must be carried forward indefinitely to reduce this income for future years.

4. The amounts are treated as a distribution of trust corpus. For these purposes, the term *corpus* means the net fair market value of the trust's assets less the total undistributed income (but not loss) in each of the just-described categories.

The character of a charitable remainder trust's income is determined at the time the income is realized by the trust. Changes in the law in 1997, 1998, and 2003 caused qualified dividend income to be taxed at the rates applicable to long-term capital gain and altered and reduced the rates for the taxation of capital gain. These developments affected the tax treatment of distributions of certain dividends and capital gain from charitable remainder trusts, requiring the IRS to revise the tax regulations in 2005 to encompass these new classes of ordinary income and capital gain.

Calculation of Charitable Deduction

Calculation of the charitable contribution deduction for a gift to a charitable remainder trust involves several factors; this is almost always accomplished using software. The elements to take into account in determining the deduction for a contribution to a charitable remainder annuity trust are the amount of the gift, the amount and frequency of payment of the income interest, the duration of the income interest, the month and year of the gift, the age of the donor, the federal government's *applicable federal interest rate* for the month, and the *annuity factor* (found in IRS actuarial tables). As an illustration, an individual who has attained the age of 65 contributes $100,000 to a charitable remainder annuity trust, in a month in which the government's interest rate is 4.2 percent. The annuity amount, paid annually and at the end of each year, is $5,000. The income interest is for the donor's life. The annuity factor is 11.3067. Under these facts, the present value of the annuity interest is $56,533.50; the value of the remainder interest—and thus the resulting charitable contribution deduction—is $43,466.50.

In an instance of a gift to a standard charitable remainder unitrust, the elements to take into account in determining the deduction are the amount of the gift, the percentage on which the income interest is based, the frequency of payment of the income interest, the duration of the income interest, the month and year of the gift, the age of the donor, the applicable federal rate for the month, and items derived from IRS tables: the payout sequence factor, the payout rate, and the life remainder factor. As an illustration, an individual who has attained the age of 70 contributes $100,000 to a standard charitable remainder unitrust, in a month in which the applicable federal rate is 4.2 percent. The unitrust amount, to be paid annually, is based on 5 percent. The unitrust interest is for the donor's life. The payout sequence factor is 0.959693; the adjusted payout rate is 4.798465; the life remainder factor is 0.540940. Under these facts, the present value of the unitrust interest is $45,906; the value of the remainder interest is $54,094.

One obvious fact: The longer the income interest is to be paid (usually because of the younger age of the income interest beneficiary) from a charitable remainder trust, the smaller the amount of the remainder interest that will be available for the charity (and the charitable deduction).

Spousal Elective Share Law Issue

The law in most states protects spouses from disinheritance by the other spouse, by means of elective share statutes. These laws provide spouses with the right to elect to receive a statutory share of the other spouse's estate, irrespective of whether the deceased spouse made any bequests to the surviving spouse. For these purposes, the spouse's share of the grantor's estate is referred to as an *elective share*; the right to elect to receive an elective share is referred to as the *right of election*.

In some states, the elective share is based solely on the value and elements of the probate estate. In other states, the estate involved is the *augmented estate*, which may include assets of a charitable remainder trust. The distribution limitations as to permissible income recipients applicable to these trusts, in situations where the surviving spouse may elect to receive an elective share including assets in a charitable remainder trust, are violated where this right of election exists—even if not exercised.

In an effort to ameliorate this matter, the IRS issued guidance providing a safe harbor procedure pursuant to which the agency will disregard certain state law rights of election for purposes of determining whether charitable remainder trusts satisfy their distribution rules. This procedure generally required the surviving spouse to irrevocably waive the right of election with regard to the assets of a charitable remainder trust.

This guidance generated considerable controversy and manifold requests that it be withdrawn. Complaints about the guidance were that: Donors are being required to be knowledgeable about state spousal election laws (including situations where donors change their place of residence); obtaining the waivers is too unwieldy; and it is chilling the establishment of charitable remainder trusts. Proposed solutions include generally disregarding a right of election as long as the surviving spouse does not exercise the right, use of the private foundation termination-of-status rules, application of the private foundation self-dealing rules, and/or application of the private foundation taxable expenditures rules. As a practical matter, although the charitable contribution deduction is available for the year in which a charitable remainder trust is created and funded, many years could elapse before there is a distribution to an electing spouse; by that time, the statute of limitations would have run on any opportunity to recapture the tax benefit obtained from funding the charitable remainder trust. In any event, the IRS succumbed to outcries from the planned giving community, withdrew this guidance, and is contemplating its next move in this regard.

Other Considerations

Nearly any kind of property can be contributed to a charitable remainder trust. Typical gift properties are cash, securities, and/or real estate. Yet a charitable remainder trust can accommodate gifts of artworks, collections, and just about any other forms of property. One of the principal considerations, however, must be the ability of the property (or successor property, if sold) to generate sufficient income to satisfy the payout requirement with respect to the income interest beneficiary or beneficiaries.

All categories of charitable organizations—public charities and private foundations (see Chapter 1)—are eligible to be remainder interest beneficiaries of as many charitable remainder trusts as they can muster. The amount of the charitable deduction will vary for contributions to different types of charitable organizations, however, because of the percentage limitations (see Chapter 4).

Often a bank or other financial institution serves as the trustee of a charitable remainder trust. The financial institution should have the capacity to administer the trust, make appropriate investments, and timely adhere to all income distribution and reporting requirements. It is not unusual, however, for the charitable organization that is the remainder interest beneficiary to act as trustee. If the donor or a related person is named the trustee, the grantor trust rules (see Chapter 1) may apply: The gain from the trust's sale of appreciated property is taxed to the donor.

Conventionally, once the income interest expires, the assets in a charitable remainder trust are distributed to the charitable organization (or organizations) that is the remainder interest beneficiary. If the assets (or a portion of them) are retained in the trust, the trust will be classified as a private foundation, unless it can qualify as a public charity (most likely, a supporting organization) (see Chapter 1).

There have been some abuses in this area in recent years. One problem has been the use of short-term (such as a term of two years) charitable remainder trusts to manipulate the use of assets and payout arrangements for the tax benefit of the donors. Certain of these abuses were stymied by legislation creating some of the previously referenced percentage rules. The tax regulations have been revised in an attempt to prevent transactions by which a charitable remainder trust is used to convert appreciated property into money while avoiding tax on the gain from the sale of the assets. (Some of these arrangements were so audacious in their flaunting of the law that the vehicles garnered the informal name *chutzpah trust.*)

Inasmuch as charitable remainder trusts are split-interest trusts, they are subject to at least some of the prohibitions that are imposed on private foundations, most notably the rules concerning self-dealing and taxable expenditures. The IRS has an informal procedure (reflected only in private letter rulings) for the premature termination of a charitable remainder trust, where the termination does not give rise to self-dealing because the procedure devised for allocation of the trust's assets to beneficiaries is reasonable.

A qualified charitable remainder trust generally is exempt from federal income taxation. In any year, however, in which it has unrelated business taxable income, the trust loses its tax-exempt status.

EARLY TERMINATION OF REMAINDER TRUSTS

There is no formal procedure for prematurely terminating a charitable remainder trust. Traditionally, the IRS has frowned on the practice, largely fearful of self-dealing (that is, of one or more income interest beneficiaries obtaining an allocation of economic benefits that is more extensive than would have been the case had the trust continued in existence until all income interests expired). Recently, however, the IRS has been informally tolerating these terminations, privately ruling that the procedure devised by the parties for allocation of the trust assets among the income and remainder interest beneficiaries is reasonable. In this context, *reasonable* means that the charitable beneficiary receives its full benefit consistent with the charitable deduction allowed to the donor.

Here is a typical scenario: Twenty years ago, A, as the donor, and B, as the initial trustee, executed a charitable remainder trust. The trust provided income to A during her lifetime. A dies; the income is to be distributed to B and C, and thereafter the trust is to terminate and transfer income and assets to a charitable organization. C is also a trustee. The parties decided to terminate the trust; B and C do not need the money and want the charity to receive its trust share early. (This change requires state court approval.) The physician of B and C signed an affidavit, under penalties of perjury, that neither B nor C has a medical condition expected to result in a shorter-than-average longevity.

In a circumstance such as this, the IRS rules that there is no excessive distribution of trust assets to the income beneficiaries. (Were that to occur, as noted, the distribution would be self-dealing.) The proposed allocation method is considered reasonable because the income beneficiaries have no knowledge of a medical condition or other circumstance likely to result in a shorter life expectancy than that predicated by the actuarial tables. This was proven to be the case by the physician's affidavit.

One of the problems with an early termination of a charitable remainder trust is that the income beneficiary generally is required to treat the entirety of the distribution to him or her as capital gain, with no offset for any basis. In rare instances, both the income beneficiary or beneficiaries and the remainder interest beneficiary or beneficiaries are able to sell their interests in the trust to a third party. When that happens, the income beneficiary can use basis to reduce the capital gains tax.

POOLED INCOME FUNDS

Another planned giving technique involves gifts to charity via a *pooled income fund*. Like a charitable remainder trust, a pooled income fund is a form of split-interest trust.

A donor to a qualified pooled income fund receives a charitable deduction for giving the remainder interest in the donated property to charity. The gift creates income interests in one or more noncharitable beneficiaries; the remainder interest in the gift property is designated for the charity that maintains the fund.

Pooling Requirement

The pooled income fund's basic instrument (a trust agreement or a declaration of trust) is written to facilitate gifts from an unlimited number of donors, so the essential terms of the transactions must be established in advance for all participants. The terms of the transfer cannot be tailored to fit any one donor's particular circumstances (as is the case with the charitable remainder trust). The pooled income fund constitutes, literally, a pool of charitable gifts.

Contributions to a pooled income fund may be considerably smaller than is practical for those to a charitable remainder trust. Gifts to pooled income funds are generally confined to cash and readily marketable securities (other than tax-exempt bonds).

Income Interests

Each donor to a pooled income fund contributes an irrevocable remainder interest in the gift property to (or for the use of) an eligible charitable organization. Each donor creates an income interest for the life of one or more beneficiaries, who must be living at the time of the transfer. The properties transferred by the donors must be commingled in the fund (thereby creating the necessary pool of gifts).

Each income interest beneficiary must receive income at least once each year. The pool amount is determined by the rate of return earned by the fund for the year. Beneficiaries receive their proportionate share of the fund's income. The dollar amount of the income share is based on the number of units owned by the beneficiary; each unit must be based on the fair market value of the assets when transferred. Thus, a pooled income fund is essentially an investment vehicle whose funding is motivated by charitable intents.

As an illustration of the determination of units assigned to a donor, on April 1 of a year, the fair market value of the property in a pooled income fund is $100,000, at which time 1,000 units of participation are outstanding (thus having a value of $100 each). On April 15 of that year, a donor transfers $50,000 to the fund, retaining an income interest. On May 1 of that year, the fair market value of the property in the fund was $160,000. No other gifts were made during this period. The average of the fair market values of the property in the fund (excluding the $50,000 gift) on April 1 and May 1 was $105,000. Accordingly, the fair market value of a unit of participation in this fund on April 15 was $105. The donor was assigned 476.19 units in the fund ($50,000/$105).

An illustration of the determination of the charitable deduction for a gift to a pooled income fund is an individual who has attained age 66 who makes a $50,000 contribution to a pooled income fund. The gift is made in a month where the applicable federal rate is 4.2 percent. The highest rate of return experienced by the fund in the most recent three years was 7 percent. The estimated annual return to the donor is $3,500. The life estimate factor is 0.384960. The remainder interest is 38.496 percent of the gift. The donor's charitable deduction for this gift is $19,248 (38.496% of $50,000).

Maintenance Requirement

A pooled income fund must be maintained by one or more charitable organizations. Usually there is only charity per fund. The charity must exercise control over the fund; it does not have to be the trustee of the fund (although it can be), but it must have the power to remove and replace the trustee. A donor or an income beneficiary of the fund may not be a trustee. A donor may be a trustee or officer of the charitable organization that maintains the fund, however, as long as he or she does not have the general responsibilities with respect to the fund that are ordinarily exercised by a trustee.

Unlike other forms of planned giving, a pooled income fund is restricted to only certain categories of charitable organizations. Most types of public charities can maintain a pooled income fund; private foundations and some other charities cannot (as to these differences, see Chapter 1).

Other Considerations

Pooled income funds are subject to at least some of the prohibitions that are imposed on private foundations, most particularly the rules concerning self-dealing and taxable expenditures.

A qualified pooled income fund is not treated as an association for tax purposes, nor does such a fund have to be a trust under local law. Generally, a pooled income fund is subject to federal income taxation. In actuality, however, a pooled income fund usually is not taxable, because it receives a deduction for amounts paid out to income interest beneficiaries and a set-aside deduction for the remainder interests reserved for the charitable beneficiary.

Pooled income funds currently are somewhat out of favor due to declines in interest rates and bond yields. These declines are causing a reduction in the investment return of these funds and, thus, a reduction in the amount of income paid to the income beneficiaries. Donors are avoiding pooled income funds, thereby increasing the costs to the charities of maintaining them. Some charities have terminated their pooled income fund(s), although many funds at the larger institutions continue to perform adequately.

CHARITABLE GIFT ANNUITIES

Still another form of planned giving is the *charitable gift annuity*. It is not based on use of a split-interest trust; instead, the annuity is the subject of an agreement between the donor and the charitable donee. The donor agrees to make a gift and the donee agrees, in return, to provide the donor (and/or someone else) with an annuity.

With one payment, the donor is thus engaging in two transactions: the purchase of an annuity and the making of a charitable gift. The contribution gives rise to the charitable deduction. One sum is transferred; the money in excess of the amount necessary to purchase the annuity is the charitable gift portion. Because of the dual nature of the transaction, the charitable gift annuity transfer constitutes a bargain sale (see Chapter 7).

The annuity resulting from the creation of a charitable gift annuity arrangement (like an annuity generally) is a fixed amount paid at regular intervals. The exact amount paid depends on the age of the beneficiary, which is determined at the time the contribution is made. Frequently, the annuity payment period begins with the creation of the annuity payment obligation. The initiation of the payment period can, however, be postponed to a future date; this type of arrangement is termed the *deferred payment charitable gift annuity*.

A portion of the annuity paid is tax-free because it constitutes a return of capital. Where appreciated securities (or other capital gain property) are contributed, there will be capital gain on the appreciation that is attributable to the value of the annuity. If the donor is the annuitant, the capital gain can be reported ratably over the individual's life expectancy. The tax savings occasioned by the charitable contribution deduction may, however, shelter the capital gain (resulting from the creation of a charitable gift annuity) from taxation.

As an illustration, an individual of thc age of 72 purchased a charitable gift annuity using appreciated property with a value of $10,000 and a basis of $5,000; the annuity is $800 annually for life (an 8 percent return). The charitable contribution deduction arising from this gift is $4,888. The annual annuity is taxable in this way: ordinary income of $447.46, capital gain of $176.27, and tax-free income of $176.27.

Inasmuch as the arrangement is by contract between the donor and donee, all of the assets of the charitable organization are subject to liability for the ongoing payment of the annuities. (With most planned giving techniques, the resources for payment of the income are confined to those in a split-interest trust.) That is why some states impose a requirement that charities must establish a reserve for the payment of gift annuities—and why many charitable organizations are reluctant to embark on a gift annuity program. Charities that are hesitant to commit to the ongoing payment of annuities can eliminate that risk by reinsuring them.

OTHER GIFTS OF REMAINDER INTERESTS

The law is specific as to the circumstances in which a charitable deduction arises, particularly when the charitable gift is made using a trust. Basically, there is no federal income tax charitable contribution deduction unless the gift meets one of a variety of stringent tests. Related to this point is the rule of law that a charitable contribution consisting of a transfer of a future interest in tangible personal property is treated as made only when all intervening interests in, and rights to the actual possession or enjoyment of, the property have expired or are held by persons other than the donor or those related to the donor (see Chapter 6).

Otherwise, there are few situations in which a federal income tax charitable contribution deduction is available for a gift of a partial interest. (The rules in this regard are essentially the same in the gift and estate tax setting [see Chapter 5].) One exception is a set of rules concerning certain gifts of works of art, as distinct from the copyrights in them, which can lead to an estate and gift tax charitable deduction (see Chapter 6).

Indeed, there are only three of these situations:

1. Qualified conservation contributions
2. Contributions of remainder interests in a personal residence or farm
3. Contributions of an undivided portion of the donor's entire interest in the property

Conservation Contributions

Special federal tax rules pertain to contributions to charity of real property for conservation purposes. These rules are an exception to the general rule that there is no charitable contribution deduction for contributions of partial interests in property. This exception involves the qualified conservation contribution (see Chapter 6).

Contributions of Remainder Interests in Personal Residence or Farm

A federal income tax charitable contribution deduction may arise from a gift of a remainder interest in a personal residence or farm, even though the gift is not made in trust and is irrevocable. This deduction is based on the value of the remainder interest. In determining this value, depreciation (computed on the straight-line method) and depletion of the property may be taken into account. If the property is contributed subject to a mortgage, the transfer must be treated as a bargain sale (see Chapter 7).

A *personal residence* is a property that is used by its owner as a personal residence; it does not have to be the owner's principal residence. For example, a vacation home would likely qualify under this definition. Indeed, there is no restriction on the form a personal residence may take. All that is required for something to qualify as a personal residence is that it contain facilities for cooking, sleeping, and sanitation. (The IRS had occasion to rule that a yacht that "contains all of the amenities found in a house" qualified as a personal residence.)

The term *personal residence* also includes stock owned by a donor as a tenant-stockholder in a cooperative housing corporation, if the dwelling that the donor is entitled to occupy as a stockholder is used by the donor as his or her personal residence.

In general, a personal residence does not include household furnishings that are not fixtures. Thus, there is no charitable deduction for a contribution of a remainder interest in household furnishings contained in a decedent's personal residence at the time of death.

In this context, the charitable remainder interest must be in the residence itself and not simply in the proceeds to be derived from sale of the residence at a future date. The IRS so held in the setting of a contribution of a remainder interest in a decedent's personal residence bequeathed to charity, under a will that provided that the property was to be sold upon the life tenant's death and the entire proceeds of the sale to be paid to a charitable organization. A charitable deduction is, however, allowed for the value of a remainder interest in a personal residence when the residence is to be sold and the proceeds distributed to a charitable organization, as long as local law permits the charity to elect distribution of the residence itself. The charitable deduction is allowed, because a gift of a remainder interest in a personal residence is given to charity and to an individual as tenants in common, for the value of the interest received by the charity. The deduction is also allowed, notwithstanding the fact that the applicable law (known as a *mortmain act*) requires the charitable recipient to dispose of the property within 10 years of the date of acquisition. In the last of these situations, the IRS noted that the "circumstance does not lend itself to abuse" because the charitable organization is receiving the . . . [property] in its original form and can sell the property for itself in the way that is most advantageous and most likely to realize the full value of the property."

The charitable organization must be given the right to possession, dominion, and control of the property. The deduction is not defeated simply because the charitable organization that is the donee fails to take actual possession of the property.

A *farm* is any land used by the donor or a tenant of the donor for the production of crops, fruits, or other agricultural products or for the sustenance of livestock. A farm includes the improvements on it. The term *livestock* includes cattle, hogs, horses, mules, donkeys, sheep, goats, captive fur-bearing animals, chickens, turkeys, pigeons, and other poultry. The words *any land* does not mean the entire farm acreage owned and used by the donor or his or her tenant for the production of crops or the sustenance of livestock; it can include any portion of farm acreage so used. It can be property that is subject to a conservation easement.

As noted, this type of gift, to be deductible, cannot be made in trust. A contribution not in trust to a charitable organization of a remainder interest in a farm, with retention of an estate in the farm for life or for a term of years, gives rise to a charitable deduction for the value of the remainder interest not transferred in trust.

The various points of law concerning the charitable contribution deduction for gifts of remainder interests in personal residences also apply in the setting of gifts of remainder interests in farms.

Undivided Portions of Entire Interests in Property

A federal income tax charitable contribution deduction is available for a gift of an undivided portion of the donor's entire interest in an item of property. This type of deduction is available only when the gift is not in trust.

An undivided portion of a donor's entire interest in property must both:

- Consist of a fraction or percentage of each and every substantial interest or right owned by the donor in the property
- Extend over the entire term of the donor's interest in the property and in other property into which the property may be converted

A charitable deduction is allowable under these rules if the charitable organization is given the right, as a tenant in common with the donor, to possession, dominion, and control of the property for a portion of each year appropriate to its interest in the property.

Also, an income tax charitable contribution is allowed:

- If a person owns 100 acres of land and makes a contribution of 50 acres to a charitable organization
- For a contribution of property to a charitable organization when the organization is given the right, as a tenant in common with the donor, to possession, dominion, and control of the property for a portion of each year appropriate to its interest in the property

A charitable contribution in perpetuity of an interest in property not in trust, when the donor transfers some specific rights and retains other substantial rights, is not considered a contribution of an undivided portion of the donor's interest in property under this rule.

CHARITABLE LEAD TRUSTS

Most forms of planned giving have a common element: The donor transfers to a charitable organization the remainder interest in an item of property, and one or more noncharitable beneficiaries retain or obtain the income interest. A reverse sequence may occur, however—and that is the essence of the *charitable lead trust.*

The property transferred to a charitable lead trust is apportioned into an income interest and a remainder interest. Like the charitable remainder trust and the pooled income fund, this is a split-interest trust. An income interest in property is contributed to a charitable organization, either for a term of years or for the life of one individual (or the lives of more than one individual). The remainder interest in the property is reserved to return, at the expiration of the income interest (the lead period), to the donor or pass to some other noncharitable beneficiary or beneficiaries. Often the property passes from one generation (the donor's) to another.

There are limits on the types of individuals whose lives can be used as measuring lives for determining the period of time the charity will receive the income flow from a charitable lead trust. The only individuals whose lives can be used as measuring ones are those of the donor, the donor's spouse, and/or a lineal ancestor of all the remaining beneficiaries. These regulations are intended to eliminate the practice of using the lives of seriously ill individuals to move assets and income away from charitable beneficiaries prematurely and, instead to private beneficiaries. (These trusts were informally referred to as *vulture trusts* or *ghoul trusts.*)

The charitable lead trust can be used to accelerate into one year a series of charitable contributions that would otherwise be made annually. There can be a corresponding single-year deduction for the "bunched" amount of charitable gifts.

In some circumstances, a charitable deduction is available for the transfer of an income interest in property to a charitable organization. There are stringent limitations, however, on the deductible amount of charitable contributions of these income interests.

APPLICATION OF SECURITIES LAWS

At the federal level, the principal securities laws are the Securities Act of 1933, the Securities Exchange Act of 1934, and the Investment Company Act of 1940. These laws are administered and enforced by the Securities Exchange Commission (SEC). Generally, this body of law is designed to preserve a free market in the trading of securities, provide full and fair disclosure of the character of securities sold in interstate commerce and through the mails, and prevent fraud and other abuse in the marketing and sale of securities. State securities laws have the same goal.

The federal securities law broadly defines the term *security* as including not only stocks and bonds but also notes, debentures, evidences of indebtedness, certificates of participation in a profit-sharing agreement, investment contracts, and certificates of deposit for securities. It is rare for a charitable organization to offer a financial benefit or package to the public where that benefit or package is considered a security, but some nonprofit organizations offer *memberships* that, technically, constitute securities. There are, however, exceptions from federal securities laws for these types of securities.

Nonetheless, a charitable organization may find itself at least within the potential applicability of the securities laws if it maintains one or more charitable income funds. The federal securities laws include rules that are designed to shield charities against the allegation that these funds are investment companies subject to the registration and other requirements of the Investment Company Act. This legislation, introduced by the Philanthropy Protection Act of 1995, provides exemptions under the federal securities laws for charitable organizations that maintain these funds.

A *charitable income fund* is a fund maintained by a charitable organization exclusively for the collective investment and reinvestment of one or more assets of a charitable remainder trust or similar trust, a pooled income fund, an arrangement involving a contribution in exchange for the issuance of a charitable gift annuity, a charitable lead trust, the general endowment fund or other funds of one or more charitable organizations, or certain other trusts in which the remainder interests benefit or are revocably dedicated to one or more charitable organizations. The SEC has the authority to expand the scope of these exemption provisions to embrace funds that may include assets not expressly defined.

A fund that is excluded from the definition of an investment company must provide at the time of the contribution, to each donor to a charity by means of the fund, written information describing the material terms of operation of the fund. This disclosure requirement, however, is not a condition of exemption from the Investment Company Act. Thus, a charitable income fund that fails to provide the requisite information to donors is not subject to the securities laws, although the fund may be subject to an enforcement or other action by the SEC.

This exemption is also grafted onto the Securities Act and the Securities Exchange Act. Thus, for example, the exemption in the Securities Act from registration and other requirements is available for "any security issued by a person organized and operated exclusively for religious, benevolent, fraternal, charitable, or reformatory purposes and not for pecuniary profit, and no part of the net earnings of which inures to the benefit of any person, private stockholder, or individual."

The Securities Exchange Act provides that a charitable organization is not subject to the act's broker-dealer regulation rules solely because the organization trades in securities on its behalf, or on behalf of a charitable income fund, or the settlors, potential settlors, or beneficiaries of either. This protection is also extended to trustees, directors, officers, employees, or volunteers of a charitable organization, acting within the scope of their employment or duties with the organization.

Exemptions similar to those available in the broker-dealer setting are provided for charitable organizations and certain persons associated with them, in connection with the provision of advice, analyses, or reports, from the reach of the Investment Advisors Act.

Interests in charitable income funds excluded from the definition of an investment company, and any offer or sale of these interests, are exempt from a state law that requires registration or qualification of securities. A charitable organization or trustee, director, officer, employee, or volunteer of a charity (acting within the scope of his or her employment or duties) is not subject to regulation as a dealer, broker, agent, or investment advisor under any state securities law because the organization or person trades in securities on behalf of a charity, charitable income fund, or the settlors, potential settlors, or beneficiaries of either.

APPLICATION OF ANTITRUST LAWS

Charitable organizations using the same annuity rate in the issuance of charitable gift annuities do not violate the antitrust laws. That is, agreeing to use, or using, the same annuity rate for the purpose of issuing one or more charitable gift annuities is not unlawful. This exemption extends to both federal and state law. The protection is not confined to charities: It extends to lawyers, accountants, actuaries, consultants, and others retained or employed by a charitable organization when assisting in the issuance of a charitable gift annuity or the setting of charitable annuity rates. This legislation defines *charitable gift annuity* by cross-reference to the federal tax law definition of the term.

Moreover, this antitrust exemption also sweeps within its ambit the act of publishing suggested annuity rates. Thus, organizations—most notably, the American Council on Gift Annuities—are not in violation of the antitrust laws when they publish actuarial tables or annuity rates for use in issuing gift annuities.

A report from a committee of the U.S. House of Representatives contains a discussion of the applicability of the antitrust laws to charitable organizations: Essentially, these laws apply when an organization is engaged in a "commercial transaction" with a "public service aspect." This committee was not certain whether charitable gift annuities involve these types of transactions or are "pure charity." In any event, the committee concluded that giving by means of these annuities is "legitimate," particularly since the IRS "approves and regulates" these instruments.

SUMMARY

This chapter provided a summary of the federal tax rules pertaining to the partial interest and certain other types of contributions involved in planned giving. The chapter summarized the principles underlying the concept of planned giving and the use of charitable remainder trusts, pooled income funds, charitable gift annuities, other forms of gifts of remainder interests, and charitable lead trusts. The chapter concluded with brief summaries of the applicable securities and antitrust laws. The nonlawyer may be surprised to find that something as seemingly simple as giving to charity can spawn these exceedingly complex bodies of law.

CHAPTER 10

Gifts of and Using
Life Insurance

Life insurance can be the subject of a charitable gift. It can be considered part of the panoply of planned gifts, although a split-interest trust is not usually involved (see Chapter 9). A gift of life insurance is a particularly good way for a younger donor to make a major gift to a charitable organization. The purpose of this chapter is to summarize this aspect of the law. Specifically, this chapter will:

- Provide an introduction to life insurance concepts
- Discuss charitable giving using life insurance
- Examine the insurable interest requirement
- Summarize the unrelated debt-financed income considerations
- Explain the law concerning charitable split-dollar insurance plans
- Analyze the applicability of the gift substantiation rules in this context

INTRODUCTION

A person may make a gift of life insurance to a charitable organization. Where a federal income tax charitable contribution deduction is desired, the donor must make the charity both the owner and the beneficiary of the insurance policy.

An individual can contribute a fully paid-up life insurance policy or a single-premium policy to a charitable organization and deduct, for federal income tax purposes, its replacement value.

Alternatively, an individual can acquire a life insurance policy, contribute it to a charitable organization, pay the premiums, and create a charitable contribution deduction for each premium payment made.

For an income tax deduction for a gift of life insurance to be available, the insurance contract must be enforceable. (A contribution by means of a contract that is void or likely to be voidable is a gift of something without value.) For the insurance contract to be enforceable, there must be a form of insurable interest between the insured and the beneficiary (see following section).

LIFE INSURANCE CONCEPTS

Prior to examining the uses of life insurance in the charitable giving context, it is appropriate to briefly summarize the basics of life insurance.

Basics

Life insurance is represented by a contract—known as an *insurance policy*—that involves at least three parties: an insured person, the owner of the insurance policy (usually the purchaser of the policy), and the insurer (the insurance company that provides the policy).

Another party to this arrangement is the beneficiary of the insurance proceeds. The owner of the insurance policy may be the beneficiary, or the beneficiary may be another person. Also, two or more persons may be beneficiaries of an insurance policy.

If the insured qualifies, and if the requisite consideration for the insurance contract—the *premium*—is paid by the policy owner, the insurance company promises to pay a cash benefit (death benefit) if the insured dies while the policy is in force. Depending on the type of life insurance, a portion of the premium may go into a cash account (and accumulate as cash value). The cash value is available to the policy owner at any time during the insured's lifetime, by canceling (*cashing in*) the insurance policy.

The insured and the owner of the policy may be the same person, or they may be different persons. For example, one may purchase a policy on his or her life. Alternatively, a spouse may purchase an insurance policy on the other spouse's life. When one spouse purchases a policy on the other spouse's life, the purchasing spouse is the policy owner and the other spouse is the insured.

The distinction between the insured and the policy owner is also important for tax reasons. At one's death, all of one's property is tabulated for the purpose of determining if one's estate must pay estate taxes (see Chapter 5). Property includes the death benefits from life insurance unless the decedent was merely the insured but not the policy owner. If the decedent was not the policy owner, and if he or she had no rights (e.g., to use the cash value or to name the beneficiary), the death benefit paid at death will not be included in the estate for estate tax purposes.

Types of Life Insurance

Broadly, there are two categories of life insurance: term insurance and permanent insurance. Each has many different types. For example, term insurance can be classified as level term, decreasing term, and increasing term. Permanent insurance can be categorized as whole life, variable life, adjustable life, and universal life.

Term insurance is analogous to renting a house. One agrees to pay a regular payment in exchange for the protection afforded by the house. Each year the landlord raises the rent as expenses increase. No matter how long an individual rents, he or she receives nothing back in the event of a move. With term insurance, in exchange for a "rent payment" (premium), the insurance company provides protection (the death benefit). Each year (typically) the rent payment (premium) is increased. If the tenant (policy owner) "leaves" (cancels the insurance policy), he or she receives nothing back, no matter how long the premium payments were made.

Permanent insurance is analogous to purchasing a house. The same protection as a rented house is provided, but the monthly payments are (usually) higher. The monthly payments are fixed. In addition, each month the house is owned, the value may increase (at least over the long term). This value is called *equity*, which can be used during lifetime by borrowing, by using the property as collateral, or by selling the house and receiving the net equity in a lump sum.

Under a permanent insurance contract, a person pays the mortgage payments (premiums) in exchange for both protection (death benefit) and equity (cash value). If an individual dies while insured, the death benefit is paid. If an individual wants to use the cash value while alive, he or she may do so by borrowing or by canceling the policy and taking the cash value. Some policies also allow for withdrawals without borrowing or surrendering. Premium payments are generally fixed during lifetime.

To summarize, term insurance is initially less expensive, offers death protection, and does not build up any cash value during an individual's lifetime. Permanent insurance is more expensive in the early years, provides the same death benefit, and also builds cash value during lifetime.

One type of permanent insurance is *universal life*. To understand this form of insurance, visualize a bucket with two spigots, one on each side. The insurance owner deposits premium dollars into the bucket; each month the insurance company turns on one of the spigots and drains off the dollars necessary to pay all of one month's cost of death protection, expense charges, and administrative charges. The spigot is then turned off; the dollars remaining in the bucket are invested and earn interest. These excess dollars and the interest earned make up the policy's cash value.

As the owner continues to deposit more premium dollars, and as more interest is earned, the cash value becomes larger. At any time, a person may cease depositing premium dollars, as long as there are enough dollars in the bucket to pay for the cost of insurance and the expense and administrative charges. Conversely, if the owner wants the cash value to build faster, he or she may pay more premium dollars.

The cash value can be taken out of the policy during lifetime in three ways:

1. Some of the money can be borrowed at a rate of interest; if the money is borrowed, it reduces the death benefit by the same amount. The money may be paid back at any time.
2. One can withdraw some of the money without incurring a loan. This method also reduces the death benefit, but it cannot be paid back without satisfying certain requirements.
3. One can surrender the policy (terminate the insurance) and take all of the cash value. The money available in all three methods may, however, be reduced by a surrender charge, illustrated by the second spigot. In the first 10 to 15 years, the insurance company imposes this charge on a sliding scale and it reduces to zero by the 10th to 15th policy year.

Universal life offers additional flexibility in that it allows an individual to select either of two death benefit options: a level death benefit or an increasing death benefit.

Two other types of insurance contracts have evolved. One is called *survivorship whole life*. It is unique in that it simultaneously insures two or more lives. The second type is group-term life insurance provided by an employer to an employee. An employee may be provided up to $50,000 of this type of insurance without having to recognize taxable income. The cost of any coverage over that amount provided by the employer must be recognized as income.

Valuation

A life insurance policy can be valued in three ways:

1. The replacement value, which is the amount the issuer of the insurance would charge to issue an identical policy to a person of the same age as the insured. This value is usually used in the gift and estate context.
2. The cash surrender value, which is the amount the insurance company is willing to pay if the policy is surrendered. This value has been applied in the income tax context.
3. The potential net death benefit amount, which is the amount the beneficiary would receive if the insured died immediately; this would be the difference between the face amount and any loan(s) outstanding.

Because the potential net death benefit value is relevant only when special circumstances suggest that, because of ill health, the insured's death is imminent, the values usually are the replacement value and the cash value (or an intermediate amount).

CHARITABLE GIVING AND LIFE INSURANCE

Essentially, a contribution of life insurance can give rise to a charitable deduction in three situations:

1. An individual may have an existing whole life insurance policy that is fully paid up, or is a single-premium policy, and is not needed for the protection of his or her family. A gift of the policy to a charitable organization would, in general, occasion a charitable deduction in an amount equal to the replacement value of the policy, as noted. A gift of a single-premium whole life insurance policy to a charitable organization, when the donor has paid the premium, gives rise to a charitable contribution deduction, with the amount of the deduction equal to the amount of the premium. An exception to this rule is derived from the fact

that a disposition of the insurance policy would not be a transaction generating long-term capital gain, so the charitable deduction cannot be greater than the donor's basis in the policy (see Chapter 2). A court held that, when valuing a paid-up life insurance policy that was contributed to a charitable organization, but was subject to a substantial loan, the proper valuation is the cash surrender value of the policy on the date it was contributed. In so holding, the court was influenced by the fact that no party had any interest in maintaining the life insurance policy as an investment.

2. An individual may own an insurance policy on which premium payments are still being made. The charitable deduction for a gift of a policy in this instance is an amount equal to the *interpolated terminal reserve value* of the policy on the date of the sale, plus the proportionate part of any premium paid by the donor prior to the date of the gift that is applicable to a period subsequent to the date of the gift. As in the prior situation, the deduction in any event cannot exceed an amount equal to the donor's basis in the property. When all other requisite conditions are met, a charitable deduction is available for the remaining premium payments.

3. The insurance policy that is donated is a new one. Thus, there is no charitable deduction for the gift of the policy but, as in the previous circumstance, there is a charitable deduction for the premium payments as made.

If the donor of a life insurance policy retains any incidents of ownership in the policy during lifetime, he or she is not permitted to deduct, for federal income tax purposes, the cost of the premiums as a charitable gift. For example, the IRS ruled that the irrevocable assignment of the cash surrender value of a life insurance policy to a college, with the donor retaining the right to designate the beneficiary and to assign the balance of the policy, whether the policy is paid up and the college is given possession or the policy is not fully paid up and the donor retains possession, constituted a charitable contribution of a partial interest for which a deduction is not allowable (see Chapters 7 and 9). *Incidents of ownership*, in this context, means the right of the insured, or of his or her estate, to the economic benefits of the policy and includes the power to:

- Change the beneficiary
- Surrender the policy
- Cancel the policy
- Assign the policy
- Revoke an assignment
- Pledge the policy for a loan
- Obtain from the insurer a loan against the surrender value of the policy
- Hold a reversionary interest in the policy or its proceeds, whether arising by the express terms of the policy or other instrument or by operation of law, but only if the value of the reversionary interest immediately before the death of the decedent exceeded 5 percent of the value of the policy

If the individual has not changed his or her mind on the subject prior to death, the charitable organization will receive the death benefit. This death benefit will be included in the estate for estate tax calculation purposes, but the estate will receive an estate tax charitable deduction for gifts to charitable organizations (see Chapter 5). Therefore, the death benefit will not create any estate tax burden.

It is not enough, for an income tax charitable deduction to come into existence, simply to cause a charitable organization to be named as the (or a) beneficiary of a life insurance policy. Full ownership rights in the policy must be conveyed for a charitable deduction to be allowed.

If one gives an amount equal to a premium payment to a charitable organization and authorizes the charity to purchase an insurance policy on the donor's life, the value of the gift is greatly multiplied. The charitable organization can use the annual gifts to purchase an insurance policy having a face value that is greater than the annual amounts combined. In this instance, because the charitable organization is the policy owner and the beneficiary, and the donor is merely the insured, the annual gift is a deductible charitable contribution.

From the charitable organization's point of view, two transactions occur each year:

1. Premium dollars plus investment earnings are added to the cash value.
2. The costs of insurance, expense charges, and administrative charges are deducted from the cash value.

The net cash value is available to the charitable organization if there is a current need for cash. Borrowing or withdrawing cash value will, however, reduce the death benefit and require additional future premium payments to keep the policy in force.

This concept can also be utilized effectively when a donor wishes to make a single large contribution. If the amount given is used to purchase life insurance, a much greater gift is likely to result.

The foregoing discussion focused on the direct use of life insurance in the context of charitable giving. One or more donors make a substantial gift to charity (via the insurance death benefit) with relatively small incremental gifts. The charity benefits in that it can use the policy cash values while the donor is alive, although the major portion of the gift is received at the death of the donor.

There are, however, instances of the indirect use of life insurance in the charitable giving setting. An individual may have a valuable parcel of property that produces little income and is not important to his or her financial welfare; at the same time, sale of the property might generate a significant capital gains tax liability. An illustration of this is a tract of raw land that originally had a small cost but has grown substantially in value. Another example is highly appreciated securities that pay little or no dividends. If the individual were to sell this type of property, he or she would have to pay capital gains tax on the gain (the difference between the original cost and the current fair market value of the property).

If this individual made an outright gift of the property to a public charity, the donor's federal income tax charitable deduction would be based on the fair market value of the property (see Chapter 2). The capital gains tax would be avoided. In general, regarding this gift, the individual could deduct an amount up to 30 percent of his or her adjusted gross income, with any excess carried forward up to five immediately succeeding years (see Chapter 4). The tax savings may offset the gift cost; the donor's estate is reduced by the amount of the contribution, so the estate tax burden is reduced.

One major deterrent to a gift of this nature is that the property itself is contributed to charity and is not passed on to the donor's heirs. Life insurance can solve this problem, however, and make it possible for the donor to make a current gift of property to charity. The individual in this situation can make tax-free gifts (currently, up to $11,000 per year per donee) of part or all of the tax savings (see Chapter 5). Adult heirs (assuming they have an insurable interest [see next section]) can purchase life insurance on the donor's life in an amount equal to or greater than the value of the property given to charity. The cost of the insurance is paid by the tax-free gifts they received from the donor.

Two purposes are served by this approach:

1. The heirs receive the same (or approximately the same) economic benefit (by means of life insurance) that they would have received if the gift had not been made.
2. Neither the property given nor the life insurance purchased on the life of the donor by the heirs will be included in the estate of the donor.

The same result can be achieved by the donor's creation of an irrevocable life insurance trust. The donor makes tax-free gifts of the tax savings to an irrevocable trust for the benefit of his or her heirs. The trust purchases life insurance on the donor with the money received from the donor. At the donor's death, the insurance is paid to the trust free of income or estate taxes; it replaces the property given to charity by the donor. (The insurance may be includible in the decedent's estate if the death occurs within three years of the transaction.)

The donor, however, may need income from the property during lifetime. This can be accomplished by the creation of a charitable remainder trust (see Chapter 9). Instead of making an outright gift of property to the charity, the donor transfers the property to this type of a trust. During the donor's lifetime, the donor retains the right to a certain amount of annual income, but at the donor's death, the amount remaining in the trust is paid to the charitable organization or organizations that are the remainder interest beneficiaries. The annual amount payable to the donor must be either a fixed amount of money or a fixed percentage of the trust assets. Payments can be made to the donor for his or her lifetime or for a term of years. If appropriate, the trust can provide for payments for the donor's lifetime and the lifetime of the donor's spouse.

The donor in this circumstance receives a current income tax deduction for the present value of the future gift of trust assets to the charity. A small annual income payment to the donor (and spouse) during lifetime will result in a larger gift to charity, inasmuch as the trust assets will not be as depleted. As a result, the current income tax charitable deduction will be higher. If larger income payments are desired, the current tax deduction will be lower.

To preserve the assets passing to the donor's heirs, the donor can create an irrevocable life insurance trust, make tax-free gifts of the donor's tax savings to the trust, and allow the trust to insure the donor's life. This use of the survivorship whole life policy is ideal if the charitable remainder trust pays an income to both the donor and his or her spouse.

Perhaps an individual cannot afford to contribute a major asset to charity at the time yet wants to provide for income to his or her spouse for life and would like to make a major gift to charity. Life insurance can assist an individual in this situation.

The individual first establishes a charitable remainder unitrust. This trust provides for payment of a fixed percentage of income for the life of the individual and his or her spouse. Then the trust purchases insurance on the donor's life. The trust pays the insurance premiums from annual gifts that the donor makes to the trust. During the donor's lifetime, there is little if any payment to the donor and spouse, since the trust asset is the life insurance policy on the donor. At the donor's death, the trust receives the death proceeds and pays income to the surviving spouse for his or her lifetime. At the death of the spouse, the trust distributes the remaining assets to the charity or charities that are the remainder interest beneficiaries.

This arrangement benefits the donor in two ways. The spouse receives a guaranteed income, and, because a remainder interest is paid to charity, the donor is allowed to deduct a portion of the annual gift of premium payments to the charitable remainder unitrust. In effect, it is a way to purchase life insurance on a partially tax-deductible basis. During his or her lifetime, the donor may be allowed to change the charitable remainder beneficiaries and may revoke the spouse's income interest by a provision to that effect in the donor's will.

Mention was made earlier of the rule concerning employer-provided group-term life insurance. The point was made that such coverage in excess of $50,000 of insurance gives rise to gross income for the employee recipient. There is, however, an exception to that rule pertaining to situations in which a charitable organization is named as the beneficiary of any insurance in excess of the $50,000 threshold.

INSURABLE INTEREST

A contract of insurance—that is, an insurance policy—is valid (enforceable) only when there is an insurable interest between the insured and the beneficiary. Basically, one person has an *insurable interest* in another person when the person who is the beneficiary of the insurance is better off economically with the insured alive rather than dead. Thus, the concept of insurable interest is that the beneficiary would suffer an economic loss if the insured were to die. (Without putting too fine a point on the subject, the insurable interest doctrine emanated from the common law, to prevent an individual from purchasing insurance on the life of another and then seeing to it that the other person's life was terminated soon thereafter. The law evolved the idea of insurable interest to prevent "gambling" on the duration of individuals' lives.) The most common example of a relationship involving insurable interest is the marital relationship; likewise, key individuals are often insured by their companies.

The IRS held that a charitable contribution deduction was not available, for federal income tax purposes, for a donor's payment of premiums for a life insurance policy donated to a charitable organization, when the charity was the sole beneficiary of the policy proceeds. The donor was characterized by the IRS as conceding that the charitable organization involved lacked an insurable interest in the donor's life.

The IRS view in this regard was based on two doctrines of law. One is that the transfer of the policy to the charitable organization was not a transfer of all of the donor's rights associated with it. The IRS characterized the donation as a gift of a partial interest in the policy, not in trust, so a charitable deduction was not available (see Chapters 7 and 9). The interest retained was portrayed as the donor's ability, through a will, to name the heirs who would benefit if the proceeds of the policy were returned to the estate. That is, the IRS relied on the fact that the personal representative of the estate could successfully maintain an action to recover the benefits of the policy and distribute them to others.

The second doctrine of law relied on the by IRS in this case was that a deduction for this type of charitable gift will not be disallowed merely because the interest that passes to, or is vested in, the charity may be defeated by the performance of some act or the happening of some event, if on the date of the gift it appears that the possibility that the act or event will occur is negligible. In the case, the potential for exercise of rights to be retained by the insurance company and by the personal representative of the estate was found to not be remote. Also, the IRS pointed out that the donor could discontinue payments of the premiums on the insurance, causing the policy to lapse unless the charitable organization paid them.

The facts underlying this ruling involved an individual who had previously made gifts to the charitable organization. This individual intended to apply for a life insurance policy and name the charity as the sole beneficiary of the policy proceeds. On receipt of the policy from the insurance company, the individual intended to irrevocably assign the policy to the charity and to continue payment of the insurance policy premiums.

The governing state (New York) insurance law prohibited anyone, without an insurable interest in an insured, from obtaining an insurance policy on the life of another person unless the benefits are to be paid to someone with an insurable interest. As noted, it was conceded that the charitable organization did not have an insurable interest in the donor's life. The intent of the donor to procure the policy and transfer it to the charity, rather than have the charity obtain it directly, was seen as a circumvention of the state law prohibition.

If the transaction was a violation of a state law, then, on the death of the donor, the insurance company might not have had to pay the proceeds of the policy to the charity. Also, if it did, the representative of the estate might have been able to bring a lawsuit to recover the proceeds from the organization and distribute them to other beneficiaries of the estate.

The facts of this ruling involved, as noted, a concession that the charitable organization lacked the requisite insurable interest in the donor. At first thought, it may appear that a charitable organization in these circumstances would benefit more financially with an insured dead than alive—that the charity would be in a preferential position with the insurance proceeds in hand. In many instances, however, this is not so, and a charitable organization will have an insurable interest in the life of a donor of a life insurance policy. For example, the donor may be a valuable volunteer and/or a major donor in other and ongoing respects. There should not always be an assumption that a charitable organization that is the owner (by gift) and beneficiary of a life insurance policy is always economically better off with that donor deceased.

The statutory law of some states has been amended to invest an insurable interest in charitable organizations that are the owners and beneficiaries of donated insurance policies. Indeed, the state involved in this ruling subsequently amended its law, on a retroactive basis, to provide for an insurable interest in charitable organizations with respect to donors of life insurance policies. Thereafter, the IRS revoked its ruling, noting that the individual was not proceeding with the gift.

A state court held that an ex-spouse had an insurable interest in the life of the other ex-spouse, even though the beneficiary ex-spouse also had a substantial interest in the insured's death. This opinion is of particular applicability in connection with the continuing uncertainty as to whether a charitable organization can have an insurable interest in the life of a contributor of a life insurance policy. In this case, the ex-wife wished to purchase insurance on the life of her ex-husband, who was paying alimony to her, to continue a stream of income to her in the event of his demise. The former husband refused to cooperate, however, fearful that his former wife would soon see to his passing; he indicated that he did not want to be "worth more dead than alive" to his former wife. She sued to force him to consent to the purchase of the insurance.

The court found that the ex-wife had an insurable interest in the life of the ex-husband, based on the state's statutory law. The court also decided that, divorce notwithstanding, a former wife who is entitled to alimony has an insurable interest in her former husband's life. The court recognized that the "primary purpose of the prohibition [on life insurance absent insurable interest] is to prevent wagering on the life of another, . . . although, as other authorities recognize, . . . the prevention of murder is another rationale." It quoted another court as writing that the rule as to insurable interest stems from the need to "avoid extending to the beneficiary the temptation to hasten by improper means the time when he [or she] will receive the benefits of the policy." (The court noted the "rancorous history" between the parties, which was cited by the ex-husband as the basis for his position.) The court also found, however, that this ex-wife would have, should she become the beneficiary of the policy, an interest in the ex-husband's death. Instead of finding that that interest obviated any insurable interest, the court recognized a "conflict of interest." That is, the ex-wife was held to have both an interest in the insured's continued life (the insurable interest) and an interest in his death. The court wryly observed that "this conflict might be a fruitful source of crime." This conflict of interest was held to be resolvable by the consent of the would-be insured. The putative insured was said to be able to "evaluate the risk to his own interest" in deciding whether to become an insured. Thus, the case turned on a state statute requiring consent by an insured to the insurance coverage even when the potential beneficiary has an insurable interest in the life of the insured. In the case, the court said that the former husband "empathetically does not consent" to this insurance and that he cannot be compelled to consent; the ex-wife thus was unable to obtain the insurance coverage.

This opinion has a substantial bearing on the matter of insurable interest in the setting of charitable giving. As noted, in the instance of an individual who is a valued volunteer and a major annual contributor to a charitable organization, it would seem that the organization has an insurable interest in this individual's life, at least in connection with the gift of a life insurance policy by him or her. Certainly the charity has an economic interest in the ongoing life of the individual. Being the beneficiary of an insurance policy is not likely to cause someone representing the charity to succumb to, to paraphrase the preceding court opinion, the temptation to hasten by improper means the time when the charity will receive the benefits of the policy.

There is nearly always an interest for a charitable organization in the death of an individual, particularly when that individual is the insured on a life insurance policy of which the charity is the owner and beneficiary. But one of the important aspects of this opinion is that the court did not find that the interest in the beneficiary's death undercut or eliminated the insurable interest; rather, it found that the interest in death *conflicted* with the insurable interest. Thus, this case is authority for the thought that a charity's interest in receiving the proceeds of an insurance policy is not automatically a basis for a finding that there is no insurable interest. As noted, the court found that this conflict of interest can be cured through consent. Obviously, a contributor of an insurance policy to a charity has consented to being an insured when the charity is the beneficiary. Thus, it would seem that if an ex-spouse can have an insurable interest in the life of the other ex-spouse, when the beneficiary ex-spouse also has an economic interest in the demise of the other ex-spouse (that is, when the potential decedent ex-spouse is "worth more dead than alive"), a charitable organization that is an owner/beneficiary of an insurance policy by gift would have an insurable interest as well.

UNRELATED DEBT-FINANCED INCOME CONSIDERATIONS

The investment income resulting from life insurance gift programs has been held to be unrelated business income, which is taxable to otherwise tax-exempt (including charitable) organizations. A court held that loans against the accumulated cash value of life insurance policies constituted indebtedness; therefore, the income derived from reinvestment of the proceeds in marketable securities was treated as income from debt-financed property. The court decided, on the basis of court opinions finding that insurance policy loans are generally regarded as a form of indebtedness and that this type of borrowing has been held sufficient to support a federal income tax interest deduction, that the withdrawals were a form of indebtedness for purposes of the debt-financed income rules.

The court placed great emphasis on the legislative history of the revision of the federal tax law, which disallows a deduction for certain insurance loans. The court wrote, however, that because Congress thus intended to preserve the interest deduction for payments on other types of insurance loans, Congress implicitly considers loans against accumulated cash value of life insurance policies as indebtedness. The court noted that, at the time, federal tax law allowed a deduction for all interest paid or accrued on indebtedness. Consequently, the court reasoned that if a life insurance loan involves an indebtedness in one tax context, it must be an indebtedness in all tax contexts, including the rules for taxation of unrelated debt-financed income.

Universal life insurance offers (or appears to offer) a solution to this problem. As noted, cash value may be withdrawn from universal life policies without creating a policy loan. Thus, a charitable organization could withdraw cash value, reinvest it, and avoid the problem of having the property considered debt-financed property that generates unrelated business income.

CHARITABLE SPLIT-DOLLAR INSURANCE PLANS

Another way in which charitable giving and life insurance interrelate, albeit adversely, is the *charitable split-dollar insurance plan.*

Plans in General

There are several variations of these plans, essentially all of which are now effectively outlawed by the federal tax law, whereby life insurance became the basis for a form of endowment-building in-vestment vehicle for a charitable organization. Under the typical arrangement, one or more contributions of money were made to a charity; the organization used some or all of these funds to pur-chase premiums in connection with a split-dollar insurance policy. The death benefits were shared between the family members of the insured and the charitable organization. Often charities considered this type of arrangement to be a basis for an endowment-building program.

Critics of these plans argued that (1) there was no true gift (and thus no charitable contribution deduction) by reason of the step transaction doctrine (see Chapter 2), because the charity was, as a matter of fact, obligated by the donor to purchase the insur-ance; and (2) the split-dollar arrangement resulted in an unwar-ranted amount of private benefit.

The IRS described the typical charitable split-dollar insurance transaction in this way. There was a transfer of funds by a taxpayer to a charitable organization, with the *understanding* that the charity would use the funds to pay premiums on a cash value life insurance policy that benefited both the charity and the taxpayer's family. Generally the charity or an irrevocable life insurance trust formed by the taxpayer (or a related person) purchased the insurance pol-icy. The designated beneficiaries of the policy included the charity and the trust. Members of the taxpayer's family (and perhaps the taxpayer) were beneficiaries of the trust.

In a "related transaction," the charity entered into a split-dol-lar agreement with the trust. The agreement specified what portion of the insurance policy premiums was to be paid by the trust and what portion was to be paid by the charity. The agreement stated the extent to which each party could exercise standard policy-holder rights, such as the right to borrow against the cash value of the policy, to partially or completely surrender the policy for cash, and to designate beneficiaries for specified portions of the death benefit.

The agreement also specified the manner in which the arrangement could be terminated and the consequences of the ter-mination. Although the terms of these split-dollar agreements var-ied, a common feature was that, over the life of the split-dollar agreement, the trust had access to a "disproportionately high per-centage" of the cash surrender value and death benefit under the policy, compared to the percentage of premiums paid by the trust.

As part of the charitable split-dollar insurance transaction, the taxpayer (or a related person) transferred funds to the charity. Although there might have been no legally binding obligation expressly requiring the taxpayer to transfer funds to the charity to assist in making premium payments or expressly requiring the charity to use the funds for premium payments, both parties usually understood that this will be the outcome.

The structure of charitable split-dollar insurance transactions varied. In some cases, a member of the taxpayer's family, a family limited partnership, or another type of intermediary related to the taxpayer was used as an intermediary rather than an irrevocable life insurance trust.

Charitable Deduction Denial Rules and Penalties

The federal tax law denies an income tax charitable contribution deduction for, and imposes excise tax penalties on, transfers associated with the use of charitable split-dollar insurance plans.

General Rules

There is no federal charitable contribution deduction for a transfer to or for the use of a charitable organization if, in connection with the transfer:

- The organization directly or indirectly pays, or has previously paid, any premium on any personal benefit contract with respect to the transferor, or
- There is an understanding or expectation that any person will directly or indirectly pay any premium on this type of a contract with respect to the transferor.

It is intended that an organization is considered as indirectly paying premiums if, for example, another person pays premiums on its behalf.

A *personal benefit contract* with respect to a transferor is any life insurance, annuity, or endowment contract, if any direct or indirect beneficiary under the contract is the transferor, any member of the transferor's family, or any other person (other than a charity) designated by the transferor. For example, this type of beneficiary includes a trust having a direct or indirect beneficiary who is the transferor or any member of the transferor's family, and includes an entity that is controlled by the transferor or any member of the transferor's family. It is intended that a beneficiary under the contract include any beneficiary under any side agreement relating to the contract.

If a person contributes a life insurance contract to a charity and designates one or more charities as the sole beneficiaries under the contract, generally it is not intended that this deduction denial rule apply. If, however, there is an outstanding loan under the contract as of the transfer of the contract, the person is considered a beneficiary. The fact that a contract also has other direct or indirect beneficiaries (persons who are not the transferor or a family member, or designated by the transferor) does not prevent it from being a personal benefit contract. These rules are not intended to adversely affect situations in which an organization pays premiums under a legitimate fringe benefit plan for employees.

A person is considered an indirect beneficiary under an insurance contract if, for example, the person receives or will receive any economic benefit as a result of amounts paid under or with respect to the contract.

For this purpose, the term *charitable organization* means the same as in the federal income tax charitable deduction setting. Thus, it includes *charities* as that term is used in the tax exemption context, but also encompasses entities such as veterans' organizations and certain fraternal groups.

Charitable Gift Annuities

In the case of a charitable gift annuity (see Chapter 9), if the charitable organization purchases an annuity contract issued by an insurance company to fund its obligation to pay the gift annuity—a practice known as *reinsurance*—a person receiving payments under the annuity arrangement is not treated as an indirect beneficiary as long as these three requirements are met:

1. The charity possesses all of the incidents of ownership under the annuity contract purchased by the charity;
2. The charity is entitled to all the payments under the contract; and
3. The timing and amount of payments under the contract are substantially the same as the timing and amount of payments to each person pursuant to the organization's obligation under the charitable gift annuity contract (as in effect at the time of the transfer to the charity).

In order for the charitable gift annuity to be exempt from insurance regulation by a state, a charitable gift annuity obligation may be issued under the laws of a state that requires each beneficiary under the gift annuity to be named as a beneficiary under an annuity contract issued by an insurance company authorized to transact business in that state. In this situation, the first two requirements just mentioned are deemed met as long as:

- The state law requirement was in effect on February 8, 1999 (see next section);
- Each beneficiary under the charitable gift annuity contract was a bona fide resident of the state at the time the charitable gift annuity was issued; and
- The only persons entitled to payments under the charitable gift annuity contract are persons entitled to payments as beneficiaries under the obligation on the date the obligation is entered into.

Charitable Remainder Trusts

If a charitable remainder trust (see Chapter 9) holds a life insurance, endowment, or annuity contract issued by an insurance company, a person is not treated as an indirect beneficiary under the contract held by the trust solely by reason of being a recipient of income paid by the trust, as long as the trust possesses all of the incidents of ownership under the contract and is entitled to all the payments under the contract. No inference should be made as to the applicability of other provisions of the Internal Revenue Code with respect to the acquisition by the trust of a life insurance, endowment, or annuity contract, or the appropriateness of this type of an investment by a charitable remainder trust.

Nothing in this legislation is intended to suggest that a life insurance, endowment, or annuity contract would be a personal benefit contract solely because an individual who is a recipient of income from a charitable remainder trust uses an income payment to purchase a life insurance, endowment, or annuity contract, and a beneficiary under the contract is the recipient, a member of his or her family, or another person he or she designates.

Excise Tax

This legislation imposes an excise tax on a charitable organization that pays the premiums of any life insurance, annuity, or endowment contract in connection with a transfer for which a deduction is not allowable under the deduction denial rule already described. The tax is equal to the amount of the premiums paid by the organization on any life insurance, annuity, or endowment contract. The tax applies even if all of the direct and indirect beneficiaries under the contract (including any related side agreement) are charities.

Payments are treated as made by the organization if they are made by any other person pursuant to an understanding or expectation of payment. The excise tax is to be applied taking into account rules ordinarily applicable to excise taxes in other exempt organization contexts, such as statute of limitation rules.

Reporting

The legislation requires that the charitable organization annually report the amount of premiums paid during the year that are subject to the excise tax. It must also report the name and taxpayer identification number of each beneficiary under the life insurance, annuity, or endowment contract to which the premiums relate. The IRS has the authority to require the provision of other information. It is intended that a beneficiary include any beneficiary under any side agreement to which the charitable organization is a party or of which it is otherwise aware.

Penalties applicable with respect to tax returns in general apply to returns under this reporting requirement. Returns required under this legislation have to be furnished at such time and in such manner as the IRS requires.

Regulations

The legislation provides for the Treasury Department to promulgate regulations necessary or appropriate to carry out the purposes of the proposal, including regulations to prevent avoidance of the purpose of the proposal. For example, it is intended that the regulations will prevent avoidance of these purposes by inappropriate or improper reliance on the limited exceptions provided for certain beneficiaries under bona fide charitable gift annuities and for certain noncharitable recipients of an annuity or unitrust amount paid by a charitable remainder trust.

No Inference

No inference is intended that a charitable contribution deduction was allowed under preexisting law with respect to a charitable split-dollar insurance arrangement. The legislation did not change the rules with respect to fraud, or civil or criminal penalties under existing law.

IRS Notice

The IRS issued a notice to "alert" taxpayers and charitable organizations about "certain" charitable split-dollar insurance transactions that "purport" to give rise to federal income and gift tax charitable contribution deductions. The IRS advised that "these transactions will not produce the tax benefits advertised by their promoters." The IRS added that promoters of these transactions, and those participating in them (including charities), "may be subject to other adverse tax consequences, including penalties."

The IRS said that, in instances of these transactions, it will apply the *substance-over-form* doctrine. This means that the IRS rejects the contention that the funds transferred to a charity constitute unrestricted gifts, on the ground that no obligation legally binds the charity to make the insurance investment-that is, to pay the policy premiums with the funds. Instead, the IRS presumes a "mutual understanding" among the taxpayer, the charity, and any other related intermediary (such as a life insurance trust).

Thus, the IRS will treat such a transaction as one in which the taxpayer obtains an insurance policy, pays premiums with respect to the policy, and transfers some of the rights under that policy to the intermediary entity and the remaining rights to charity. A person in this context is treated as dividing the rights in the insurance policy between the trust and charity. This is cast as a violation of the partial-interest gift rules, causing disallowance of the charitable deduction (see Chapters 7 and 9). (The argument against application of the partial interest rule is that the donor is not a party to the split-dollar arrangement with the charity.)

The IRS stated that this notice applies to any charitable split-dollar insurance transaction, regardless of whether a trust or some other type of related intermediary is used in the transaction.

Here are the potential sanctions—a formidable array, to be sure—proffered by the IRS:

- Challenge to the tax-exempt status of a participating charity on the basis of private inurement
- Challenge to the tax-exempt status of a participating charity on the ground of impermissible private benefit

- Imposition of the intermediate sanctions penalties on a disqualified person who benefits from the split-dollar insurance transaction, and perhaps on the charity's managers
- Imposition of the private foundation self-dealing rules
- Assessment of the private foundation's taxable expenditures penalties on participating foundations, and perhaps on their managers
- Penalties on the charity if it provides substantiation of a charitable contribution in connection with one of these transactions, on the ground that it is aiding and abetting an understatement of tax liability
- Imposition of the accuracy-related penalty
- Imposition of the return-preparer penalty
- Imposition of the promoter penalty
- Imposition of the penalty for aiding and abetting an understatement of tax liability on participants other than charities

Charitable organizations are required to report participation in these transactions on their annual information returns.

Gift Substantiation

In the case of a charitable contribution of $250 or more, there is no federal charitable income tax deduction unless the donor receives from the charity written substantiation of the gift (see Chapter 12). This document must include various statements, including (assuming it is true) that the donor did not receive from the donee charity, in exchange for the gift, any goods or services. If goods or services were provided by the charity, only the difference between their value and the amount transferred is a deductible charitable gift.

A court held, in a case concerning a charitable split-dollar insurance arrangement (entered into when they were lawful), that the *understanding* between the donor and the charity that amounts of money given to the charity would be invested in one of these arrangements was a *service* for purposes of the gift substantiation rules. The substantiation letter provided to the donor in this case was silent as to this understanding. For that reason, the donor was not allowed any charitable deduction for the transfers of money to the charity. (This decision is of considerable [and understandable] concern to fundraisers in the charitable context, who now apparently must divine the intent of donors, glean the motive for the making of gifts, and reference that intent in the substantiation letters. Compounding this dilemma is the requirement that these goods or services must be assigned—by the charitable donee—a value.)

This aspect of the law remains confusing. This fact was highlighted by a ruling issued by the IRS in 2005. The case concerned a wealthy individual who was instrumental in establishing a tax-exempt school. Part of his assistance to the school was a substantial loan. As time went by, the school became modestly successful but not to the point where this debt could be paid. Desiring repayment, this individual caused a private foundation that he controlled to make a grant to the school, in the precise amount of the debt, with the understanding (that word again) that the school would use the funds to satisfy the debt. The school did precisely that. On the face of it, and following the reasoning of the court decision just described, this would seem to be blatant self-dealing (use of foundation funds for the personal benefit of an insider). Yet the IRS ruled that the transaction did not amount to self-dealing, because the "understanding" was not legally binding on the school, so that legally the school could have expended the grant funds any way it wished. While this is the correct legal analysis, it is diametrically opposite to the position taken by the IRS (and adopted by the court) in the litigation just described.

SUMMARY

This chapter provided a summary of the uses of life insurance in the charitable giving context. The chapter began with an introduction to the concepts involved in life insurance and followed that with a discussion of the charitable giving rules in connection with life insurance. The chapter examined the requirement of insurable interest and also explained the law concerning charitable split-dollar insurance plans. The chapter concluded with an analysis of the applicability of the gift substantiation requirements in this context.

CHAPTER 11

International Charitable Giving

The purpose of this chapter is to describe the legal requirements underlying the U.S. income, gift, and estate tax charitable deductions for gifts to foreign charities made by American individuals. Also described are the methods by which an American company can obtain tax benefits through the practice of overseas corporate giving. Particular attention is given to the utility of a corporate foundation. In this sense, the chapter also discusses the rules governing overseas activities of American private foundations (see Chapter 1), inasmuch as corporate grant-making foundations are generally technically classified as private foundations.

Specifically, this chapter will:

- Explain why in general U.S.-based donors cannot deduct, for income tax purposes, contributions to foreign charities
- Discuss the earmarking and conduit rules
- Summarize applicable law in tax treaties
- Explain the estate and gift tax rules in this context
- Discuss corporate gifts to foreign charities
- Explain the rules pertaining to grants by corporate foundations to foreign charities

INTRODUCTION

National borders do not confine the charitable impulse; persons may contribute to charities located in countries other than their own. Individuals, businesses, private foundations, and other charitable and noncharitable organization in the United States increasingly find the means by which to transfer materials and funds to needy, troubled, and otherwise deserving areas of the world. Although not as simple as domestic giving, international charitable giving is certainly feasible; increases in this type of giving are clearly the way of the future, as both individuals and organizations strive to meet large global social, cultural, and environmental needs.

Some say that the nations of the world are uniting. Others insist that a process of balkanization is under way. Few would deny that the frontiers of the world are being redefined. Attendant to geopolitical changes are internal national restructurings, which are weakening sovereignties that have traditionally financed all social needs. Nearly everyone has been impressed by the deep and critical needs in all sectors of life within, for example, the Central and Eastern European countries. Yet the rise of charitable organizations and the necessity for them is truly an international phenomenon.

In general, contributions by individuals during their lifetime to overseas organizations do not result in a U.S. income tax charitable deduction, because of historic policies that restrict deductibility to charitable activities that essentially relieve (and reduce) expenditures of U.S. public funds. Nonetheless, in certain situations, international gifts will be deductible if the requisite control over their disbursement to foreign charitable organizations and activities is strictly controlled and managed by U.S.–based charitable entities.

The increase in the mobility of managers of multinational companies and the tendency toward retirement in foreign countries have led to greater foreign property ownership. These facts, coupled with the increase in transborder philanthropic activity by residents and businesses in industrialized countries, have greatly expanded the likelihood that transborder charitable mechanisms will be an important part of estate planning.

The extent to which gifts by bequest to foreign charitable organizations will be deductible under the American estate and gift tax schemes (see Chapter 5) is discussed later. These tax provisions do not prohibit the use of funds overseas. Gifts to foreign corporations serving charitable purposes and donations to governmental entities that act as trustees in directing the funds to charitable purposes may be deductible.

BACKGROUND

Prior to passage of the Revenue Act of 1938, U.S. individual taxpayers were allowed to make deductible contributions to charitable organizations irrespective of where the organizations had been created or were located. Corporations did not enjoy this freedom: The Revenue Act of 1936, which first allowed a deduction for corporate charitable contributions, limited that deduction to contributions to organizations established in the United States that used the contributions within the country.

The Revenue Act of 1938 modified the rule regarding contributions by individuals. The act provided that contributions by individuals were deductible only when the recipient was a domestic organization. A congressional committee report declared that the rationale for allowing these deductions was that any loss of tax revenue was seen to be offset by relief of an obligation that otherwise would require public funds. Obviously, gifts to foreign institutions did not produce any of these benefits.

The Revenue Act of 1939 changed the requirement that a qualifying organization be "domestic" to the requirement that it have been "created or organized in the United States or in any possession thereof." In virtually identical form, this requirement was reenacted as part of the subsequent and today's version of the Internal Revenue Code.

Since 1939, the IRS has consistently held that contributions by individuals to or for the use of domestic charitable organizations are deductible even though they are entirely used abroad (subject to the conduit and earmarking restrictions to be discussed). In contrast, gifts made directly to foreign charities are not deductible as charitable contributions because of the requirement that the recipient organization be a domestic entity, that is, a corporation, trust or community chest, fund, or foundation that is established in the United States.

The classification of domestic versus foreign organizations is not necessarily obvious. For example, a court denied a charitable deduction for a direct gift from an American to the First Church of Christ, Scientist, in Berne, Switzerland, a Swiss corporation. The organization's claim to U.S. provenance was grounded on the fact that it was an affiliate of the First Church of Christ, Scientist, in Boston, Massachusetts, a Massachusetts corporation. The court reviewed the organizational documents of the Swiss organization and determined that they negated the contention that the mother church and the Berne branch were inseparable. The Swiss organization was thus held to be legally independent of the American church. Therefore, the individual's contribution to the First

Church of Christ, Scientist, Berne (Switzerland), was held not to be deductible.

In another situation, however, the same court decided in favor of the American donor. In this instance, a school had been created in France under French corporation laws and had operated there for many years before incorporating in Delaware. The IRS maintained that the U.S. corporation had no activities and was merely a shell created to attract tax-deductible American contributions. The court found that the organization was created in the United States by virtue of the Delaware incorporation. Further, the court observed that the organization did not distribute any of its funds to a foreign organization operating a school in France. Rather, the organization itself was found to be operating the Paris school and applied contributions received toward operation of that school. This was sufficient to characterize the entity as a domestic charity for U.S. law purposes, notwithstanding the school's foreign origin. The operational nexus with the U.S. organization, even though essentially technical, was sufficient to distinguish the domestic organization from a mere shell (discussed in the following section).

EARMARKING AND CONDUIT RESTRICTIONS

As discussed, an American individual is not permitted to deduct, for federal income tax purposes, a charitable deduction for a gift that flows directly to a foreign charitable organization, because of fundamental policies underlying the charitable deduction framework. Nonetheless, an American individual may be permitted to make a contribution to an incorporated American charity that devotes some or all of its funds to overseas activities. The ability to claim the deduction depends on the degree of control exerted by the American charitable organization and the lack of control imposed by the donor in directing that the gift be applied to foreign charitable activities.

Following a basic American tax law principle, deductibility of a contribution does not necessarily depend on its payment to a qualifying organization. If the gift is *earmarked* for a further destination, it is appropriate to look beyond the immediate recipient (although a qualifying organization) to determine whether the payment is a charitable contribution that will bring an income tax deduction to the donor.

In one instance, a court considered the question of whether amounts paid to a foster home for the care of a named individual were furnished for the use and benefit of the home and hence qualified as deductible charitable contributions. The earmarking in this instance transformed the gift to the foster home into a gift to a particular individual. In the eyes of the court, the "contributions" were not to be used in any manner as deemed appropriate by the home, but were for the use of a single individual in whom the "donor" felt a keen fatherly and personal interest. The charitable contribution deduction was denied in this circumstance.

The IRS, in applying this principle to transfers of contributions from U.S. sources to foreign organizations, concluded: "A given result at the end of a straight path is not made a different result because reached by following a devious path. Moreover, it seems clear that the requirements of [the federal income tax law] would be nullified if contributions inevitably committed to a foreign organization were held to be deductible solely because, in the course of transmittal to a foreign organization, they came to rest momentarily in a qualifying domestic organization. In such case the domestic organization is only nominally the donee; the real donee is the ultimate foreign recipient."

IRS ruling policy permits a U.S. charitable organization to fund a foreign charitable organization and/or individual when:

- The domestic organization's purpose can be furthered by granting funds to one or more foreign entities;
- The domestic organization has reviewed and approved of the foreign entity's purposes; and
- The grants are paid from general funds rather than from special funds solicited on behalf of the foreign organization

Difficulty arises, from the IRS's point of view, when a domestic charity is empowered in such a way that it is no more than an agent of or trustee for a participating foreign organization; has purposes so narrow that its funds can go only to a particular foreign organization; or solicits funds on behalf of a particular foreign organization.

The IRS has analyzed five situations:

1. A foreign organization that caused a domestic organization to be formed to conduct a fundraising campaign in the United States, pay administrative expenses from the collected funds, and remit any balance to the foreign organization.

2. Certain persons in the United States, desirous of furthering the work of a foreign organization, who formed a domestic charitable organization to receive contributions and
   send them periodically to the foreign organization.

3. A foreign organization and a domestic organization that
   had previously received a ruling from the IRS that contributions to it would be deductible as charitable gifts entered
   into an agreement under which the domestic organization
   was to conduct a fundraising campaign in the United States
   on behalf of the foreign organization, representing to
   prospective contributors that the raised funds would go to
   the foreign organization.

4. A domestic organization that conducts a variety of charitable activities in a foreign country sometimes grants funds
   to a foreign charitable organization to further the domestic organization's purposes. These grants are made for purposes that the domestic organization has reviewed and
   approved, and the grants are made from the organization's
   general funds rather than from a special fund raised on
   behalf of the foreign organization.

5. A domestic organization that does work in a foreign country forms a subsidiary in that country to facilitate its
   operation. The subsidiary was formed for purposes of administrative convenience, and the domestic organization
   controls all facets of its operations. The domestic organization will solicit funds for the specific purpose of carrying
   out its charitable activities in the foreign country, as it did
   before forming the foreign subsidiary, but will not transmit
   the funds directly to the foreign subsidiary.

A common theme in the first three of these cases is that the organizations are charitable organizations nominally created in the
United States. They are organized or operated solely to solicit funds
on behalf of preexisting foreign entities. The domestic entities are effectively agents or *conduit* organizations for the foreign beneficiaries.
As such, contributions to them are not deductible under U.S. law as
charitable gifts. Examples 4 and 5 describe organizations that solicit
funds without any express understanding that the donations will be
forwarded to foreign entities. They are independent organizations
with their own charitable programs. These organizations exercise *discretion and control* over the funds solicited from U.S. sources.
Consequently, gifts to them are deductible. The IRS's view is that the

real donees in the first, second, and third of these situations are the
foreign organizations; hence, contributions ostensibly to the domestic organization are not deductible under U.S. law. In contrast, the
IRS has concluded that contributions to the domestic organizations
in the fourth and fifth situations are deductible as charitable gifts because the domestic organizations in these situations actually received
and essentially controlled the use of the funds.

Thus, the problem of earmarking that arises when the
American donee organization acts as a conduit for the American
donor is resolved when the American organization exercises mean-
ingful *discretion and control* as to the ultimate use of the contributions.

An important test in this regard is who solicited whom: Did
the individual taxpayer seek out the recipient organization's coop-
eration to facilitate application of the funds to a designated project, or did the American donee organization seek the donor's
support of a project identified by the organization? When the recipient charitable organization designates the overseas use of the
funds, the donor's contribution produces an allowable deduction.
The donor may choose from among overseas uses presented as options by the charitable organization. When, however, the donor
identifies a desired overseas use, and employs the charitable organization as a funding agent or conduit, the gift is not allowed as
a charitable deduction to the donor.

The IRS, in its private letter rulings, is attempting to add another criterion in this context, which is that the grantor of funds is
expected to undertake some form of *expenditure responsibility*. For example, in one of these rulings, the IRS observed that the board of
directors of the grantor organization was to "review" and "monitor"
the use of the granted charitable funds. In another private ruling,
the IRS wrote of a requirement of "periodic accounting" for the
monies granted; in this ruling, the IRS found the requisite control,
in part because of a monitoring procedure. Monitoring is also mentioned in other private letter rulings. Since this series of private letter rulings began, the IRS has mentioned the control element as
the singular factor on only one occasion.

CONTROL OVER FOREIGN DONEES

The IRS clarified the matter of what constitutes adequate control
of the donated funds. This guidance discussed a situation in which
a domestic charitable organization solicited contributions in the

United States for a specific project of a foreign counterpart organization. The charity's charter provided that, in furtherance of its educational, scientific, and charitable purposes, it had the power to receive and to allocate contributions—within the discretion of the board of directors—to any organization organized and operated exclusively for charitable or educational purposes within the meaning of the U.S. tax law. The board of directors exercised effective review of the project before approving any funding. The board monitored the foreign distributing organization's ongoing adherence to the domestic charity's goals. Notwithstanding that the donations were technically "earmarked," the domestic organization demonstrated that it exercised full control over the donated funds and retained substantial responsibility as to their use. These standards entail more than merely being able to decide whether to contribute and being able to require the foreign recipient to furnish a periodic accounting. In its decision, the IRS referred to an earlier ruling holding that, when gifts to a charitable organization were not earmarked by the donor for a particular individual, the deduction would be allowable if it was established that a gift was intended by the donor for the use of the organization and not actually as a gift to a specific individual for whose benefit the gift would be used by the donee organization. The test, said the IRS, is whether the organization retains full control of the donated funds to ensure that they will be used to carry out the organization's own charitable purposes.

The conclusion in another IRS pronouncement was that, because the trustees of the subject organization were unable to state that all the funds would be used in the United States, they did not have sufficient control and discretion over the use of any contributions made to foreign distributees. The problem in this case was that the domestic organization did not seem to have any formal operating system by which it could control the selection of projects to be funded—it had no means of effective supervision over the use of the funds for a project, nor the ability to withhold or control the funds once committed. In this regard, the IRS concluded that it appeared that the domestic organization was intending to remit the monies to the foreign distributee before even considering possible projects and then discussing with the foreign organization the possible uses of its funds. Thus, the operating procedures and inability of the domestic organization to supervise the use of funds by the foreign organization did not evidence that degree of control and discretion required under the law.

The IRS presented another analysis of the control and accountability requirement. This ruling discussed a domestic charity formed to address the problem of plant and wildlife ecology in a foreign country through programs that included grants to foreign private organizations. The domestic charity maintained control and responsibility over the use of any funds granted to a foreign organization by first making an investigation of the purpose to which the funds were to be directed; by then entering into a written agreement with the recipient organization; and ultimately by making site visits to see that the agreement was being followed. Any foreign organization that received financial assistance from the charitable organization had to be organized and operated in a manner analogous to a U.S. tax-exempt charitable organization and be completely independent of foreign governments. The charitable organization exercised accountability for the funds dispensed to these programs. Accordingly, it was held that contributions to the organization were deductible as charitable gifts.

In yet another illustration of this form of control and accountability, the IRS considered a domestic association that was organized for the relief of poor, distressed, and displaced persons of certain countries. This domestic association was incapable of listing in advance the names of the ultimate recipients of the monies it would turn over to a foreign organization. Even though the foreign organization promised to use the funds for humanitarian purposes, such as furnishing food, clothing, shelter, and medical supplies and services for distressed persons, and even though both the foreign organization and its distributees were required to account for the use of the funds, there was too little discretion and control by the domestic organization to meet these standards.

Conversely, a tax-exempt charitable organization does not jeopardize its exemption by making controlled distributions assuredly in furtherance of its own exempt purposes to organizations that are not themselves tax-exempt as charitable entities. "We do not believe this [tax-exempt] status of the distributees is a requirement for the distributor's qualifications" as a charitable organization, the lawyers for the IRS observed. They added: "It can be readily understood that such status for the foreign distributee is a safeguard for insuring that charitable funds will be expended solely in furtherance of charitable purposes."

In reaching its conclusion in this particular case, the IRS emphasized that the domestic organization did not know how the funds would be used. This IRS pronouncement additionally stated that it may not be necessary for a domestic charitable organization to know in advance the precise nature of ultimate distributees to ensure that its qualification as a charitable entity is not jeopardized, if it can establish that its methods of operation include these types of procedures:

- The domestic charitable organization apprises its agents, at the outset, of the limitations imposed by U.S. law with respect to eligible recipients of its funds and makes clear to its agents that they are subject to the same limitations in distributing its funds.
- The domestic charitable organization reviews proposed projects in detail, and approves those reasonably calculated to accomplish one or more of its qualified charitable objectives, before turning over any funds to its agents for expenditure for these purposes.
- The domestic charitable organization turns over funds to its agents only as needed for specific projects. This form of expenditure control encourages compliance with the dictates of the domestic organization.
- The domestic charitable organization, or an independent agent selected by it for the purpose, makes periodic audits of programs and requires periodic financial statements by its agents. This continuing review assures that the charitable funds in question are not being misspent.

Adoption of these guidelines, as subsequently cited with approval by the IRS, can strengthen the case for the deductibility of contributions as charitable gifts.

Consequently, although the requirements of the U.S. tax law with respect to tax exemption as a charitable organization and deductibility of charitable gifts are parallel in many respects (see Chapter 1), they are not identical. In some situations, contributions to or for the use of a foreign organization are not deductible for income tax purposes because the domestic organization requirement is not met. As for a domestic organization that serves as a conduit for a foreign charitable organization, contributions to the domestic organization are no more deductible as charitably gifts than if they had been made directly to the foreign organization.

In most other situations, these two provisions operate in parallel. If a domestic organization transmits its funds to a foreign private organization but retains the required control and discretion over the funds—as detailed in examples 4 and 5 of the IRS ruling discussed earlier—contributions to the domestic organization will be deductible as charitable gifts. Conversely, a domestic organization otherwise qualified as a charitable entity forfeits its qualification for tax-exempt and charitable donee status if it regularly transmits its funds to any organization that is not described in the U.S. rules for charitable organizations, because it then cannot demonstrate that it is operated exclusively for charitable purposes. Further, if the domestic organization fails to exercise discretion and control over the use of funds transmitted to a foreign organization, to assure their use exclusively for purposes that qualify as charitable under U.S. law, those contributions to it will not be deductible.

INCOME TAX TREATIES

In connection with the international law aspects of the federal income tax, income tax treaties often must be considered, in addition to the principles of U.S. tax law as set forth in the Internal Revenue Code, regulations, rulings, and court opinions. The United States is a party to more than 50 income tax treaties, although most of them do not contain provisions relevant to the deductibility of cross-border contributions. Indeed, the U.S. prototype income tax treaty is silent on the subject.

    The income tax treaty between the United States and Canada provides that contributions by a citizen or resident of the United States to an organization that is resident in Canada and is generally exempt from Canadian tax are treated as charitable contributions, but only if the organization could qualify in the United States to receive deductible contributions if it were organized in the United States. Generally, the amount of these contributions made deductible by the treaty is limited to the income of the U.S. citizen or resident arising in Canada. The percentage limitations applicable to the deductibility of charitable contributions (see Chapter 4) apply after the limitations established by the treaty. Any amounts treated as charitable contributions that are in excess of amounts deductible in a tax year may generally be carried over and deducted in subsequent tax years.

    The income tax treaty between the United States and Mexico has similar rules as to deductibility of charitable contributions. This treaty also contains rules by which charitable organizations in

Mexico can be recognized, for U.S. law purposes (including charitable giving), as public charities. The U.S. Department of the
Treasury's technical explanation of the treaty includes this statement: "The provisions [of the treaty] were considered a desirable
way to encourage contributions by U.S. residents to small Mexican
charities that would have difficulty in organizing a U.S. entity
through which contributions could be directed." This explanation
added that the treaty "also enables taxpayers living and operating
at the border to support organizations across the border from
which they derive benefits," and observed that the "physical proximity of Mexico and the United States provides a unique circumstance for the reciprocal recognition of tax-exempt organizations."

ESTATE AND GIFT TAX CONSIDERATIONS

The treatment of gifts and bequests under U.S. estate and gift tax
provisions does not limit the use of funds overseas. The federal estate tax deduction and the federal gift tax deduction (see Chapter 5)
permit bequests and gifts by U.S. residents to foreign organizations
for charitable purposes. For estate and gift tax purposes, an individual is considered to be a resident of the Unite States if that individual maintains his or her domicile in the United States at the time of
death or at the time of the gift, whichever is applicable.

The federal estate tax charitable deduction provision is similar to the federal income tax charitable deduction provisions in allowing deductions for gifts to U.S. governmental entities but not to
foreign governmental units. Unlike the income tax rule, however,
the federal estate tax rule permits deductions for bequests to charitable trusts without the requirement that the trusts be domestic
organizations.

In the case of a nonresident who is not a U.S. citizen, gifts will
be subject to the gift tax if they are not made to a domestic charitable corporation. A gift made to any charitable trust, community
chest, fund, or foundation, by a nonresident who is not a citizen
must be used exclusively within the United States.

ESTATE TAX RULES

Federal tax law allows an unlimited charitable deduction from the
gross estate of a U.S. citizen or resident decedent for transfers to
qualifying donees for public, charitable, educational, religious, and

other similar purposes. The estate tax provisions do not restrict qualifying donees to domestic charitable organizations. Under certain circumstances, transfers to foreign governments for charitable purposes may be allowed.

Transfer to Foreign Corporation Serving Charitable Ends

An estate tax deduction is allowed for transfers to or for the use of "any corporation" organized and operated exclusively for religious, charitable, scientific, literary, or educational purposes, including the encouragement of art, or to foster national or international amateur sports competition, and the prevention of cruelty to children or animals.

It is significant to note that this provision of law refers to transfers "to or for the use of any corporation" and does not limit the contemplated transfers to American corporations. The accompanying regulations reflect this provision in referring to "any corporation or association."

To qualify as a suitable donee corporation, the foreign organization must meet certain standards. For example, the foreign organization must satisfy the prohibitions against private inurement and political campaign activities. The lobbying restriction applicable to domestic tax-exempt charitable organizations extends to foreign associations as well.

This body of law does not define with precision when an organization will be considered "organized and operated exclusively for religious, charitable, scientific, literary or educational purposes." The statutory language of the estate tax deduction provision is, however, parallel to that of the income tax deduction provision.

Generally, the term *charitable* is construed in its common law sense and includes, among other concepts:

- Relief of the poor and distressed or of the underprivileged
- Advancement of religion
- Advancement of education or science

The concept of what constitutes a foreign charitable corporation was discussed in a court opinion. A charitable deduction had been claimed for a proportional residuary bequest to a governmentally owned Canadian hospital, as a nonprofit organization operated exclusively for the purpose of providing care for the sick and for medical educational facilities. The gift was determined to qualify for an estate tax charitable deduction under the provision that allows a deduction for bequests to charitable corporations. In this case, involving a private hospital that had been turned over to a city, the hospital was found not to be a political subdivision in the sense that it was either a political unit or an integral governmental instrumentality exercising sovereign powers. Rather, the court determined that the hospital was a nonintegral governmental instrumentality, a clear counterpart of a private charitable corporation organized and operated exclusively for charitable purposes.

The IRS, from time to time, issues rulings concerning the qualification of a charitable contribution to a foreign corporation for the federal estate tax charitable deduction. When a decedent is not a resident or citizen of the United States, the estate is subject to a tax on the transfer of the taxable estate that is situated in the United States at the time of death. There is a deduction from the value of the taxable estate for bequests to a corporation organized and operated for charitable purposes; this deduction is limited to transfers to entities created in, and to trustees for use within, the United States. This deduction may not exceed the value of the transferred property required to be included in the gross estate. The statutory law on this subject is not overridden by U.S. tax conventions with other countries.

Transfer to Foreign Government Serving Public Purposes

An estate tax charitable deduction is allowed for transfers to or for the use of the United States, any political subdivision thereof, or the District of Columbia, for exclusively public purposes. Although a transfer to a U.S. governmental subdivision for its general or public purposes would qualify for the deduction, the same gift to a foreign government would not.

In the facts of one court case, an individual died, having bequeathed his entire estate to the Hammer School District of Vrads Parish in Denmark, "to be used by said school district in any manner it may wish for the betterment of the schools or aid to the students of said district." In determining whether a U.S. estate tax deduction for the gift was allowable, the court referred to the statutory language. The court specifically chose to determine whether the Danish school district was a political subdivision of a foreign government, not whether it was a corporation. Although the

Danish school district was a corporation operated exclusively for educational purposes, the law limits deductible bequests to political subdivisions to those that are subdivisions of the American government. Thus, the court held that this bequest was not deductible for estate tax purposes.

Transfer to Trustee

An estate tax charitable deduction is allowed for "contributions or gifts to a trustee or trustees . . . to be used by such trustee or trustees . . . exclusively for religious, charitable, scientific, literary or educational purposes, or for the prevention of cruelty to children or animals." The question of whether a bequest to a foreign governmental body, to be used exclusively for charitable purposes, could be deductible as a bequest to a foreign charitable trust has arisen. A growing body of federal case law holds that a bequest to a foreign governmental entity can be instilled with a charitable purpose. In such a case, it would be deductible under the rule concerning bequests to a trustee for charitable purposes.

The two courts that have considered this matter subsequent to this court opinion have expressly rejected the first court's rationale and have adopted another approach to statutory construction. Both cases involved bequests to foreign governmental units. Both courts applied this rule, allowing a deduction for a bequest to a trustee for exclusively charitable purposes. The precedent was therefore set that a transfer to a foreign government, subdivision, or instrumentality may qualify for the estate tax charitable deduction, provided it is restricted exclusively for charitable purposes and the government subdivision acts in a fiduciary capacity.

In another case, the question was whether a clause in the will of an individual constituted a charitable trust and thus qualified as an allowable deduction in the computation of New York state taxes. A controversial paragraph in the decedent's will provided for a gift of valuable coins to the State of Israel on the condition that they be exhibited in a museum. The State of Israel, of course, is not a domestic governmental body as defined under the law, nor is it a corporation organized and operating exclusively for charitable purposes as described in the law. Thus, the claimed deduction had to stand under the rule concerning gifts to a trustee for a charitable purpose. Whereas the bequest in the earlier case had been given outright to a Danish city school district, the coin collection in this case had been donated to a governmental subdivision to be maintained in trust for the decedent. In drawing a line between what Congress may have intended in limiting an estate tax deduction for gifts made directly to foreign governments and those given "in trust" to foreign governments for charitable purposes, the court in this case relied on the reasoning in another court opinion.

In that case, a devise (bequest) had been made to the "mayor and magistratsraete of Fuerth, Bayern, Germany to be used and expended for the benefit of said City of Fuerth." A majority of the court refused to apply the reasoning of the prior court opinion and, although the court disallowed the deduction because the bequest was left to a foreign city outright and not in trust, it noted in its ruling that "contributions and gifts to foreign cities for exclusively charitable purposes are deductible," notwithstanding the political nature of the trustee.

The majority and dissent in this case emphasized that Congress logically could have differentiated between public purposes that could be advanced only under the general estate tax deduction rule and the charitable purposes contemplated under the rule concerning bequests to a charitable trustee. The court wrote that the use of the word *public* showed a "Congressional intention to bring within the statutory exemption gifts which could be used for such standard governmental functions as the payment of salaries to policemen and firemen." The court added: "We think there is a clear indication that Congress considered that many contributions which would benefit domestic municipalities are not charitable, because the exemption permits different and broader uses of a bequest than those which are exclusively for charitable purposes."

Following these court decisions, the IRS announced that a deduction is allowable under the estate tax rules with respect to a transfer of property to a foreign government or political subdivision thereof for exclusively charitable purposes. The IRS noted the earlier court decision but looked to the more recent decisions, which had concluded that when the use of property is limited to exclusively charitable purposes, a gift by bequest to a foreign government body or political subdivision will qualify for a charitable deduction.

The essence of this IRS announcement was the basis of a subsequent court opinion involving the reformation of a provision in a will. The decedent, according to the court, had intended the municipality of Kerasitsa, Greece, rather than his children, to be the ultimate heir of a hospital, built there from proceeds of the sale of his U.S. real estate. The court generally restated the IRS position: The IRS "makes no argument that if we find the remainder interest vested in some entity other than decedent's heirs that the bequest is still outside the bounds of . . . [the federal estate tax charitable deduction]. Petitioner asserts that the decedent intended for the hospital to pass to the village government upon its completion and that this intent establishes the charitable nature of the bequest."

A further demonstration of the utility of the IRS position appears in an IRS private letter ruling. A court attempted to reform a bequest to meet the estate tax law requirements. The IRS determined, however, that for the taxpayer to be able to re-form a nonqualifying charitable remainder trust, the beneficiary designated in the will had to be an organization or purpose described or defined in the law of charity. The State of Israel had been named as the beneficiary. The IRS announced: "If the beneficiary designated in the will had been a . . . [charitable] organization or purpose, the trust established under the decedent's will, as conformed by a probate court order, would have constituted a charitable remainder annuity trust."

In another instance, an executor of an estate attempted to salvage a bequest of residuary property given in trust to a foreign government. The foreign country acknowledged that the bequest would be used for an agricultural high school in that country. The issue was whether the actual charitable use to which the funds were to be applied would qualify the gift for the deduction when in fact the will had not specifically so directed. The IRS concluded that the "fact [that the foreign country] has agreed to use its gift for charitable purposes does not convert an otherwise general gift into a charitable gift."

Testamentary Charitable Remainder Trusts

A charitable organization to or for the use of which the remainder interest passes must meet the requirements for the estate tax deductions as well as the remainder trust rules (see Chapter 9). Therefore, the charitable entity to which the remainder interest in a charitable remainder trust passes may not be a foreign corporation.

GIFT TAX RULES

The federal tax law allows an unlimited gift tax charitable deduction for gifts to qualifying donees. This deduction is not subject to the percentage limitations applicable to the income tax charitable deduction.

Although a donor may be willing to forgo an income tax charitable deduction in order to benefit a foreign charitable organization, care should be taken to ensure that the donor does not inadvertently make a taxable gift. The rules governing the gift tax charitable deduction are similar to those applicable to the estate tax charitable deduction: A gift tax deduction is not limited to gifts to or for the use of domestic charitable corporations.

CHARITABLE GIVING BY NONCITIZEN NONRESIDENTS

Estate Tax Rules

When the decedent is a nonresident who is not a citizen of the United States, the federal tax law allows a charitable deduction from the nonresident's U.S. gross estate for transfers to qualifying donees "to or for the use of the United States, any political subdivision thereof, or the District of Columbia" for exclusively public purposes: "charitable, educational, religious and other similar purposes." The deduction is limited to transfers to domestic charitable corporations and transfers to trustees for use in the United States.

Transfers to a foreign government for exclusively charitable purposes do not qualify for the federal estate tax deduction. Transfers to foreign organizations, including foreign governments, exclusively for charitable purposes may be deductible as a transfer to a trustee, provided the funds are restricted to use within the United States.

An individual (a citizen and resident of Ontario, Canada) provided in his will for a bequest to be used to pay tuition and related expenses of Canadian students at a college in the United States. The court held that the bequest was "to a trustee or trustees . . . to be used within the United States," since the funds were to be expended in the United States. Hence the decedent's estate was held to be entitled to the claimed deduction for a charitable contribution.

Gift Tax Rules

A gift of real property or tangible personal property situated in the United States, made by a nonresident who is not a citizen, is subject to the federal gift tax. The gift tax charitable deduction provisions that apply to nonresidents who are not citizens parallel the estate tax provisions. A gift tax charitable deduction is allowed for gifts to domestic organizations for charitable purposes and gifts to trustees for charitable purposes within the United States.

CORPORATE GIFTS TO U.S. CHARITY FOR OVERSEAS USE

A dynamic aspect of the global market environment is the extension of corporate philanthropy practiced by American companies doing business abroad. U.S. tax law imposes certain limitations on overseas charitable giving, depending on the character of the donor and the donee. These constraints are by no means barriers to transborder corporate giving. A U.S. corporation that is planning to conduct philanthropic activities in a foreign country has several methods available for transferring contributions abroad.

A U.S. corporation may deduct up to 10 percent of its pretax net profits for gifts made to U.S. charitable corporations, as charitable contributions (see Chapter 4), even though the gift may ultimately be used overseas. Certain adjustments to pretax net profits are required for purposes of this computation. A corporate charitable contribution may be used for overseas purposes if it is made to an organization that is incorporated under American laws and qualified as a charitable entity. In contrast, a gift to an unincorporated trust, chest, fund, or foundation is deductible only if it is to be used within the United States or its possessions. A corporate contribution that is made directly to a tax-exempt organization established under the laws of any foreign country, even if the recipient has charitable status under U.S. law, does not qualify for a charitable deduction.

Because organizations such as the American National Red Cross, the United Way, and the Salvation Army were established and incorporated in the United States, they are frequently used by corporations for facilitating foreign giving objectives. Overseas giving achieved through the mechanism of support of U.S. organizations with charitable status raises no legal or procedural questions not already contemplated in a domestic giving program.

Another category of international agencies that is useful for this purpose are the *private voluntary organizations*, which receive their principal support from the U.S. Agency for International Development. Agencies such as CARE, Save the Children Fund, American Friends Service Committee, Overseas Education Fund, and the Population Council are private voluntary organizations.

Typically, these agencies address large problems in developing countries, such as disaster relief and food aid. Because they are qualified as tax-exempt charitable organizations under U.S. law, they are able to receive charitable donations to be applied to their foreign charitable activities.

GIFT OF GOODS OR SERVICES TO BENEFIT
FOREIGN CHARITY

A company may choose to support charitable endeavors by making expenditures from its marketing or advertising budgets. In this situation, funds benefiting charitable organizations overseas may be able to flow through the business expense budget category and be deductible as a business expense under U.S. tax law. This law, however, disallows a business expense deduction of any amount that meets the definition of a charitable contribution but cannot be deducted under that section because of the percentage limitations, dollar limitations, or time-of-payment requirements. These expenditures are sponsorship of broadcasts or concerts of performing arts groups, museum exhibits, public service advertising in support of a charitable cause, purchase of tickets to fundraising events, and other activities that directly or indirectly promote sales of a company's products or services through association with cultural or other charitable activities. To qualify for deduction as business expenses, the corporation must be prepared to justify how the expenditures in fact promote the corporation's business interests.

In-kind gifts of company products are also deductible. Examples include pharmaceutical products that are sent to an overseas hospital or computer equipment that is given to a school. The amount of the deduction for such gifts is governed by the general rules applicable to gifts for use outside the United States. There are special rules relating to gifts of inventory, by virtue of which the deduction may be as great as twice the cost basis inherent in the donated property (see Chapter 6). In general, the rules concerning gifts of tangible personal property allow a donor to deduct only the acquisition cost of the property, rather than the current fair market value, if the property is of a type the donor normally sells in its business.

Another method of supporting a charity is to make in-kind gifts of the use of a corporation's facilities or personnel. This type of charitable giving includes occupancy of surplus office space, use of corporate printing or computer facilities, and loan of corporate staff services. As expenses of these facilities and personnel would have been incurred regardless of the donation, the expenses associated with this type of giving are deductible under U.S. law as business expenses. (There is no U.S. charitable deduction for gifts of the use of property or for gifts of services [see Chapters 7 and 8].)

GRANTS OF FUNDS FROM U.S. CORPORATION–RELATED FOUNDATIONS TO FOREIGN CHARITY

Large American corporations often consider establishing overseas foundations. The current practice, however, is that an American company with an established philanthropic program makes its outbound grants through its U.S. corporate foundation. A corporate foundation is almost always a private foundation under U.S. law (see Chapter 1). Nothing in the U.S. tax statutes or regulations prohibits overseas grant-making by private foundations.

Taxable Expenditures

Of considerable concern to a private foundation is avoidance of making a taxable expenditure while engaging in grant-making. U.S. law categorizes certain types of expenditures as taxable ones if made by private foundations, and it levies significant penalties for engaging in these practices.

The term *taxable expenditure* means any amount paid or incurred by a private foundation

1. As a grant to an organization unless:

   The organization is a public charity or an exempt operating foundation, or

   The private foundation exercises *expenditure responsibility* with respect to the grant, or
2. For any purpose other than a charitable purpose.

The penalty for making a taxable expenditure begins at 10 percent of the expenditure against the foundation and 2.5 percent (maximum $5,000) against any foundation manager (such as a trustee or officer) who agreed to the expenditure. If the expenditure is not timely *corrected*, the penalty increases to 100 percent against the foundation and 50 percent (maximum $10,000) against the foundation manager.

To avoid exposure to taxable expenditure liability, a private foundation must make two preliminary determinations with regard to an overseas grant:

1. Whether the grant is for a charitable purpose
2. Whether the private foundation must exercise expenditure responsibility with respect to the grantee organization because it is not a public charity

Charitable Purpose

The U.S. regulatory scheme surrounding transborder grant-making parallels the rules concerning domestic grant-making. The most basic concept in this regard is that of *charitable purpose.* A grant to a charitable organization will not, in itself, satisfy the requirement. A grant that is specifically designated for a charitable purpose, however, but made to an organization that is not charitable can qualify.

To qualify as an eligible grantee, an organization must be organized and operated exclusively for religious, charitable, scientific, literary, or educational purposes; to foster amateur sports competition; or for the prevention of cruelty to children or animals. The emphasis is not on the structure of the organization; it is on the charitable purposes served.

Expenditure Responsibility

The U.S. tax law requires *expenditure responsibility* of private foundations to ensure that their grants are spent solely for the purpose for which they were made, and that full and complete reports on how the funds were spent are submitted to the grantor by the grantee. This body of law requires private foundations to exercise expenditure responsibility with respect to grants to certain organizations.

As noted, foundation grants to public charities need not be the subject of expenditure responsibility. If the prospective grantee is a charitable organization other than a public charity or qualified operating foundation, though, expenditure responsibility must always be exercised.

In making the determination that the prospective grantee organization is publicly supported, a private foundation must obtain documentation of the sources of the prospective grantee's financing. The prospective grantee must also inquire whether the proposed grant would reduce the general public and/or government support below the required level of public support to qualify as a publicly supported charity, thus changing (or *tipping*) the grantee from status as a public charity to a private charity.

If the grantee is a public charity and will remain so even with the proposed grant, the answer to the question as to whether the private foundation will have to exercise expenditure responsibility depends on the nature of the organization under several categories established in U.S. tax law.

Determination of whether expenditure responsibility is required for grants to overseas donees takes these five forms:

1. When the grant is made to a governmental unit, expenditure responsibility is generally not required.
2. When the IRS has determined that an organization is publicly supported, expenditure responsibility is generally not required.
3. Whether or not the organization has been classified by the IRS as publicly supported or substantiated by its legal counsel as the equivalent of a publicly supported organization, expenditure responsibility is generally not required if two conditions are met:

    The organization, according to the reasonable judgment of the foundation manager, establishes that it is the equivalent of a publicly supported organization.

    Supporting data are in the form of an affidavit or legal opinion provided by the donee organization's legal counsel.

4. If the organization is a tax-exempt charitable organization by virtue of an IRS determination, but is not publicly supported, or if legal counsel has submitted an opinion that the organization is an equivalent of a tax-exempt charitable organization but does not qualify as the equivalent of a publicly supported organization, expenditure responsibility must be exercised.
5. Otherwise, expenditure responsibility is mandatory. A further safeguard is required: Grant funds must be segregated into a separate accountable fund.

If the determination is made that expenditure responsibility must be exercised, the foundation must conduct a pregrant inquiry of the potential grantee. This requirement entails a "limited inquiry . . . complete enough to give a reasonable man assurance that the grantee will use the grant for the proper purposes." Six criteria are usually sufficient to satisfy the pregrant inquiry:

1. Basic institutional character (such as educational institution and research institution)
2. Names and titles of officers and managers
3. Tax status of the proposed grantee in its country of origin
4. Any previous grant history with the private foundation
5. Summary of information reflecting the proposed grantee's accountability
6. Private foundation's analysis of the suitability of the proposed grantee for the requested funds

When a foundation is satisfied that the grantee will use the grant for its stated purposes, the actual grant must be accompanied by an agreement to be signed by an officer of the grantee organization, specifically covering limitations on the grant and providing the grantee's assurance of its intended compliance with all conditions.

Overseas Grantee Categories

For both the *charitable purpose* determination and the analysis as to whether expenditure responsibility is necessary, the character of the grantee organization is important. Fundamentally, four categories of grantee organizations may be recipients of grants from U.S. private foundations:

1. Foreign governmental units that do not have the status of tax-exempt charitable entities under U.S. law
2. Foreign organizations that have obtained recognition as tax-exempt charitable organizations under U.S. law
3. Foreign organizations that are recognized as "equivalent to" American tax-exempt charitable organizations
4. Foreign organizations that are within none of the preceding three categories

Governmental units are entities such as agencies and instrumentalities of foreign governments and other international agencies. The terms *foreign government* and *agency of a foreign government* are used throughout U.S. tax law in their generally accepted sense, including a state or local ministry or department or a bureau or office of a ministry or department. An *instrumentality* of a government unit is slightly more complex. Taken in its generally accepted meaning, an *instrumentality* would be an entity furthering the purposes financed by a government unit, such as a school or university.

To document the classification of an organization as an instrumentality of a government, a foundation manager is advised to obtain information in three areas:

1. A copy of the document by which the organization was created (termed *articles of organization*), describing its purposes.
2. A copy of documentation stating that the organization is exempt from taxation. In some cases, this documentation will consist of a certificate from an appropriate ministry. When the organization is exempt from taxation because it belongs to a general class of organizations, a written statement from the taxation authorities acknowledging tax exemption is recommended. In systems where this is unobtainable, a legal opinion describing the nexus between this particular grantee organization and the classification of tax-exempt organizations will be satisfactory.
3. Further documentation provided by the organization's legal counsel in affidavit form that details the source(s) of the organization's operating funds.

The term *public international organizations* is used to describe international organizations that are composed of governments as members and are designated as international organizations by executive order. Examples of these organizations are the United Nations, the International Chamber of Commerce, the World Bank, and the World Health Organization. Should a private foundation seek to make a grant to an organization composed of governments but not so designated, it is advised to follow the procedure for establishing that the organization is an instrumentality of a government, as summarized previously.

An American private foundation should not automatically assume that a governmental unit's use of a proposed grant will be for a charitable purpose. This must be established by documents supporting the grant application.

Grants to governmental units are generally made for the purpose of carrying out educational, charitable, or social programs. The fact that the grant is made to a governmental unit supervising the pursuit of these activities is not necessarily conclusive, and care should be taken to ascertain that the particular grant supports the stated charitable purpose.

U.S. law provides that expenditure responsibility is not required if the grant is made to "a foreign government, or any agency or instrumentality thereof, or an international organization designated as such by [e]xecutive [o]rder . . . , even if it is not" a tax-exempt charitable organization. Nonetheless, this body of law also states that "any grant to an organization referred to in this subparagraph must be made exclusively for charitable purposes."

Grants to Charitable Organizations and Equivalents

The determination letter issued by the IRS, recognizing an organization to be a tax-exempt charitable entity, establishes that the IRS has found the organization to be in pursuit of charitable purposes. This letter reflects the IRS's findings that:

- The organization is organized and operated exclusively for religious, charitable, scientific, testing for public safety, literary, or educational purposes; to foster national or international amateur sports competition; or for the prevention of cruelty to children or animals
- No part of the net earnings of the organization inures to the benefit of any private shareholder or individual
- No substantial part of the organization's activities is the carrying on of propaganda programs or otherwise attempting to influence legislation
- No part of the organization's activities is participating in or intervening in any political campaign on behalf of or in opposition to any candidate for public office

U.S. law permits foreign organizations to qualify for recognition of tax exemption. The tax exemption provision merely refers to "an organization described in" appropriate categories as being tax-exempt, and another provision of law refers specifically to restrictions on foreign organizations that can obtain tax exemption as charitable organizations. U.S. law defines *private foundation* as "a domestic or *foreign* organization" that is a charitable entity.

According to the IRS, more than 500 foreign organizations, predominantly in the fields of education, agriculture, and health, have sought determination of exempt organization status.

As with domestic charitable organizations, a private foundation may in large part rely on the tax exemption determination of the overseas exempt organization to support the determination that a grant to that organization is for a charitable purpose. This strong presumption is permissible because the recipient organization is itself answerable to the IRS (as is any charitable organization) on the question of whether the funds are used for a charitable purpose.

Typically, however, a foreign organization will not have obtained recognition of tax exemption as a charitable entity from the IRS. Thus, an American private foundation that is a prospective grantor must establish that the potential donee organization is organized and operated in a manner consistent with a tax-exempt charitable organization, thus constituting the equivalent of a tax-exempt charitable organization.

Charitable organization *equivalents* are foreign organizations that have not obtained determination letters from the IRS but that are organized and operated in such a manner that they can quite easily be determined to be equivalent to public charities under U.S. law. A private foundation is well advised, in these circumstances, to develop its own form modeled after the IRS's application for recognition of tax-exempt status, because the foundation itself is assuming the burden of determining with convincing documentary evidence that the prospective grantee meets the essential requirements for public charity status. Private foundations thus should gather evidence of the prospective grantee's nonprofit status and charitable purposes, copies of organizational documents, relevant statutory decrees, evidence (if any) of local tax standing, description of the intended uses of the grant, identification of the organization's directors and officers, and certification by an officer as to the correctness of the information (and compliance with the standards listed previously). This documentation must be retained by the grant-maker to defend the grant in the case of an audit by the IRS.

According to U.S. law, if a grant is made to an organization that does not have a ruling or determination letter that it is a public charity, the grant will be considered as made to a public charitable organization if the grantor foundation has made a "good faith determination" that the grantee organization is a public charity. The determination is based on an affidavit of the grantee organization or an opinion of either the grantee's counsel or the grantor's counsel that the grantee is a public charitable organization, setting forth sufficient facts concerning the operations and support of the grantee for the IRS to determine that the grantee would be likely to qualify as a public organization.

If an organization has been determined to be organized for charitable purposes and to be a public charity under U.S. law, there will be a strong presumption that grants to it are made for charitable purposes. Thus, a private foundation is allowed to rely on the IRS letter of determination in satisfying this portion of its inquiry. The presumption also follows when the foundation has made a good faith determination that the organization is organized and operated for purposes that render it equivalent to a public charitable organization.

U.S. law requires expenditure responsibility concerning grants made to charitable organizations and their equivalents unless these organizations can be classified as public charities. Several categories of public charitable organizations are embraced by this section, including various educational organizations, hospitals and medical research organizations, churches and associations of churches, organizations that receive sufficiently wide financial support from a governmental unit or from the "public," and organizations that support one of the preceding types of organizations and meet certain other criteria.

IRS Simplified Procedure

The IRS developed a simplified procedure enabling private foundations in the United States to make grants to foreign charitable organizations, relying solely on an appropriate affidavit. Essentially, this simplification is accomplished by eliminating the need for a lawyer's opinion as to the tax status of the foreign grantee. This procedure is not available when the grant is a transfer of assets pursuant to a liquidation, merger, redemption, recapitalization, or other similar adjustment, organization, or reorganization.

The procedure is engrafted onto the previously described regulations, which set forth ways in which a U.S. private foundation can make a grant to a foreign charitable organization without contravening the qualifying distribution rules or the taxable expenditure limitations. These circumstances relate to foreign charitable organizations that do not have an IRS determination letter recognizing them as charitable organizations but are equivalent to U.S. public charitable organizations or private operating foundations (which is usually the case). Absent these rulings, the management of a private foundation must make a "reasonable judgment" that the prospective grantee is a charitable organization and a "good faith determination" that the potential recipient is a public charity or operating foundation.

Under this procedure, both this reasonable judgment and good faith determination may be made on the basis of a "currently qualified" affidavit prepared by the grantee for the prospective grantor or for another grantor or prospective grantor. This procedure requires that the affidavit be written in English and state the required substantive information. An affidavit is considered current when it reflects the grantee's latest complete accounting year or (in the case of public charitable organizations whose public charity status is not dependent on public support) if the affidavit is updated at the request of the prospective grantor to reflect the grantee's current data.

Grants to Other Organizations

When a private foundation decides to make a grant to an organization that is not a governmental unit, tax-exempt charitable organization, or charitable organization equivalent, the grant must be highly nondiscretionary and clearly identified with a specific charitable purpose. In this situation, the grant supports a purpose that is determined to qualify as a charitable purpose. The structure of the organization carrying out this purpose is therefore overlooked.

When public charity status equivalency cannot be established, the private foundation may nonetheless make the grant, but the grant must be clearly identified for a precise charitable purpose. The U.S. tax laws do not provide a procedure for making this type of determination as to a specific charitable purpose. Foundations that have experience in this area have followed a practice of securing from the prospective grantee a project description demonstrating how the grant is to be used for a charitable purpose and/or securing a written commitment that the grantee will use the grant only for its stated purposes.

Whenever a grant is made to a tax-exempt charitable organization or to an organization that is a charitable organization equivalent and is a public charity, the presumption that the grant will be used for charitable purposes is so strong that a foundation is well advised to seek public charity status equivalency for grants to foreign nongovernmental organizations, whenever possible. An additional advantage of establishing this equivalency is that operating or general support grants may be made to these organizations.

Expenditure responsibility must be exercised when a grant is made to this category of donee organization. Further, the grantee organization must agree to segregate the grant funds in a separate account designated for financing a charitable purpose.

SUMMARY

This chapter provided a summary of the rules that generally preclude donors in the United States from deducting, for federal income tax purposes, contributions to charities located in other countries. Then the chapter explained the exceptions to these rules, captured in the conduit and earmarking laws. The chapter summarized applicable law in tax treaties, explained the workings of the estate and gift tax rules in this context, and discussed the law pertaining to contributions to foreign charities by U.S.–based corporations. The chapter concluded with an explanation of the law governing grants by corporate foundations to foreign charities.

CHAPTER 12

Administration of Charitable Giving Programs

The purpose of this chapter is to summarize the law in connection with charitable giving that is too often overlooked: the rules concerning the administration, by charitable organizations, of their charitable giving program. Recent years have brought much new law in this regard, at both the federal and state levels. Specifically, this chapter will:

- Describe the burden of proof rules
- Summarize the charitable gift substantiation requirements
- Summarize the property appraisal requirements
- Summarize the various reporting and disclosure requirements
- Explain the law pertaining to tax shelters
- Summarize the quid pro quo contribution rules
- Describe the disclosure rules applicable to noncharitable organizations
- Summarize the state fundraising regulation laws

BURDEN OF PROOF RULES

As a general proposition, a person—as a taxpayer—has the burden of proving the amount or value of a charitable contribution that he, she, or it wants to deduct. Thus, for example, in one (admittedly extreme) case, a charitable contribution deduction for a gift of computer equipment and related lease rights to a school was denied by a court because the donors failed to offer any evidence of the transactions or the value of the (ostensibly) contributed items. In some instances, a court, convinced that a charitable contribution in fact occurred, will estimate the amount or value involved.

As part of this responsibility, it is incumbent on a donor to prove that the donee organization is in fact charitable in nature (see Chapter 1). Thus, as an illustration, amounts contributed to an entity were held nondeductible, as charitable contributions, by a court because the donors failed to prove that the entity qualified as a charitable organization.

GIFT SUBSTANTIATION REQUIREMENTS

As to contributions of at least $250, a set of substantiation rules imposed by statute applies. Under these rules, donors who make a separate charitable contribution of $250 or more in a year, for which they claim a charitable contribution deduction, must obtain written substantiation from the donee charitable organization.

More specifically, the charitable deduction is not allowed for a *separate contribution* of $250 or more unless the donor has written substantiation from the charitable donee of the contribution in the form of a *contemporaneous written acknowledgment*. Thus, donors cannot rely solely on a cancelled check as substantiation for a gift of $250 or more. (A cancelled check will suffice as substantiation for gifts of less than $250.)

An acknowledgment meets this requirement if it includes this information: (1) the amount of money and a description (but not value) of any property other than money that was contributed; (2) whether the donee organization provided any goods or services in consideration, in whole or in part, for any money or property contributed; and (3) a description and good faith estimate of the value of any goods or services involved or, if the goods or services consist solely of intangible religious benefits, a statement to that effect.

The phrase *intangible religious benefit* means "any intangible religious benefit which is provided by an organization organized exclusively for religious purposes and which generally is not sold in a commercial transaction outside the donative context." An acknowledgment is considered to be *contemporaneous* if the contributor obtains the acknowledgment on or before the earlier of (1) the date on which the donor filed a tax return for the taxable year in which the contribution was made or (2) the due date (including extensions) for filing the return. Even when no good or service is provided to a donor, a statement to that effect must appear in the acknowledgment.

As noted, this substantiation rule applies with respect to *separate payments*. Separate payments generally are treated as separate contributions and are not aggregated for the purpose of applying the $250 threshold. When contributions are paid by withholding from wages, the deduction from each paycheck is treated as a separate payment.

The written acknowledgment of a separate gift is not required to take any particular form. Thus, acknowledgments may be made by letter, postcard, electronic mail, or computer-generated form. A donee charitable organization may prepare a separate acknowledgment for each contribution or may provide donors with periodic (such as annual) acknowledgments that set forth the required information for each contribution of $250 or more made by the donor during the period.

It is the donor's responsibility to obtain the substantiation documentation and maintain it in his or her records. (Again, the charitable contribution deduction depends on compliance with these rules.) The substantiation rules do not impose on charitable organizations any requirement as to the reporting of gift information to the IRS.

Tax regulations pertain to contributions made by means of withholding from individuals' wages and payment by individuals' employers to donee charitable organizations. (The problems in this setting include the fact that the donee charity often does not know the identities of the donors/employees, nor the amounts contributed by each.) These regulations state that gifts of this nature may be substantiated by both:

- A pay receipt or other document (such as Form W-2) furnished by the donor's employer, setting forth the amount withheld by the employer for the purpose of payment to a donee charity
- A pledge card or other document prepared by or at the direction of the donee organization that includes a statement to the effect that the organization does not provide goods or services in whole or partial consideration for any contributions made to the organization by payroll deduction

For purposes of the $250 threshold in relation to contributions made by payroll deduction, the amount withheld from each payment is treated as a separate contribution. Thus, the substantiation requirement does not apply to contributions made by means of payroll deduction unless the employer deducts $250 or more from a single paycheck for the purposes of making a charitable gift. The preamble to these regulations contains a discussion of this question: Can a Form W-2 that reflects the total amount contributed by payroll deduction, but does not list each contribution of $250 or more, be used as evidence of the amount withheld from the employee's wagers to be paid to the donee charitable organization? The IRS noted that the statute provides that an acknowledgment must reflect the amount of cash and a description of property other than cash contributed to a charitable organization. When a person makes multiple contributions to a charitable organization, the law does not require the acknowledgment to list each contribution separately. Consequently, an acknowledgment may substantiate multiple contributions with a statement of the total amount contributed by a person during the year, rather than an itemized list of separate contributions. Therefore, said the IRS, a Form W-2 reflecting an employee's total annual contribution, without separately listing the amount of each contribution, can be used as evidence of the amount withheld from the employee's wages. (The IRS determined that the regulations need not address this point.)

A charitable organization, or a principal combined fund organization for purposes of the combined federal campaign and acting in that capacity, that receives a payment made as a contribution is treated as a donee organization for purposes of the substantiation requirements, even if the organization (pursuant to the donor's instructions or otherwise) distributes the amount received to one or more charitable organizations.

The term *good faith estimate* means the donee charitable organization's estimate of the fair market value of any goods or services, "without regard to the manner in which the organization in fact made that estimate."

A charitable organization is considered as providing goods or services *in consideration for* a person's payment if, at the time the person makes the payment, the person receives or expects to receive goods or services in exchange for the payment. Goods or services a donee charity provides in consideration for a payment by a person would include goods or services provided in a year other than the year in which the payment is made.

Certain goods or services may be disregarded when applying these substantiation rules:

- Those that have an insubstantial value, in that the fair market value of all the benefits received is not more than 2 percent of the contribution or $50 (indexed for inflation), whichever is less.
- Those that have an insubstantial value, in that the contribution is $25 or more (indexed for inflation) and the only benefits received by the donor in return have an aggregate cost of not more than a low-cost article, which generally is one with a cost not in excess of $5 (indexed for inflation).
- Annual membership benefits offered to an individual for a payment of no more than $75 per year that consist of rights or privileges that the individual can exercise frequently during the membership period. This exception is not available with respect to payments made in exchange for the opportunity to preferred seating at athletic events of educational institutions, for which there are special rules. Examples of these rights and privileges include free or discounted admission to the organization's facilities or events, free or discounted parking, preferred access to goods or services, and discounts on the purchase of goods or services.
- Annual membership benefits offered to an individual for a payment of no more than $75 per year that consist of admission to events during the membership period that are open only to members of the donee organization. For this rule to apply, the organization must reasonably project that the cost per person (excluding any allocable overhead) for each event is within the limits established for low-cost articles. The projected cost to the donee organization is determined at the time the organization first offers its membership package for the year.
- Goods or services provided by a charitable organization to an entity's employees in return for a payment to the organization, to the extent the goods or services provided to each employee are the same as those covered by the previous two exceptions. When one or more of these goods or services are provided to a donor, the contemporaneous written acknowledgment may indicate that no goods or services were provided in exchange for the donor's payment.

These regulations illustrate the rules pertaining to membership benefits, rights, and privileges. An example is offered concerning a charitable organization that operates a performing arts center. In return for a payment of $75, the center offers a package of basic membership benefits, which includes the right to purchase tickets to performances one week before they go on sale to the general public; free parking in its garage during the evening and weekend performances; and a 10 percent discount on merchandise sold in its gift shop. In exchange for a $150 payment, the center offers a package of preferred membership benefits, which includes all of the benefits in the $75 package as well as a poster that is sold in the center's gift shop for $20. The basic membership and the preferred membership are each valid for 12 months, and there are approximately 50 performances of various productions at the center during a 12-month period. The gift shop is open for several hours each week and at performance times. An individual is solicited by the center to make a contribution, being offered the preferred membership option. This individual makes a payment of $300. This individual can satisfy the substantiation requirement by obtaining a contemporaneous written acknowledgment from the center that includes a description of the poster and a good faith estimate of its fair market value ($20), and disregards the remaining membership benefits.

Another example concerns a charitable organization that operates a community theater organization that performs four plays every summer; each is performed twice. In return for a membership fee of $60, the organization offers its members free admission to any of its performances. Nonmembers may purchase tickets on a performance-by-performance basis for $15 a ticket. An individual, being solicited by the organization to make a contribution, is advised that the membership benefit will be provided for a payment of $60 or more. This individual chooses to make a payment of $350 to the organization and receives in exchange the membership benefit. This membership benefit does not qualify for the exclusion because it is not a privilege that can be exercised frequently (due to the limited number of performances offered). Therefore, to meet the substantiation requirements, a contemporaneous written acknowledgment of the $350 payment would have to include a description of the free admission benefit and a good faith estimate of its value. (The example does not continue to state that that value is $60 and the charitable deduction thus is $290.)

If a person makes a contribution of $250 or more to a charitable organization and, in return, the charity offers the person's employees goods or services (other than those that may be disregarded), the contemporaneous written acknowledgment of the person's contribution does not have to include a good faith estimate of the value of the goods or services, but must include a description of those goods or services.

An individual who incurred unreimbursed expenditures incident to the rendition of services is treated as having obtained a contemporaneous written acknowledgment of the expenditures if the individual:

- Has adequate records to substantiate the amount of the expenditures, and
- Timely obtains a statement prepared by the donee charity containing (1) a description of the services provided; (2) a statement as to whether the donee provides any goods or services in consideration, in whole or in part, for the unreimbursed expenditures; and (3) the information summarized in the third and fourth of the items that must be reflected in the written acknowledgment.

The substantiation rules do not apply to a transfer of property to a charitable remainder trust or a charitable lead trust (see Chapter 9). They do, however, apply with respect to transfers by means of pooled income funds. The reason for this distinction is grounded in the fact that the grantor of a remainder trust or lead trust is not required to designate a specific organization as the charitable beneficiary at the time property is transferred to the trust, so in these instances there is no designated charity available to provide a contemporaneous written acknowledgment to the donor. Also, even when a specific beneficiary is designated, the identification of the charity can be revocable. By contrast, a pooled income fund must be created and maintained by the charitable organization to which the remainder interests are contributed.

If a partnership or S corporation makes a charitable contribution of $250 or more, the partnership or corporation is treated as the taxpayer for gift substantiation purposes. Therefore, the partnership or corporation must substantiate the contribution with a contemporaneous written acknowledgment from the donee charity before reporting the contribution on its information return or income tax return for the appropriate year, and must maintain the contemporaneous written acknowledgment in its records. A partner of a partnership or a shareholder of an S corporation is not required to obtain any additional substantiation for his or her share of the partnership's or S corporation's charitable contribution.

If a person's payment to a charitable organization is matched, in whole or in part, by another payor, and the person received goods or services in consideration for the payment and some or all of the matched payment, the goods or services are treated as provided in consideration for the person's payment and not in consideration for the matching payment.

The required substantiation may be provided by a properly authorized agent of the charitable donee. For example, when the contribution is of a vehicle (see Chapter 6), a for-profit fundraising company or other entity licensed to sell vehicles may act as the charitable donee's agent. The IRS approved of an arrangement whereby a charitable organization that engaged in the solicitation, processing, and sale of donated vehicles denominated a for-profit corporation that was in the business of buying, maintaining, dismantling, and selling used vehicles as the charity's agent for the acceptance of contributed vehicles.

To reiterate, these rules apply with respect to the making of *contributions*; the donor's deduction is not available unless there is full compliance with the rules. By making the requisite acknowledgment, the charitable organization involved is acquiescing in or concurring with the donor's position that the payment is in fact a contribution. There may, however, be an issue as to whether the payment is a gift (see Chapter 1). A charitable organization that certifies in this fashion that a payment is a gift, when the transaction is not in law a gift, may be subject to one or more tax penalties, such as for participating in an understatement of income tax or promotion of a tax shelter (see Chapter 8).

DISCLOSURE OF GIFTS OF PROPERTY

A donor to a charitable organization is required to disclose to the IRS, by means of the appropriate federal income tax return, certain information in the case of a claimed deduction for noncash contributions in excess of $500. This filing requirement is applicable in the case of contributions by individuals, partnerships, personal service corporations, closely held corporations, and other corporations. C corporations (that are not personal service corporations or closely held corporations) are required to make this disclosure only if the amount claimed as a charitable deduction is more than $5,000.

This disclosure is made by means of IRS Form 8283. The form consists of Sections A and B. A donor may need to complete one of these sections or the other, or both, depending on the type of property contributed and the amount claimed as a charitable deduction. This form is filed with the donor's tax return for the year of the gift.

The donor includes in Section A only references to items (or groups of similar items for which the donor claimed a deduction of $5,000 or less per item (or group of similar items). This information is required in Part I:

- The name and address of the donee organization
- A description of the donated property in sufficient detail
- The date of the contribution
- The date the donated property was acquired by the donor
- How the property was acquired by the donor
- The donor's cost or adjusted basis in the property
- The fair market value of the property
- The method used to determine this fair market value

Also, the donor is required to list these publicly traded securities even if the claimed deduction is more than $5,000:

- Securities listed on an exchange in which quotations are published daily
- Securities regularly traded in national or regional over-the-counter markets for which published quotations are available
- Securities that are shares of a mutual fund for which quotations are published on a daily basis in a newspaper of general circulation throughout the United States

The donor must respond to questions in Part II about any partial interest gifts (see Chapter 5) and/or any conditions placed on contributed property. If this part applies to more than one item of property, a separate statement must be attached to the return, providing the required information for each property.

The donor references in Section B (appraisal summary) only items (or groups of similar items) for which the donor claimed a deduction of more than $5,000 per item (or group). (This rule does not apply with respect to publicly traded securities that are reportable in Section A.) Generally, the donor must have a written appraisal from a qualified appraiser that supports the information provided in Section B, Part I. If the total deduction for art is

$20,000 or more, the donor must attach a complete copy of the signed appraisal; a photograph of the artwork must be provided to the IRS on request.

A separate qualified appraisal and a separate Form 8283 are required for each item of property, except for an item that is part of a group of similar items. If the donor gave similar items to more than one charitable donee for which the donor claimed a total deduction of more than $5,000, the donor must attach a separate form for each donee.

The donor should complete Part II of Section B for each item included in Part I of the section that has an appraised value of $500 or less. Because the donor does not have to show the value of these items in Part I of the donee's copy of the Form 8283, these items should be identified for the donee in Part II. Then the donee does not have to file with the IRS if the property is sold within two years of the gift.

If the donor was required to obtain an appraisal, the appraiser must complete Part III of Section B to be qualified. The charitable organization that received the property is required to complete Part IV of the section. The donor must provide a copy of Section B of Form 8283 to the donee.

DISPOSITIONS OF CONTRIBUTED PROPERTY

Charitable organizations that dispose of certain charitable deduction property within two years of the gift must disclose the transaction to the IRS. This is accomplished by filing Form 8282. The charitable donee is required to file the form within 125 days after the date of disposition of the property.

This form does not have to be filed if, at the time the original donee signed the appraisal summary, the donor signed a statement on Form 8283 that the appraised value of the specific item was not more than $500. If the Form 8283 references more than one similar item, this rule applies only to those items that are clearly identified as having a value of $500 or less. Also, the charitable donee is not required to file this form if an item is consumed or distributed, without consideration, in fulfillment of its exempt purpose or function.

If the gift property is transferred by the donee charitable organization (the *original donee*) to another charitable organization (the *successor donee*) within the two-year period, the original donee must provide the successor donee with the name, address, and tax identification number of the organization; a copy of the appraisal summary; and a copy of the Form 8282 involved, within 15 days of filing by the original donee.

The first two of these items must be furnished to the successor donee within 15 days after the latest of the date the original donee transferred the property, the original donee signed the appraisal summary, or the original donee received a copy of the appraisal summary from the preceding donee if the charity is also a successor donee.

A successor donee must provide the original donee with the successor organization's name, address, and tax identification number within 15 days after the later of the date the property was transferred by the original organization or the date the successor organization received a copy of the appraisal summary.

A charitable organization must provide a copy of the completed Form 8282 to the original donor of the property.

A charitable organization may be subject to a penalty if it fails to timely file Form 8282, fails to include all of the information required to be shown on the form, or fails to include correct information on the form. Generally, this penalty is $50.

APPRAISAL REQUIREMENTS

There are disclosure requirements in connection with the substantiation of deductions claimed by an individual, a closely held corporation, a personal service corporation, a partnership, or an S corporation for charitable contributions of certain property.

Property to which these rules apply is termed *charitable deduction property*. If the contributed property is a partial interest in an item of property (see Chapter 5), the appraisal must be of the partial interest. These requirements apply to contributions of property (other than money and publicly traded securities) if the aggregate claimed or reported value of the property—and all similar items of property for which deductions for charitable contributions are claimed or reported by the same donor for the same tax year whether donated to the same charitable donee—is in excess of $5,000.

The phrase *similar items of property* means property of the same generic category or type, such as stamp collections, coin collections, lithographs, paintings, photographs, books, non–publicly traded securities, parcels of land, buildings, clothing, jewelry, furniture, electronic equipment, household appliances, toys, everyday kitchenware, china, crystal, or silver.

For this type of gift, the donor must obtain a qualified appraisal and attach an appraisal summary to the federal income tax return on which the deduction is claimed. In the case of non-publicly traded stock, however, the claimed value of which does not exceed $10,000 but is greater than $5,000, the donor is not required to obtain a qualified appraisal but must attach a partially completed appraisal summary form to the federal income tax or information return on which the deduction is claimed.

A *qualified appraisal* is an appraisal document that relates to an appraisal that is made not earlier than 60 days prior to the date of contribution of the appraisal property; is prepared, signed, and dated by a qualified appraiser (or appraisers); contains the requisite information; and does not involve a prohibited type of appraisal fee.

The qualified appraisal must include:

- A description of the property in sufficient detail for a person who is not generally familiar with the type of property to ascertain that the property that was appraised is the property contributed; the physical condition of the property (in the instance of tangible property)
- The date of contribution of the property
- The terms of any agreement between the parties relating to any subsequent disposition of the property, including restrictions on the charitable organization's use of the gift property
- The name, address, and tax identification number of the appraiser
- The qualifications of the qualified appraiser (or appraisers)
- A statement that the appraisal was prepared for income tax purposes
- The date or dates on which the property was appraised
- The appraised fair market value of the property on the date of contribution
- The method of valuation used to determine the fair market value of the property
- The specific basis for the valuation

The qualified appraisal must be received by the donor before the due date (including extensions) of the return on which the deduction for the contributed property is first claimed or, in the case of a deduction first claimed on an amended return, the date on which the amended return is filed.

A separate qualified appraisal is required for each item of property that is not included in a group of similar items of property. One qualified appraisal is required for a group of similar items of property contributed in the same tax year, as long as the appraisal includes all of the required information for each item. The appraiser may select any items the aggregate value of which is appraised at $100 or less, for which a group description (rather than a specific description of each item) is adequate.

The tax regulations provide that the appraisal must be retained by the donor "for so long as it may be relevant in the administration of any internal revenue laws."

The *appraisal summary* must be made using Section B of Form 8283, signed and dated on behalf of the charitable donee and by the qualified appraiser (or appraisers), and attached to the donor's federal income tax return on which a deduction with respect to the appraised property is first claimed or reported. The signature by the representative of the charitable donee does not represent concurrence by the donee in the appraised value of the contributed property.

The appraisal summary must include:

- The name and taxpayer identification number of the donor (such as the social security number of an individual)
- A description of the donated property in requisite detail
- A brief summary of the condition of the property at the time of the gift (in the case of tangible property)
- The manner and date of acquisition of the property by the donor
- The cost basis of the property
- The name, address, and taxpayer identification number of the charitable donee
- The date the donee received the property
- A statement explaining whether the charitable contribution was made by means of a bargain sale and amount of any consideration received from the donee for the contribution
- The name, address, and taxpayer identification number of the qualified appraiser (or appraisers)
- The appraised fair market value of the property on the date of contribution
- A declaration by the appraiser

The rules pertaining to separate appraisals also apply with respect to appraisal summaries. A donor who contributed similar items of property to more than one charitable donee must, however, attach a separate appraisal summary for each donee.

Every donor who presents an appraisal summary to a charitable organization for signature must furnish a copy of the appraisal summary to the charitable organization. If the donor is a partnership or S corporation, the donor must provide a copy of the appraisal summary to every partner or shareholder who receives an allocation of a deduction for a charitable contribution of property described in the appraisal summary. The partner or shareholder must attach the appraisal summary to the partner's or shareholder's federal income tax return. If a donor (or partner or shareholder of a donor) fails to attach the appraisal summary to the return, the charitable deduction will not be disallowed if the donor (or partner or shareholder of a donor) submits an appraisal summary within 90 days of being requested to do so by the IRS, as long as the failure to attach the appraisal summary was a good faith omission and certain other requirements are met (including timely completion of the appraisal).

An appraisal summary on Section B of Form 8283 must be filed by contributors where the total value of all noncash contributions exceeds $500 and is less than $5,000. This portion of the form must also be used to report contributions of publicly traded securities, even where the value of them is in excess of $5,000.

The term *qualified appraiser* means an individual who includes on the appraisal summary a declaration that:

- He or she holds himself or herself out to the public as an appraiser to perform appraisals on a regular basis.
- Because of the appraiser's qualifications as described in the appraisal, he or she is qualified to make appraisals of the type of property being valued.
- The appraiser is not one of the persons excluded by these rules from being a qualified appraiser.
- The appraiser understands that an intentionally false or fraudulent overstatement of the value of the property described in the qualified appraisal or appraisal summary may subject the appraiser to a civil penalty for aiding and abetting an understatement of tax liability, and consequently the appraiser may have appraisals disregarded.

Notwithstanding these requirements, an individual is not a qualified appraiser if the donor had knowledge of facts that would cause a reasonable person to expect the appraiser to falsely overstate the value of the donated property. Also, the donor, donee, or certain other related persons cannot be a qualified appraiser of the property involved in the gift transaction.

More than one appraiser may appraise the donated property, as long as each appraiser complies with these requirements, including signing the qualified appraisal and appraisal summary. If more than one appraiser appraises the property, the donor does not have to use each appraiser's appraisal for purposes of substantiating the charitable deduction.

Generally, no part of the fee arrangement for a qualified appraisal can be based on a percentage of the appraised value of the property. If a fee arrangement is based, in whole or in part, on the amount of the appraised value of the property that is allowed as a charitable deduction, after an IRS examination or otherwise, it is treated as a fee based on a percentage of the appraised value of the property. (This rule does not apply in certain circumstances to appraisal fees paid to a generally recognized association that regulates appraisers.)

In any situation involving a gift of property, the charitable organization that is the recipient of the gift must value the property for its own record-keeping, reporting, and (if applicable) financial statement purposes. The charitable donee, however, is not required to share that valuation amount with the donor.

These rules are subject to the *doctrine of substantial compliance*. Pursuant to this doctrine, where the rules involved are procedural or directory in nature, strict adherence to them is not required; substantial compliance is sufficient. It has been held that in this context, the requirement that certain documentation be attached to the donor's federal income tax return is directory rather than mandatory.

A separate set of rules applies appraisal requirements to regular corporations (that is, corporations other than those referenced earlier, termed *C corporations*). These rules, in general, require these corporations to obtain a qualified independent appraisal to validly claim a charitable contribution deduction for gifts of most items of property, other than money, having a value in excess of $5,000.

There are special rules concerning contributions of inventory. C corporations are required to include summary information in their annual federal income tax return, such as a description of the inventory contributed and the valuation method used. This information is to be embodied in a *partially completed appraisal summary*.

These substantiation requirements must be complied with if the charitable contribution deduction is to be allowed.

OFFERING OF INFORMATION OR SERVICES

A tax-exempt organization is required to adequately disclose that information or services it is offering to the public are available without charge from the federal government, assuming that is in fact the case.

This disclosure requirement is violated in these three instances:

1. A tax-exempt organization offers to sell (or solicits money for) specific information or a routine service for an individual that could be readily obtained by that individual without charge (or for a nominal charge) from an agency of the federal government.
2. The exempt organization, when making the offer (or solicitation), fails to make an express statement in a "conspicuous and easily recognizable format" that the information or service can be so obtained.
3. The failure is due to intentional disregard of these requirements.

This disclosure requirement applies only if the information to be provided involves the specific individual solicited. Thus, for example, the requirement applies with respect to obtaining the social security earnings record or the social security identification number of an individual solicited, while the requirement is inapplicable in connection with the furnishing of copies of newsletters issued by federal agencies or providing copies of or descriptive material concerning pending legislation.

This requirement is also inapplicable to the provision of professional services (such as tax return preparation, assistance with respect to the submission of an application for a grant, or medical services), as opposed to routine information retrieval services, to an individual even if they may be available from the federal government without charge (or at a nominal charge).

There is a penalty for failure to comply with this rule, which is applicable for each day on which the failure occurred. It is the greater of $1,000 or 50 percent of the aggregate cost of the offers and solicitations that occurred on any day on which the failure occurred and with respect to which there was this type of failure.

TAX SHELTERS

There is considerable interest in tax shelters, by promoters and users of them, by the media, and by federal and state regulators.

Much attention is being given to inversions, conversions, improper use of trusts, inflated business expense deductions, off-sheet financing schemes, unfounded constitutional law or other legal arguments, frivolous refund claims, and the like. This matter of tax shelters is not confined to for-profit businesses and the for-profit sector in general; tax shelter activity is also taking place in the nonprofit sector.

There is no single, and certainly no simple, definition of the term *tax shelter*. Basically, however, a tax shelter has two elements:

1. It can be an entity (such as a partnership or trust) or a plan, transaction, or other arrangement (investment or otherwise).
3. The sole or principal purpose of the entity or arrangement is avoidance or evasion of taxes. An *abusive tax shelter* is a scheme created and used to obtain, or to try to obtain, tax benefits that are not allowable by law.

Disclosure obligations are imposed on taxpayers who participate in *reportable transactions*. There are several types of these transactions, including *listed transactions*. These are transactions that the IRS has identified as having a tax avoidance purpose and whose tax benefits are subject to disallowance under existing law. The IRS, from time to time, identifies these transactions, some of which involve or are used by (sometimes as accommodation parties tax-exempt organizations.

Examples of tax shelters in the exempt organizations context include the accelerated charitable remainder trust (see Chapter 5), overvaluation of property contributed to charity, certain trust arrangements that purport to qualify as multiple-employer welfare benefit funds in order to deduct what would otherwise be nondeductible life insurance premiums, and misuse of the tax exemption afforded small insurance companies (see Chapter 2). A tax-exempt organization may be an *accommodation party* in a tax shelter, such as a type of abusive tax avoidance transaction, structured to improperly shift taxation away from taxable S corporation shareholders to an exempt entity, such as a charitable organization, for the purpose of deferring or avoiding taxes.

Indeed, depending on the definition of the term that is applied, tax shelters may embrace certain supporting organizations (see Chapter 3), certain donor-advised fund arrangements (see Chapter 3), charitable split-dollar insurance plans (largely outlawed) (see Chapter 10), and charitable family limited partnerships. The IRS observed that it is being "confronted" with a number of "aggressive tax avoidance schemes," citing these four subjects as examples.

Bodies of law that may be brought to bear in connection with these transactions (particularly where the tax-exempt organization is a charitable entity) include the private inurement or private benefit doctrines, the intermediate sanctions rules, denial of a charitable deduction because of lack of a completed gift (see Chapter 1), or denial of the deduction because of an absence of donative intent.

Various statutory provisions limit tax benefits in certain transactions. Also, various penalties and sanctions are applicable to tax shelters:

- Accuracy-related penalty
- Fraud penalty
- Penalty for understatement of a taxpayer's liability by an income tax return preparer
- Penalties with respect to the preparation of income tax returns for others
- Penalty for promoting abusive tax shelters
- Penalty for aiding and abetting an understatement of tax liability
- Penalty for failure to register tax shelters
- Penalty for failure to maintain lists of investors in potentially abusive tax shelters

The IRS also has the authority to pursue litigation to enjoin income tax return preparers from engaging in inappropriate conduct and to enjoin promoters of abusive tax shelters. The agency uses still other laws to combat unwarranted tax practices in the tax-exempt area, such as the property appraisal requirements and various anti-abuse rules in the tax regulations.

QUID PRO QUO CONTRIBUTION RULES

The federal tax law imposes certain disclosure requirements on charitable organizations that receive quid pro quo contributions. A *quid pro quo contribution* is a payment "made partly as a contribution and partly in consideration for goods or services provided to the payor by the donee organization." The term does not include a payment made to an organization, operated exclusively for religious purposes, in return for which the donor receives solely an intangible religious benefit that generally is not sold in a commercial transaction outside the donative context. Specifically, if a charitable organization (other than a state, a possession of the United States, and the District of Columbia) receives a quid pro quo contribution in excess of $75, the organization must, in connection with the solicitation or receipt of the contribution, provide a written statement that: (1) informs the donor that the amount of the contribution that is deductible for federal income tax purposes is limited to the excess of the amount of any money and the value of any property other than money contributed by the donor over the value of the goods or services provided by the organization; and (2) provides the donor with a good faith estimate of the value of the goods or services.

It is intended that this disclosure be made in a manner that is reasonably likely to come to the donor's attention. Therefore, immersing the disclosure in fine print in a larger document is inadequate.

For purposes of the $75 threshold, separate payments made at different times of the year with respect to separate fundraising events generally will not be aggregated.

These rules do not apply when only de minimis, token goods or services (such as key chains and bumper stickers) are provided to the donor. In defining these terms, prior IRS pronouncements are followed. Also, these rules do not apply to transactions that do not have a donative element (such as the charging of tuition by a school, the charging of health care fees by a hospital, or the sale of items by a museum).

A charitable organization is able to use "any reasonable methodology in making a good faith estimate, provided it applies the methodology in good faith." A good faith estimate of the value of goods or services that are not generally available in a commercial transaction may, under these regulations, be determined by reference to the fair market value of similar or comparable goods or services. Goods or services may be similar or comparable even though they do not have the "unique qualities of the goods or services that are being valued."

An example concerns a charitable organization that operates a museum. In return for a payment of $50,000 or more, the museum allows a donor to hold a private event in one of its rooms; in the room is a display of a unique collection of art. No other private events are permitted to be held in the museum. In the community, there are four hotels with ballrooms having the same capacity as the room in the museum. Two of these hotels have ballrooms that offer amenities and atmosphere that are similar to the amenities and atmosphere of the room in the museum; none of them has any art collections. Because the capacity, amenities, and atmosphere of the ballrooms in these two hotels are comparable to the capacity, amenities, and atmosphere of the room in the museum, a good faith estimate of the benefits received from the museum may be determined by reference to the cost of renting either of the two hotel ballrooms. The cost of renting one of these ballrooms is $2,500. Thus, a good faith estimate of the fair market value of the right to host a private event in the room in the museum is $2,500. Here, the ballrooms in the two hotels are considered similar and comparable facilities in relation to the museum's room for valuation purposes, notwithstanding the fact that the room in the museum displays a unique collection of art.

In another example, a charitable organization offers to provide a one-hour tennis lesson with a tennis professional in return for the first payment of $500 or more it receives. The professional provides tennis lessons on a commercial basis at the rate of $100 per hour. An individual pays the charity $500 and in return receives the tennis lesson. A good faith estimate of the fair market value of the tennis lesson provided in exchange for the payment is $100.

In this context, the regulations somewhat address the matter of the involvement of celebrities. This subject is not addressed by a separate regulation but rather by an example. A charity holds a promotion in which it states that, in return for the first payment of $1,000 or more it receives, it will provide a dinner for two followed by an evening tour of a museum conducted by an artist whose most recent works are on display there. The artist does not provide tours of the museum on a commercial basis. Typically, tours of the museum are free to the public. An individual pays $1,000 to the charity and in exchange receives a dinner valued at $100 and the museum tour. Because the tours are typically free to the public, a good faith estimate of the value of the tour conducted by the artist is $0. The fact that the tour is conducted by the artist rather than one of the museum's regular tour guides does not render the tours dissimilar or incomparable for valuation purposes.

Five types of goods or services are disregarded for purposes of the quid pro quo contribution rules. A comparable rule as to goods or services provided to employees of donors is applicable in this context.

No part of this type of a payment can be considered a deductible charitable gift unless two elements exist: (1) the patron makes a payment in an amount that is in fact in excess of the fair market value of the goods or services received, and (2) the patron intends to make a payment in an amount that exceeds that fair market value. This requirement of the element of *intent* may prove to be relatively harmless, as the patron is likely to know the charity's good faith estimate figure in advance of the payment and thus cannot help but have this intent. Still, proving intent is not always easy. This development is unfortunate, inasmuch as the law has been evolving to a more mechanical test (and thus is less reliant on subjective proof): Any payment to a charitable organization in excess of fair market value is regarded as a charitable gift.

DISCLOSURE BY NONCHARITABLE ORGANIZATIONS

Certain contribution disclosure rules are applicable to all types of tax-exempt organizations (other than charitable ones) and are targeted principally at social welfare organizations. They are designed to prevent these noncharitable organizations from engaging in gift-solicitation activities under circumstances in which donors will assume, or be led to assume, that the contributions are tax deductible, when in fact they are not. These rules do not, however, apply to an organization that has annual gross receipts that are normally no more than $100,000. Also, when all of the parties being solicited are tax-exempt organizations, the solicitation does not have to include the disclosure statement (inasmuch as these grantors have no need of a charitable deduction).

This law applies in general to any organization to which contributions are not deductible as charitable gifts and which:

- Is tax-exempt,
- Is a political organization,
- Was either type of organization at any time during the five-year period ending on the date of the solicitation, or
- Is a successor to one of these organizations at any time during this five-year period

The IRS is accorded the authority to treat any group of two or more organizations as one organization for these purposes when "necessary or appropriate" to prevent the avoidance of these rules through the use of multiple organizations.

Under these rules, each fundraising solicitation by or on behalf of a tax-exempt noncharitable organization must contain an express statement, in a "conspicuous and easily recognizable format," that gifts to it are not deductible as charitable contributions for federal income tax purposes. (The IRS has promulgated rules as to this statement; these rules are summarized in the next section.) A *fundraising solicitation* is any solicitation of gifts made in written or printed form, by television, radio, or telephone (although there is an exclusion for letters or calls not part of a coordinated fundraising campaign soliciting more than 10 persons during a calendar year). Despite the clear reference in the statute to "contributions and gifts," the IRS interprets this rule to mandate the disclosure when any tax-exempt organization (other than a charitable one) seeks funds, such as dues from members.

The IRS promulgated rules in amplification of this law, particularly the requirement of a disclosure statement. These rules, which include guidance in the form of "safe-harbor" provisions, address the format of the disclosure statement in instances of use of print media, telephone, television, and radio. They provide examples of acceptable disclosure language and methods (which, when followed, amount to the safe-harbor guidelines), and of included and excluded solicitations. They also contain guidelines for establishing the $100,000 threshold.

The safe-harbor guideline for print media (including solicitations by mail and in newspapers) is fourfold:

1. The solicitation should include language such as this: "Contributions or gifts to [name of organization] are not deductible as charitable contributions for federal income tax purposes."
2. The statement should be in at least the same type size as the primary message stated in the body of the letter, leaflet, or advertisement.
3. The statement should be included on the message side of any card or tear-off section that the contributor returns with the contribution.
4. The statement should be either the first sentence in a paragraph or itself constitute a paragraph.

The safe-harbor guidelines for telephone solicitations follow.

• The solicitation includes language such as: "Contributions or gifts to [name of organization] are not deductible as charitable contributions for federal income tax purposes."

- The statement must be made in close proximity to the request for contributions, during the same telephone call, by the same solicitor.
- Any written confirmation or billing sent to a person pledging to contribute during the telephone solicitation must be in compliance with the requirements for print media solicitations.

To conform to the guidelines, solicitation by television must include a solicitation statement that complies with the first of the print medium requirements. Also, if the statement is spoken, it must be in close proximity to the request for contributions. If the statement appears on the television screen, it must be in large, easily readable type appearing on the screen for at least five seconds.

In the case of a solicitation by radio, the statement must, to meet the safe-harbor test, comply with the first of the print medium requirements. Also, the statement must be made in close proximity to the request for contributions during the same radio solicitation announcement.

When the soliciting organization is a membership entity, classified as a trade or business association or other form of business league, or a labor or agricultural organization, this statement is in conformance with the safe-harbor guideline: "Contributions or gifts to [name of organization] are not tax deductible as charitable contributions. They may, however, be deductible as ordinary and necessary business expenses."

If an organization makes a solicitation to which these rules apply and the solicitation does not comply with the applicable safe-harbor guidelines, the IRS will evaluate all of the facts and circumstances to determine whether the solicitation meets the disclosure rule. A good faith effort to comply with these requirements is an important factor in the evaluation of the facts and circumstances. Nonetheless, disclosure statements made in "fine print" do not comply with the statutory requirement.

This disclosure requirement applies to solicitations for voluntary contributions as well as to solicitations for attendance at testimonials and similar fundraising events. The disclosure must be made in the case of solicitations for contributions to political action committees.

Exempt from this disclosure rule are:

- Billing of those who advertise an organization's publications
- Billing by social clubs for food and beverages

- Billing of attendees of a conference
- Billing for insurance premiums of an insurance program operated or sponsored by an organization
- Billing of members of a community association for mandatory payments for police and fire (and similar) protection
- Billing for payments to a voluntary employees' beneficiary association, as well as similar payments to a trust for pension and/or health benefits

General material discussing the benefits of membership in a tax-exempt organization, such as a trade association or labor union, does not have to include the required disclosure statement. The statement is required, however, when the material both requests payment and specifies the amount requested as membership dues. If a person responds to the general material discussing the benefits of membership, the follow-up material requesting the payment of a specific amount in membership dues (such as a union check-off card or a trade association billing statement for a new member) must include the disclosure statement. General material discussing a political candidacy and requesting persons to vote for the candidate or "support" the candidate need not include the disclosure statement, unless the material specifically requests either a financial contribution or a contribution of volunteer services in support of the candidate.

STATE FUNDRAISING REGULATION

The solicitation of charitable contributions in the United States involves practices that are recognized as being forms of free speech protected by federal and state constitutional law. Thus, there are limitations on the extent to which fundraising for charitable organizations can be regulated by government. Nevertheless, nonprofit organizations in the United States face considerable regulatory requirements at the federal, state, and local levels when they solicit contributions for charitable purposes.

The process of raising funds for charitable purposes is heavily regulated by the states. At this time, all but four states have some form of statutory structure by which the fundraising process is regulated. Of these states, 39 have formal charitable solicitation acts.

State Regulation in General

The various state charitable solicitation acts generally contain certain features, including:

- A process by which a charitable organization registers or otherwise secures a permit to raise funds for charitable purposes in the state
- Requirements for reporting information (usually annually) about an organization's fundraising program
- A series of organizations or activities that are exempt from some or all of the statutory requirements
- A process by which a professional fundraiser, professional solicitor, and/or commercial coventurer registers with, and reports to, the state
- Record-keeping requirements, applicable to charitable organizations, professional fundraisers, professional solicitors, and/or commercial coventurers
- Rules concerning the contents of contracts between a charitable organization and a professional fundraiser, professional solicitor, and/or a commercial coventurer
- A series of prohibited acts
- Provision for reciprocal agreements among the states as to coordinated regulation in this field
- A summary of the powers of the governmental official having regulatory authority (usually the attorney general or secretary of state)
- A statement of the various sanctions that can be imposed for failure to comply with this law (such as injunctions, fines, and imprisonment)

These elements of the law are generally applicable to the fundraising charitable organization. Nevertheless, several provisions of law are directed at the fundraising professional or the professional solicitor, thus going beyond traditional fundraising regulation.

Historical Perspective

Until the mid-1950s, the matter of fundraising practices was not addressed by state law. At that time, not much attention was paid to those practices from the legal perspective. Some counties had adopted fundraising regulation ordinances, but there was no state or federal law on the subject.

This began to change about 50 years ago as part of the disclosure and consumer protection movements. North Carolina was the first state to enact a fundraising regulation law. Others soon followed, however, generating a series of laws that came to be known as *charitable solicitation acts*. New York was the second state to enact one of these acts, and this law became the prototype for the many that were to follow.

The New York law and its progeny involved a statutory scheme based on registration and reporting. Charitable organizations are required to register in advance of solicitation and to report annually; bond requirements came later. Subsequently, forms of regulation involving professional fundraisers and professional solicitors were developed. Exceptions involved, disclosure requirements expanded, and a variety of prohibited acts were identified.

Today's typical charitable solicitation statute is far more extensive than its forebears of decades ago. When charitable solicitation acts began to develop (as noted, beginning in the mid-1950s), the principal features were registration and annual reporting requirements. These laws were basically licensing statutes. They gave the states essential information about the fundraising to be conducted, so that they would have a basis for investigation and review should there be suspicion of some abuse.

During the ensuing years, some states decided to go beyond the concept of licensing and began to affirmatively regulate charitable solicitations. This was done in part because of citizen complaints; another reason was political grandstanding. The regulation worked its way into the realm of attempting to prevent "less qualified" (including out-of-the-mainstream) charities from soliciting in the states.

Structurally, the typical charitable solicitation statute originally did not have much to do with actual regulation of the efforts of either the fundraising institution or the fundraising professional. Rather, the emphasis was on information gathering and disclosure of that information to ostensibly desirous donors. As noted, statute requirements were based on the submission of written information (registration statements, reports, etc.) by charitable organizations and their fundraising advisors; the typical statute also contained bond requirements and granted enforcement authority to the attorneys general, secretaries of state, or other governmental officials charged with administering and enforcing the law.

Later, however, law requirements began to creep in that sounded more like ethical precepts. These requirements were more than just mechanics—they went beyond registration requirements, filing due dates, and accounting principles. They went beyond telling the charity and the professional fundraisers when to do something and entered the realm of telling them how they must conduct the solicitation and what they cannot do in that regard.

From the regulators' viewpoint, the apogee of this form of regulation came when the states could ban charitable organizations with "high" fundraising costs. (As noted later in this chapter, this form of regulation ultimately was found to be unconstitutional.) This application of constitutional law rights to charitable solicitation acts left the state regulators without their principal weapon. In frustration, they turned to other forms of law, those based on the principle of "disclosure."

Soon more state fundraising law developed. The registration and annual reports became more extensive. The states tried, with limited success, to force charities and solicitors into various forms of point-of-solicitation disclosure of various pieces of information. Some states dictated the contents of the scripts of telephone solicitors. This disclosure approach failed to satisfy the regulatory impulse, and more frustration ensued.

The regulators turned to even more ways to have a role in the charitable fundraising process. They started to micromanage charitable fundraising. They began to substitute their judgment for that of donors, charities, and professional fundraisers. Thus, they engendered laws that beefed up the record-keeping requirements, spelled out the contents of contracts between charities and fundraising consultants and solicitors, stepped into commercial coventures, and even injected themselves into matters such as the sale of tickets for charitable events and solicitations by fire and police personnel.

The regulatory appetite still remained unsatisfied. Having accomplished the imposition of just about all of the *law* they could think of, they turned to principles of *ethics*. For example, in one state, charities that solicit charitable gifts and their professional fundraisers and solicitors are "fiduciaries." This is a role historically confined to trustees of charitable trusts and more recently to directors of charitable corporations.

States' Police Power

Prior to a fuller analysis of state law regulation in this field, it is necessary to briefly reference the underlying legal basis for this body of law: the *police power*. Each state (and local unit of government) inherently possesses the police power. This power enables a state or other political subdivision of government to regulate—within the bounds of constitutional law principles—the conduct of its citizens and others, so as to protect the safety, health, and welfare of its citizens.

Generally, it is clear that a state can enact and enforce, in the exercise of its police power, a charitable solicitation act that requires a charity planning on fundraising in the jurisdiction to first register with (or secure a license or permit from) the appropriate regulatory authorities and subsequently to file periodic reports about the results of the solicitation. There is nothing inherently unlawful about this type of requirement. It may also mandate professional fundraisers and professional solicitors to register and report, or empower the regulatory authorities to investigate the activities of charitable organizations in the presence of reasonable cause to do so, and impose injunctive remedies, fines, and imprisonment for violation of the statute. It appears clear that a state can regulate charitable fundraising notwithstanding the fact that the solicitation utilizes the federal postal system, uses television and radio broadcasts, or otherwise occurs in interstate commerce. The rationale is that charitable solicitations may be reasonably regulated to protect the public from deceit, fraud, or the unscrupulous obtaining of money under a pretense that the money is being collected and expended for a charitable purpose.

Despite the inherent police power lodged in the states (and local jurisdictions) to regulate the charitable solicitation process, and the general scope of the power, principles of law operate to confine its reach. Most of these principles are based on constitutional law precepts, such as freedom of speech, procedural and substantive due process, and equal protection of the laws, as well as the standards usually imposed by statutory law, which bar the exercise of the police power in a manner that is arbitrary.

Fundamental Definitions

State law regulation of this nature pertains to fundraising for charitable purposes. The use of the term *charitable* in this setting refers to a range of activities and organizations that is much broader than that embraced by the term as used in the federal tax context. That is, while the term includes organizations that are charitable, educational, scientific, and religious, as those terms are used for federal tax law purposes, it also includes (absent specific exemption) organizations that are civic, social welfare, recreational, and fraternal. Indeed, the general definition is so encompassing as to cause some of these statutes to expressly exclude fundraising by political action committees, labor organizations, and trade organizations.

Some of this regulation is applicable to a *professional fundraiser* (or similar term). The majority of the states define a *professional fundraiser* as one who, for a fixed fee under a written agreement, plans, conducts, advises, or acts as a consultant, whether directly or indirectly, in connection with soliciting contributions for, or on behalf of, a charitable organization. This definition usually excludes those who actually solicit contributions. Other terms used throughout the states include *professional fundraising counsel, professional fundraiser consultant,* and *independent fundraiser.*

Much of this regulation is applicable to those who are *professional solicitors.* Most of the states that use this term define this type of person as one who, for compensation, solicits contributions for or on behalf of a charitable organization, whether directly or through others, or a person involved in the fundraising process who does not qualify as a professional fundraiser. A minority of states define the term as a person who is employed or retained for compensation by a professional fundraiser to solicit contributions for charitable purposes.

There is considerable confusion in the law as to the appropriate line of demarcation between these two terms. Because the extent of regulation can be far more intense for a professional solicitor, it is often very important for an individual or company to be classified as a professional fundraiser rather than a professional solicitor.

Some states impose disclosure requirements with respect to the process known as *commercial coventuring* or *charitable sales promotions.* This process occurs when a business announces to the general public that a portion (a specific amount or a specific percentage) of the purchase price of a product or service will, during a stated period, be paid to a charitable organization, the amount of which depends on consumer response to the promotion by, and positive publicity for, the business sponsor.

Registration Requirements

A cornerstone of each state's charitable solicitation law is the requirement that a charitable organization (as defined in that law and not exempt from the obligation that intends to solicit—by any means—contributions from persons in that state must first apply for and acquire permission to undertake the solicitation. This permission is usually characterized as a *registration*; some states denominate it a *license* or *permit*. If successful, the result is authorization to conduct the solicitation. These permits are usually valid for one year.

These state laws apply to fundraising within the borders of each state involved. Thus, a charitable or like organization soliciting in more than one state must register under (and otherwise comply with) not only the law of the state in which it is located, but also the law of each of the states in which it will be fundraising. Moreover, many counties, townships, cities, and similar jurisdictions throughout the United States have ordinances that attempt to regulate charitable fundraising within their borders.

As noted later in this chapter, the charitable solicitation acts of most states require a soliciting charity (unless exempt) to annually file information with the appropriate governmental agency. This is done either by an annual updating of the registration or the like or by the filing of a separate annual report.

In many states, professional fundraisers and professional solicitors are required to register with the state.

Reporting Requirements

Many of the state charitable solicitation acts mandate annual reporting to the state by registered charitable organizations, professional fundraisers, and professional solicitors. This form of reporting can be extensive and may entail the provision of information concerning gifts received, funds expended for programs and fundraising, payments to service providers, and a battery of other information.

These reports are made on forms provided by the states. These forms, and the rules and instructions that accompany them, vary considerably in content. Underlying definitions and accounting principles can differ. There is little uniformity with respect to due dates for these reports. There has been progress in recent years, however, in the development of a uniform reporting form, although many states persist in adding differing reporting requirements to it.

In many states, professional fundraisers and professional solicitors are required to file annual reports with the state.

Exemptions from Regulation

Many of the states exempt one or more categories of charitable organizations from the ambit of their charitable solicitation statutes. The basic rationale for these exemptions is that the exempted organizations are not part of the objective that the state is endeavoring to achieve through this type of regulation: the protection of the state's citizens from fundraising fraud and other abuse. (Other rationales are the constitutional law limitations involved in the case of churches and the ability of one or more categories of organization to persuade the legislature to exempt them.)

The most common exemption in this context is for churches and their closely related entities. These entities include conventions of churches and associations of churches. Some states broadly exempt religious organizations. These exemptions are rooted in constitutional law principles, barring government from regulating religious practices and beliefs. Some states have run into successful constitutional law challenges when they have attempted to narrowly define the concept of *religion* for this purpose.

Some states exempt at least certain types of educational institutions from the entirety of their charitable solicitation acts. Usually this exemption applies when the educational institution is accredited. The more common practice is to exempt educational institutions from only the registration or licensing, and reporting, requirements.

Some states, either as an alternative or in addition to the foregoing approach, exempt from the registration and reporting requirements educational institutions that confine their solicitations to their constituency. That is, this type of exemption extends to the solicitation of contributions by an educational institution to its student body, alumni, faculty, and trustees, and their families. Solicitations by educational institutions of their constituency are exempt from the entirety of their charitable solicitation laws in a few states.

Many educational institutions undertake some or all of their fundraising by means of related foundations. Some states expressly provide exemption, in tandem with whatever exemption their laws extend to educational institutions, to these supporting foundations. Alumni associations are occasionally exempted from the registration requirements.

The rationale for exempting educational institutions from coverage under these laws includes:

- The public is not solicited
- There have not been any instances of abuses by these institutions of the fundraising process.
- These institutions already adequately report to state agencies.
- The inclusion of these institutions under the charitable solicitation statute would impose an unnecessary burden on the regulatory process.

Some states exempt hospitals (and, in some instances, their related foundations) and other categories of health care entities. Again, the exemption can be from the entirety of the statute or from its registration and reporting requirements. Other exemptions for organizations may include veterans' organizations; police and firefighters' organizations; fraternal organizations; and, in a few states, organizations identified by name. Exemptions are also often available for membership organizations, small solicitations (ranging from $1,000 to $10,000), and solicitations for specified individuals.

Some of these exemptions are available as a matter of law. Others must be applied for, sometimes on an annual basis. Some exemptions are not available or are lost if the organization utilizes the services of a professional fundraiser or professional solicitor.

Fundraising Cost Limitations

Once the chief weapon for state regulators in regard to fundraising cost limitations was laws that prohibited charitable organizations with "high" fundraising costs from soliciting in the states. Allegedly "high" fundraising expenses were defined in terms of percentages of gifts received. These laws proliferated, with percentage limitations extended to the compensation of professional fundraising consultants and professional solicitors. The issue found its way to the Supreme Court, where all of these percentage limitations were struck down as violating the charities' free speech rights. This application of the First and Fourteenth Amendments to the Constitution stands as the single most important bar to more stringent government regulation of the process of soliciting charitable contributions.

As noted, the states possess the police power to regulate the process of soliciting contributions for charitable purposes. The states cannot, however, exercise this power in a manner that unduly intrudes on the rights of free speech of the soliciting charitable organizations and their fundraising consultants and solicitors.

The Supreme Court first held that a state cannot use the level of a charitable organization's fundraising costs as a basis for determining whether a charity may lawfully solicit funds in a jurisdiction. Four years later, the Court held that the free speech principles apply, even though the state offers a charitable organization an opportunity to show that its fundraising costs are reasonable, despite the presumption that costs in excess of a specific ceiling are "excessive." Another four years later, the Court held that these free speech principles applied when the limitation was not on a charity's fundraising costs but on the amount or extent of fees paid by a charitable organization to professional fundraisers or professional solicitors. Subsequent litigation suggests that the courts are consistently reinforcing the legal principles so articulately promulgated by the Supreme Court during the 1980s.

Prohibited Acts

Most states' charitable solicitation laws contain a list of one or more acts in which a charitable organization (and perhaps a professional fundraiser and/or professional solicitor) may not lawfully engage. These acts may be some or all of these:

- A person may not, for the purpose of soliciting contributions, use the name of another person (except that of an officer, director, or trustee of the charitable organization by or for which contributions are solicited) without the consent of that other person. This prohibition usually extends to the use of an individual's name on stationery or in an advertisement or brochure, or as one who has contributed to, sponsored, or endorsed the organization.
- A person may not, for the purpose of soliciting contributions, use a name, symbol, or statement so closely related or similar to that used by another charitable organization or governmental agency that it would tend to confuse or mislead the public.
- A person may not use or exploit the fact of registration with the state so as to lead the public to believe that the registration in any manner constitutes an endorsement or approval by the state.
- A person may not represent to or mislead anyone, by any manner, means, practice, or device, to believe that the or-

ganization on behalf of which the solicitation is being conducted is a charitable organization or that the proceeds of the solicitation will be used for charitable purposes, when that is not the case.

- A person may not represent that the solicitation for charitable gifts is for or on behalf of a charitable organization or otherwise induce contributions from the public without proper authorization from the charitable organization.

In one state, it is a prohibited act to represent that a charitable organization will receive a fixed or estimated percentage of the gross revenue from a solicitation in an amount greater than that identified to the donor. In another state, it is a prohibited act for an individual to solicit charitable contributions if the individual has been convicted of a crime involving the obtaining of money or property by false pretenses, unless the public is informed of the conviction in advance of the solicitation.

In still another state, prohibited acts for a charitable organization (or, in some instances, a person acting on its behalf) include:

- Misrepresenting the purpose of a solicitation
- Misrepresenting the purpose or nature of a charitable organization
- Engaging in a financial transaction that is not related to accomplishment of the charitable organization's exempt purpose
- Jeopardizing or interfering with the ability of a charitable organization to accomplish its charitable organization's exempt purpose
- Expending an "unreasonable amount of money" for fundraising or for management

Some states make violation of a separate law concerning "unfair or deceptive acts and practices" a violation of the charitable solicitation act as well.

Contractual Requirements

Many of the state charitable solicitation acts require that the relationship between a charitable organization and a professional fundraiser, and/or between a charitable organization and a professional solicitor, be evidenced in a written agreement. This agreement is required to be filed with the state soon after the contract is executed. These types of requirements are clearly lawful and are not particularly unusual.

A few states, however, have enacted requirements—some of them rather patronizing—that dictate to the charitable organization the contents of the contract. For example, under one state's law, a contract between a charitable organization and a fundraising counsel must contain sufficient information "as will enable the department to identify the services the fundraising counsel is to provide and the manner of his compensation." Another provision of the same law mandates that the agreement "clearly state the respective obligations of the parties."

The law in another state requires a contract between a charitable organization and a fundraising counsel to contain provisions addressing the services to be provided, the number of persons to be involved in providing the services, the time period over which the services are to be provided, and the method and formula for compensation for the services.

Under another state's law, whenever a charitable organization contracts with a professional fundraiser or other type of fundraising consultant, the charitable organization has the right to cancel the contract, without cost or penalty, for a period of 15 days. Again, this type of law seems predicated on the assumption that charitable organizations are somehow not quite capable of developing their own contracts and tend to do so impetuously. It can be argued that these laws are forms of overreaching, in terms of scope and detail, on the part of government, and that charitable organizations ought to be mature enough to formulate their own contracts.

Disclosure Requirements

Many of the states that were forced to abandon or forgo the use of the percentage mechanism as a basis for preventing fundraising for charity utilize the percentage approach in a disclosure setting. Several states, for example, require charitable organizations to make an annual reporting, either to update a registration or as part of a separate report, to the authorities as to their fundraising activities in the prior year, including a statement of their fundraising expenses. Some states require a disclosure of a charity's fundraising costs, stated as a percentage, to donors at the time of the solicitation—although this requirement arguably is of dubious constitutionality. In a few states, solicitation literature used by a charitable organization must include a statement that, upon request, financial and other information about the soliciting charity may be obtained directly from the state.

Some states require a statement as to any percentage compensation in the contract between the charitable organization and the professional fundraiser and/or the professional solicitor. A few states require the compensation of a paid solicitor to be stated in the contract as a percentage of gross revenue; another state has a similar provision with respect to a professional fundraiser. One state wants a charitable organization's fundraising cost percentage to be stated in its registration statement.

An example of this type of law is a statute that imposed on the individual who raises funds for a charitable organization the responsibility to "deal with" the contributions in an "appropriate fiduciary manner." Thus, an individual in these circumstances owes a fiduciary duty to the public. These persons are subject to a surcharge for any funds wasted or not accounted for. A presumption exists in this law that funds not adequately documented and disclosed by records were not properly spent.

By direction of this law, all solicitations must "fully and accurately" identify the purposes of the charitable organization to prospective donors. Use of funds, to an extent of more than 50 percent, for "public education" must be disclosed under this law. The charitable organization's governing board must, under some of these laws, approve every contract with a professional fundraiser. Some of the provisions of this law probably are unconstitutional, such as the requirement that professional fundraisers or solicitors must disclose to those being solicited the percentage of their compensation in relation to gifts received.

Another example is some of the provisions of another state's law, which makes an "unlawful practice" the failure of a person soliciting funds to "truthfully" recite, on request, the percentage of funds raised to be paid to the solicitor. This state, like many other states, is using the concept of prohibited acts to impose a sort of code of ethics on all who seek to raise funds for charity.

Under one state's law, any person who solicits contributions for a charitable purpose and who receives compensation for the service must inform each person being solicited, in writing, that the solicitation is a "paid solicitation." In another state, when a solicitation is made by "direct personal contact," certain information must be "predominantly" disclosed in writing at the point of solicitation. In another state, the solicitation material and the "general promotional plan" for a solicitation may not be false, misleading, or deceptive, and must afford a "full and fair" disclosure.

In general, the typical state charitable solicitation act seems immune from successful constitutional law challenge. That is, the constitutional law attacks on these laws prevail only in relation to particularly egregious features of them. The same may be said of local fundraising regulation ordinances. The difficulty with the latter, however, is not so much their content as their number. A charitable organization involved in a multistate charitable solicitation may be expected to comply with hundreds, perhaps thousands, of these ordinances. To date, when responding to complaints by charities as to this burden of regulation, the courts review only the content of each local law, refusing to evaluate the difficulties they pose in the aggregate.

SUMMARY

This chapter opened with a description of the burden-of-proof rules in the charitable deduction context, then summarized the charitable gift substantiation and property appraisal requirements. The chapter explained the various reporting and disclosure requirements, the rules pertaining to tax shelters, and the quid pro quo contribution rules. It then reviewed the rules requiring certain disclosures by noncharitable organizations and concluded with a description of the state fundraising laws.

Glossary

The bodies of law concerning nonprofit, tax-exempt organizations and charitable giving overlap considerably. As noted in the preface, this book is a companion to *Nonprofit Law Made Easy*. Most of the terms that follow are discussed more fully in that work.

Antitrust law. This body of law is briefly referenced in Chapter 9 of this book, in the context of planned giving regulation; it is treated more fully in Chapter 11 of *Nonprofit Law Made Easy*. In general, federal and state antitrust laws are intended to advance and protect competition in economic marketplaces. These laws are directed against combinations, conspiracies, and other collective restraints of trade.

Corporation. From the standpoint of the federal tax law, a for-profit corporation is classified as a C corporation or an S corporation. These terms are derived from the applicable reference in the Internal Revenue Code. A C corporation, sometimes termed a *regular corporation*, is a corporation referenced in Subchapter C of the Code, Subtitle A, Chapter 1. A C corporation is any for-profit corporation that is not an S corporation.

Intermediate sanctions. Federal excise taxes that are imposed on one or more disqualified persons who extract an impermissible economic benefit from a public charity or a social welfare organization, such as excessive compensation or unreasonable loan and rental arrangements. This body of law is summarized in Chapter 10 of *Nonprofit Law Made Easy*.

Limited liability company. A type of entity that can be differentiated from a corporation, partnership, or trust. For federal tax purposes, however, a limited liability company is taxed in the same manner as a partnership.

Lobbying activities. Charitable organizations are limited as to the extent to which they can engage in attempts to influence legislation. Excessive amounts of lobbying activity can lead to loss of a charitable organization's tax-exempt status. This body of law is summarized in Chapter 10 of *Nonprofit Law Made Easy*.

Partnership. A form of organization recognized as a separate legal entity. By definition, this type of entity must have two or more members, known as partners. A partnership does not pay federal income tax; this tax liability flows through to the partners.

Political organization. A tax-exempt entity that has as its primary purpose the election (or perhaps opposition to the election) of one or more individuals to public office. This body of law is summarized in Chapters 2 and 11 of *Nonprofit Law Made Easy.*

Private benefit. A term that references a body of law by which a charitable organization can be denied or lose tax-exempt status if it confers an impermissible economic benefit (other than an incidental one) on one or more persons. This body of law is summarized in Chapter 10 of *Nonprofit Law Made Easy.*

Private foundation. This term is briefly discussed in Chapter 1 of this book and is treated more fully in Chapter 3 of *Nonprofit Law Made Easy.*

Private inurement. This references a body of law by which a charitable (and several other types of tax-exempt entity) organization can be denied or lose tax-exempt status if it confers an impermissible economic benefit on one or more persons who are insiders with respect to it. This body of law is summarized in Chapter 10 of *Nonprofit Law Made Easy.*

Public charity. The term is briefly discussed in Chapter 1 of this book and is treated more fully in Chapter 3 of *Nonprofit Law Made Easy.*

S corporation. An S corporation, also known as a small business corporation, is so named because it is referenced in the Internal Revenue Code, Subtitle A, Subchapter S. A for-profit corporation that is not a C corporation is an S corporation, although S corporation status must be elected. S corporations are taxed for federal income tax purposes in the same manner as partnerships.

Securities law. This topic is briefly referenced in Chapter 9 of this book, in the context of planned giving regulation. Generally, this aspect of the law is designed to facilitate the fair trading of securities and to prosecute securities trading fraud. This body of law is treated more fully in Chapter 11 of *Nonprofit Law Made Easy.*

State fundraising regulation. This body of law is briefly referenced in Chapter 12 of this book. It is treated more fully in Chapter 8 of *Nonprofit Law Made Easy.*

Unrelated business activities. Nearly all charitable (and other tax-exempt) organizations are taxable on the net income they derive from the regular conduct of business activities that are unrelated to their tax-exempt purpose (although many exceptions are available). This body of law is summarized in Chapter 7 of *Nonprofit Law Made Easy.*

Unrelated debt-financed income. A component of the law concerning unrelated business activities is the rule that net income derived by charitable (and other tax-exempt) organizations from property that was acquired or is maintained by debt financing is (with exceptions) taxable as unrelated business income.

Unrelated use. Use of property by a charitable organization, which it acquired by means of a contribution, in a manner that is inconsistent with its tax-exempt purpose.

Epilogue: 2006 Legislation

As this book was being written and set in type, Congress passed a considerable amount of legislation creating new law and amending existing laws that directly affect the law of charitable giving. This epilogue provides a summary of that new law.

SUPPORTING ORGANIZATIONS

Supporting organizations are discussed in Chapter 1 (see pages 8–9). Some of the 2006 law changes are applicable to all supporting organizations. Other changes apply only to supporting organizations that are "operated in connection with" one or more supported organizations—the so-called Type III supporting organizations. Also, there are now two types of Type III supporting organizations: functionally integrated Type III entities and those that are not functionally integrated.

The concept of the *automatic excess benefit transaction* is grafted onto the supporting organization's rules. Under this new law, if a supporting organization (Type I, II, or III) makes a grant, loan, payment of compensation, or similar payment (e.g., expense reimbursement) to a substantial contributor (or related person) of the supporting organization, the substantial contributor (defined under prior law) is regarded (for purposes of the intermediate sanctions rules) as a disqualified person. The payment is treated as an automatic excess benefit transaction—that is, the entire amount of the payment is treated as an excess benefit.

Accordingly, a substantial contributor in this position is subject to an initial 25 percent excise tax on the amount of the payment. An organization manager who knowingly participated in the making of the payment is subject to a 10 percent tax. The second-tier taxes and the other intermediate sanctions rules are also applicable to these payments.

Loans by any supporting organization to a disqualified person with respect to the supporting organization are treated as an excess benefit transaction; the entire amount of the loan is treated as an excess benefit.

A supporting organization is required to file annual information returns with the IRS, irrespective of the amount of the organization's gross receipts. A supporting organization must identify its type on its annual return. The supported organization(s) must be identified.

A supporting organization must annually demonstrate that it is not controlled, directly or indirectly, by one or more disqualified persons (other than its managers and supported organizations) by means of a certification on its annual information return.

For purposes of the intermediate sanctions rules, a disqualified person of a supporting organization is treated as a disqualified person of the (or each) supported organization.

The private foundation excess business holdings rules apply to a Type II supporting organization where the organization accepts a contribution from a person (other than a public charity) who (1) controls, directly or indirectly, either alone or together (with persons described below) the governing body of a supported organization of the supporting organization; (2) is a member of the family of such a person; or (3) is a 35-percent controlled entity.

As noted, there are now essentially four types of supporting organizations. The newest is the functionally integrated Type III supporting organization (to be defined in regulations), which basically is an entity that engages in activities that are directly related to the performance of the functions of or carrying out the purposes of one or more supported organizations.

The IRS is directed to rewrite the tax regulations as to payouts required by Type III non–functionally integrated supporting organizations. These regulations must require this type of supporting organization to make distributions of a percentage of either income or assets to its supported organization(s) to ensure that a significant amount is paid out.

The private foundation excess business holdings rules are also applicable to Type III supporting organizations that are not functionally integrated entities. In applying these rules, the term *disqualified person* is defined under the intermediate sanctions rules and includes substantial contributors, related persons, and any organization that is effectively controlled by the same person or persons who control the supporting organization or any organization substantially all of the contributions to which were made by the same person or persons who made substantially all of the contributions to the supporting organization.

The IRS has the authority not to impose the excess business holdings rules on a Type III supporting organization if the organization establishes that its excess holdings are consistent with the purpose or function constituting the basis of the organization's tax-exempt status.

In general, a Type III supporting organization cannot support an organization that is not organized in the United States. In the case of a Type III supporting organization that supports a foreign organization on August 17, 2006, this rule does not apply until the first day of the third year of the organization beginning after that date.

A Type III supporting organization must apprise each organization that it supports of information regarding the supporting organization in order to help ensure the supporting organization's responsiveness. A Type III supporting organization that is organized as a trust must establish to the satisfaction of the IRS that it has a close and continuous relationship with the supported organization such that the trust is responsive to the needs or demands of the supported organization.

If a Type I or III supporting organization accepts a gift from a person (other than a public charity) who (1) controls, directly or indirectly, either alone or together (with persons described below) the governing body of a supported organization of the supporting organization, (2) is a member of the family of such a person, or (3) is a 35-percent controlled entity, then the supporting organization is treated as a private foundation for all purposes until such time as the organization can demonstrate to the satisfaction of the IRS that it qualifies as a type of public charity other than a supporting organization.

A nonoperating private foundation may not count as a qualifying distribution an amount paid to (1) a Type III supporting organization that is not a functionally integrated Type III supporting organization or (2) any other type of supporting organization if a disqualified person with respect to the foundation directly or indirectly controls the supporting organization or a supported organization of the supporting organization. Any amount that does not count as a qualifying distribution under this rule is treated as a taxable expenditure.

The supporting organization rules generally took effect on August 17, 2006. The excess benefit transaction rules are generally effective for transactions occurring after July 25, 2006. The excess business holdings requirements are effective for years beginning after August 17, 2006. The provision relating to distributions by non-operating private foundations is effective for distributions and expenditures made after August 17, 2006. The return requirements are effective for returns filed for years ending after August 17, 2006.

DONOR-ADVISED FUNDS

Chapter 1 includes this statement: "Congress is likely to legislate limitations and requirements regarding contributions to and operations of donor-advised funds" (page 14). Congress did so.

A *donor-advised fund* is now defined by statute as a fund or account that is (1) separately identified by reference to contributions of one or more donors (2) owned and controlled by a sponsoring organization and (3) with respect to which a donor (or a person appointed or designated by a donor [a *donor advisor*]) has, or reasonably expects to have, advisory privileges with respect to the distribution or investment of amounts held in the fund or account by reason of the donor's status as a donor. A *sponsoring organization* is a charitable entity that is not a private foundation and that maintains one or more donor-advised funds.

The presence of an *advisory privilege* may be evidenced by a written document that describes an arrangement between the donor or donor advisor and the sponsoring organization by which a donor or donor advisor may provide advice to the sponsoring organization about the investment or distribution of amounts held by a sponsoring organization, even if the privileges are not exercised. The presence of an advisory privilege also may be evident through the conduct of a donor or donor advisor and the sponsoring organization.

The concept of a donor-advised fund does not include a fund or account that makes distributions only to a single identified organization, such as an endowment fund. A donor-advised fund also does not include certain funds or accounts with respect to which a donor or donor advisor provides advice as to which individuals receive grants for travel, study, or other similar purposes. The IRS may exempt a fund or account from treatment as a donor-advised fund if (1) it is advised by a committee not directly or indirectly controlled by a donor, donor advisor, or persons related to a donor or donor advisor; or (2) it benefits a single identified charitable purpose (a restricted fund).

Contributions to a sponsoring organization for maintenance in a donor-advised fund are ineligible for a federal income tax charitable contribution deduction if the sponsoring organization is a veterans' organization, a fraternal society, or a cemetery company. There is no such deduction for gift or estate tax purposes if the sponsoring organization is a fraternal society or a veterans' organization. Further, there is no such deduction for income, gift, or estate tax purposes if the sponsoring organization is a Type III supporting organization that is not a functionally integrated Type III organization.

In addition to prior-law substantiation requirements, a donor must obtain, with respect to each charitable contribution to a sponsoring organization to be maintained in a donor-advised fund, a contemporaneous written acknowledgment from the sponsoring organization providing that the sponsoring organization has exclusive legal control over the assets contributed.

The private foundation excess business holdings rules are applicable to donor-advised funds. The term *disqualified person* means, with respect to a donor-advised fund, a donor, donor advisor, a member of the family of either, or a 35-percent controlled entity of any such person.

A grant, loan, compensation, or other similar payment from a donor-advised fund to a person who, with respect to the fund, is a donor, donor advisor, or a person related to a donor or donor advisor automatically is treated as an excess benefit transaction for intermediate sanctions law purposes. This means that the entire amount paid to any of these persons is an excess benefit.

Donors and donor advisors with respect to a donor-advised fund (and related persons) are disqualified persons for intermediate sanctions law purposes with respect to transactions with the donor-advised fund (although not necessarily with respect to transactions with the sponsoring organization generally).

Certain distributions from a donor-advised fund are subject to tax. A *taxable distribution* is a distribution from a donor-advised fund to (1) a natural person, (2) to any other person for a noncharitable purpose or (3), if for a charitable purpose, the sponsoring organization does not exercise expenditure responsibility with respect to the distribution. Nonetheless, a taxable distribution does not include a distribution to a public charity and certain other charitable organizations, the sponsoring organization of the donor-advised fund, or to another donor-advised fund. This exception, however, is inapplicable with respect to a *disqualified supporting organization*, which is (1) a Type III supporting organization other than a functionally integrated one and (2) any other type of supporting organization if either (a) the donor or donor advisor of the distributing donor-advised fund directly or indirectly controls a supported organization of the supporting organization or (b) the IRS determines by regulations that a distribution to a supporting organization otherwise is inappropriate.

In the event of a taxable distribution, an excise tax equal to 20 percent of the amount of the distribution is imposed on the sponsoring organization. An excise tax equal to 5 percent of the amount of the distribution is imposed on a manager of the sponsoring organization who knowingly approved the distribution; this tax may not exceed $10,000 with respect to any one taxable distribution. These taxes are subject to abatement.

If a donor or donor advisor (or related person) with respect to a donor-advised fund provides advice as to a distribution that results in any such person receiving, directly or indirectly, a more-than-incidental benefit, an excise tax equal to 125 percent of the amount of the benefit is imposed on the person who advised as to the distribution and on the recipient of the benefit. A comparable 10 percent tax is imposed on a manager of a sponsoring organization. These taxes are also subject to abatement.

A sponsoring organization is required to disclose on its annual information return the number of donor-advised funds it owns, the aggregate value of assets held in the funds at the end of the organization's tax year, and the aggregate contributions to and grants made from these funds during the year.

When seeking recognition of tax-exempt status, a sponsoring organization must disclose whether it intends to maintain donor-advised funds. It is intended that the organization must provide information regarding its planned operation of these funds, including a description of procedures it intends to use to (1) communicate to donors and donor advisors that assets held in the funds are the property of the sponsoring organization and (2) ensure that distributions from donor-advised funds do not result in more than incidental benefit to any person.

The donor-advised funds law generally is effective for tax years beginning after August 17, 2006. The provision relating to excess benefit transactions is effective for transactions occurring after August 17, 2006. Information return requirements are effective for tax years ending after August 17, 2006. The requirements concerning disclosures on an application for recognition of tax exemption are effective for organizations applying for recognition after August 17, 2006. Requirements relating to charitable contributions to donor-advised funds are effective for contributions made after February 14, 2007.

DEPARTMENT OF TREASURY STUDIES

The Department of the Treasury is directed to undertake a study on the organization and operation of donor-advised funds and supporting organizations. This study must consider whether (1) the amount and availability of the income, gift, or estate tax charitable deductions allowed for contributions to sponsoring and supporting organizations is appropriate in consideration of the use of contributed assets or the use of the assets of these organizations for the benefit of persons making the charitable contributions; (2) donor-advised funds should be required to distribute for charitable purposes a specified amount to ensure that the sponsoring organization is operating consistent with the purposes or functions constituting the basis for its tax-exempt or public charity status; (3) the retention by donors to donor-advised funds or supporting organizations of rights or privileges with respect to amounts transferred to such entities is consistent with the treatment of such transfers as completed gifts that qualify for charitable deductions; and (4) any of these matters also raise issues with respect to other forms of charities or charitable contributions.

NOTIFICATION REQUIREMENT

In Chapter 1, it was observed that hundreds of thousands of organizations exist that are not registered with the IRS (page 22). Under new law, organizations that need not file annual information returns with the IRS because their gross receipts are normally below a $25,000 threshold must annually furnish to the IRS, in electronic form, (1) the legal name of the organization, (2) any name under which the organization operates or does business, (3) the organization's mailing address and any Web site address, (4) the organization's identification number, (5) the name and address of a principal officer, and (6) evidence of the organization's continuing basis for its exemption from the return filing requirement. Notice of termination of existence must also be provided.

If an organization fails to provide this notice for three consecutive years, its tax-exempt status is revoked. This rule is effective for notices with respect to annual periods beginning after 2006.

CONTRIBUTIONS FOR UNRELATED USE

Chapter 2 includes a summary of law concerning charitable contributions of tangible personal property that the recipient charity puts to an unrelated use (pages 33–35). Under new law, if a donee charitable organization disposes of tangible personal property (for which a deduction of more than $5,000 is claimed) within three years of contribution of the property, the donor is subject to an adjustment of the tax benefit. If the disposition is in the year of the gift, the donor's deduction generally is confined to the basis amount. In the case of a subsequent distribution, the donor must include as ordinary income any amount of the claimed deduction that is in excess of the donor's basis. There are reporting rules and a penalty. This recapture rule applies to contributions made after September 1, 2006.

VALUATION OF PROPERTY

Chapter 2 includes an observation that the penalty system in connection with property valuation abuses is not effective (page 41). Under new law, the thresholds for imposing accuracy-related penalties are lowered. A civil penalty has been created, to be imposed on any person who prepares an appraisal that is to be used to support a tax position, if the appraisal results in a substantial or gross valuation misstatement. These rules generally apply to appraisals prepared and returns filed after August 17, 2006.

GIFTS FOR CONSERVATION PURPOSES

Chapter 6 includes a summary of the law concerning contributions of real property for conservation purposes (pages 145–148). Under new law, the charitable contribution deduction limit is raised from 30 percent of adjusted gross income (AGI) to 50 percent of AGI for qualified conservation contributions (as defined under prior law). This limit is raised to 100 percent of AGI for eligible farmers and ranchers. Donors are able to carry forward these deductions for up to 15 years. This law change applies to contributions made in tax years beginning after December 31, 2005, and before January 1, 2008.

The rules for qualified conservation contributions have been revised with respect to property for which a charitable deduction is allowable by reason of a property's location in a registered historic district. A charitable deduction is not allowable with respect to a structure or land area located in such a district (by reason of its location in the district). A charitable deduction is allowable with respect to buildings but the qualified real property interest that relates to the exterior of the building must preserve the entire exterior of the building. Certain information must be attached to the donor's tax return to support the deduction. These rules are effective for contributions made after July 25, 2006.

In the case of a qualified conservation contribution, the amount of the charitable deduction is reduced by an amount that bears the same ratio to the fair market value of the contribution as the sum of the rehabilitation credits for the preceding five tax years with respect to a building that is part of the contribution bears to the fair market value of the building on the date of contribution. This rule is effective for contributions made after August 17, 2006.

S CORPORATION STOCK

Chapter 6 includes a summary of the law concerning contributions of S corporation stock (pages 149–153). Under new law, the amount of a shareholder's basis reduction in the stock of an S corporation, by reason of a charitable contribution made by the corporation, is equal to the shareholder's pro rata share of the adjusted basis of the contributed property. This rule applies to contributions made in tax years beginning after December 31, 2005, and tax years beginning before January 1, 2008.

CONTRIBUTIONS FROM RETIREMENT ACCOUNTS

Chapter 7 references a "popular proposal [that] would allow donors to exclude from gross income direct transfers from IRAs to eligible charitable organizations" (page 160). A version of this proposal has been enacted into law.

An exclusion from gross income for otherwise taxable individual retirement plan distributions from a traditional or Roth individual retirement account (IRA) is available in the case of a qualified charitable distribution. This exclusion may not exceed $100,000 per taxpayer per year. Special rules apply in determining the amount of an IRA distribution that is otherwise taxable.

A *qualified charitable distribution* is a distribution from an IRA directly by the IRA trustee to a public charity and certain other charitable organizations, other than a supporting organization or a donor-advised fund. Distributions are eligible for the exclusion only if made on or after the date the IRA owner attains the age of $70^1/_2$.

The exclusion applies only if a charitable contribution deduction for the entire distribution otherwise would be available (under prior law), determined without regard to the generally applicable percentage limitations. For example, if the deduction amount is reduced because a benefit was received in consideration for the gift, the exclusion is not available with respect to any part of the IRA distribution.

These rules do not apply to distributions made in tax years beginning after December 31, 2007.

TWICE-BASIS DEDUCTIONS

Chapter 8 includes a summary of the law concerning twice-basis deductions (pages 204–205). Under new law, a taxpayer, whether a C corporation or not, engaged in a trade or business is eligible to claim the enhanced deduction for contributions of food inventory. For taxpayers other than C corporations, the total deduction for gifts of food inventory in a year generally may not exceed 10 percent of the taxpayer's net income for the year from all sole proprietorships, S corporations, or partnerships (or other non-C corporations) from which contributions of apparently wholesome food (defined in prior law) are made. This rule is effective for contributions made after December 31, 2005, and before January 1, 2008.

An enhanced deduction for C corporations for qualified book contributions is allowed. This rule is effective for contributions made after December 31, 2005, and before January 1, 2008.

GIFTS INVOLVING INSURANCE

Chapter 10 concerns charitable gifts of and using insurance. Under new law, for reportable acquisitions of interests in certain life insurance contracts occurring after August 17, 2006, and on or before two years thereafter, an applicable exempt organization that makes such an acquisition is required to file an information return. A *reportable acquisition* means the acquisition by an applicable exempt organization of a direct or indirect interest in a contract that the exempt organization knows or has reason to know is an applicable insurance contract, if the acquisition is part of a structured transaction involving a pool of such contracts.

An *applicable insurance contract* means any life insurance, annuity, or endowment contract with respect to which both an applicable exempt organization and a person other than such an organization have directly or indirectly held an interest in the contract (whether at the same time or not). An *applicable exempt organization* generally is a tax-exempt charitable organization, a government or political subdivision of a government, or an Indian tribal government.

This reporting provision is effective for acquisitions of contracts after August 17, 2006.

TAX SHELTERS

Chapter 12 includes a discussion of the law of charitable giving as it interrelates with tax shelters (pages 315–317). Under new law, an excise tax is imposed on most tax-exempt entities and/or entity managers that participate in prohibited tax shelter transactions as accommodation parties. This tax can be triggered in three instances:

1. An exempt organization is liable for the tax in the year it becomes a party to the transaction and any subsequent year or years in which it is such a party.
2. An exempt organization is liable for the tax in any year it is a party to a subsequently listed transaction.
3. An entity manager is liable for the tax if the manager caused the exempt organization to be a party to a prohibited tax shelter transaction at any time during a year and knew or had reason to know that the transaction is such a transaction.

For this purpose, the term *tax-exempt entity* includes an organization described in the general list of tax-exempt organizations, an apostolic organization, a charitable donee other than the federal government, an Indian tribal government, or a prepaid tuition program. The term *entity manager* means, with respect to a tax-exempt entity, (1) an individual with authority or responsibility similar to that exercised by a trustee, director, or officer of the organization; and (2) with respect to any act, the person having authority or responsibility with respect to that act.

A *prohibited tax shelter transaction* is of two types: a listed transaction and a prohibited reportable transaction. A *listed transaction* is defined in preexisting law as a reportable transaction that is the same as, or is substantially similar to, a transaction specifically identified by the IRS as a tax avoidance transaction. A *reportable transaction* is a transaction with respect to which information is required to be included with a return or statement because the transaction is of a type that the IRS determines has a potential for tax avoidance or evasion.

OTHER PROVISIONS

Legislation enacted in 2006 brought these additional new laws.

Split-Interest Trust Filing Requirements

The penalty on split-interest trusts (see Chapter 9) for failure to file a return, and failure to include the information required to be shown on the return and to show the correct information, is increased. The penalty is $20 for each day the failure continues up to $10,000 for any one return. In the case of a split-interest trust with gross income in excess of $250,000, the penalty is $100 for each day the failure continues, up to a maximum of $50,000.

If a trustee, director, officer, employee, or other individual who is under a duty to file the return or include required information knowingly failed to file the return or include required information, then that person is personally liable for such a penalty, which is to be imposed in addition to the penalty paid by the trust.

These rules are effective for returns for tax years beginning after December 31, 2006.

Contributions of Fractional Interests

A donor may take a deduction for a charitable contribution of a fractional interest in tangible personal property as long as the

donor satisfies prior law requirements for deductibility and, in subsequent years, makes additional charitable contributions of interests in the same property. There is recapture of the income and gift
tax charitable deduction under certain circumstances, such as
where the donor's remaining interest in the property is not contributed to the same donee within ten years, or if the donee does
not timely take substantial physical possession of the property or
use the property for an exempt use. These rules are applicable for
contributions, bequests, and gifts made after August 17, 2006.

Gifts of Clothing and Household Items

Generally, a charitable deduction for a gift of clothing or household items is not allowed unless the gift item is in good used condition or better. A deduction may be allowed for a charitable
contribution of an item of clothing or a household item not in
good used condition or better if the amount claimed for the item
is more than $500 and the donor includes with the tax return a
qualified appraisal with respect to the property. These provisions
are effective for contributions made after August 17, 2006.

Contributions of Taxidermy

The amount allowed as a deduction for charitable contributions of
taxidermy property that is contributed by the person who prepared, stuffed, or mounted the property is the lesser of the taxpayer's basis in the property or its fair market value. Most associated
indirect costs may not be included in basis. These rules apply to
contributions made after July 25, 2006.

Record-Keeping Requirements

In the case of a charitable contribution of money, regardless of the
amount, applicable record-keeping requirements are satisfied only
if the donor maintains as a record of the contribution a bank
record or a written communication from the donee showing the
name of the charity, the date of the contribution, and its amount.
This rule applies to contributions made in tax years beginning after August 17, 2006.

Index